THE WILES LECTURES GIVEN AT
THE QUEEN'S UNIVERSITY OF BELFAST

ARISTOCRATIC CENTURY

ARISTOCRATIC CENTURY

The peerage of eighteenth-century England

JOHN CANNON
Professor of Modern History
The University of Newcastle upon Tyne

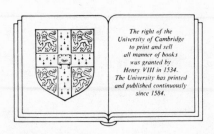

The right of the
University of Cambridge
to print and sell
all manner of books
was granted by
Henry VIII in 1534.
The University has printed
and published continuously
since 1584.

CAMBRIDGE UNIVERSITY PRESS

Cambridge
London   New York   New Rochelle
Melbourne   Sydney

Published by the Press Syndicate of the University of Cambridge
The Pitt Building, Trumpington Street, Cambridge CB2 1RP
32 East 57th Street, New York, NY 10022, USA
296 Beaconsfield Parade, Middle Park, Melbourne 3206, Australia

First published 1984

Printed in Great Britain at the University Press, Cambridge

Library of Congress catalogue card number: 84-7721

British Library Cataloguing in Publication Data

Cannon, John, *1926–*
Aristocratic century.
1. England—Nobility—History   2. Great
Britain—History—18th century
1. Title
305.5'2'0942   HT653.G7

ISBN 0 521 25729 8

CONTENTS

ACKNOWLEDGEMENTS

My first thanks are due to the Trustees of the Wiles Lectures for their very kind invitation and to Professor W. Lewis Warren and his colleagues in The Queen's University, Belfast for the warmth of their welcome. What could have been a rather daunting occasion was made extremely enjoyable by their kindness and hospitality. I received great benefit from the comments of the invited members of the discussion group – Dr Christopher Clay, Professor William Doyle, Dr Paul Langford, Mr David Large, Dr Frank O'Gorman and Dr E. A. Smith, all of whom have very kindly continued to give me assistance while preparing the Lectures for publication. I have also been given great help on ecclesiastical matters by Dr W. M. Marshall of Millfield School.

Among my Newcastle friends, I would like to mention the help I received from Mrs Eileen Inkster: I am very sorry that she did not live to see the book in print. Dr P. E. Murrell worked as a research associate with me for two years and has continued to help most generously: I owe a great deal to her meticulous scholarship and hope that she will be pleased to see the shape her work has taken. Professor Norman McCord read sections of the book and offered me, as always, splendid advice: it was made more piquant by the evident mistrust which he felt for some of my propositions. Miss Janice Cummin typed the final typescript for me with great speed, accuracy and good humour and much of the organisational side has been eased by the help of Mrs Joyce Bamlett. It is a pleasure to put my debt to them on record.

Lastly, I must acknowledge with gratitude a grant from the Social Science Research Council, which was of critical importance in enabling me to make progress at a time when there were many other distractions.

PREFACE

My defence for the inadequacy of these lectures, of which I am acutely aware, is twofold. The letter conveying the invitation of the Wiles Trustees made it clear that the work should be 'broad in character and of a pioneering nature'. I have availed myself of that loophole without mercy. Second, the preparations were not assisted by being undertaken while parts of the university world were falling about my ears. If it is true that medieval cartographers eked out their want of knowledge with 'Here be demons', I offer, as substitute, 'Here be the School of Modern Languages' and 'Here be the Department of Music saved'.

In this study I wished to attempt three things. First, to practise a little structural analysis. It has sometimes seemed to me that while the methodological debate on the virtues and defects of that technique has been hotly, indeed passionately, pursued, the technique itself has been relatively little employed: it is as though the energy devoted to the theoretical battle was enough to exhaust the combatants. Second, to help to rescue English historiography from its isolation from the continent and to look at some English developments against a continental background. To that ambition, I must offer two qualifications. First, some excellent work has already been done, most particularly by Derek Jarrett.[1] Second, the differences in composition, size and structure of nobilities is so great that, in any comparisons, great caution is to be exercised. The third objective was to draw attention to the neglect of what was, by any standards, one of the most successful of all ruling elites, the eighteenth-century English peerage. One is struck by the vast amount of work that has been done on the French nobility compared with the English and the more so in the light of their respective achievements.

---

[1] *The begetters of Revolution: England's involvement with France, 1759–1789.*

The constraints upon this enterprise are obvious. The nobility played so important a part in eighteenth-century life and left so much evidence, literary and architectural, that forty years of visiting record offices and country houses would be but a perfunctory preparation. Yet the nobility is too important to ignore. If one of the great achievements of eighteenth-century England was the creation of a period of political stability – and, in the modern world, one feels that this is a peculiarly difficult thing to attain, a kind of political Indian rope trick – what was the contribution of the nobility to that achievement? If a second great achievement was to encourage or permit an industrial revolution, which has changed the lives of half the human race, what was the relationship between these two achievements? John Kenyon drew our attention to one facet of the problem when he wrote that, during the reign of the first two Georges, 'Britain's rise to world power was matched by paralysis or deepening ossification at home', and he called it one of the most baffling periods in our history.[2] Harold Perkin, in a brilliant and thoughtful work, *The origins of modern English society, 1780–1880*, tried to relate the two by suggesting that the social structure of eighteenth-century England was unique and proved to be the decisive factor in the race for an industrial revolution.

Ever since the early 1930s, when the work of Namier and Butterfield landed like a cluster of mortar bombs on the traditional Whig/liberal interpretation of eighteenth-century England, there have been complaints that the period has been atomised, devoid of any synthesising coherence. Neither Namier nor Butterfield did very much to restore the landscape after the devastation they had caused. Much of the work of other scholars in the 1950s and 1960s made it even harder to perceive any overall pattern, partly because their interest in the role of party led them, inevitably, to emphasise the divisions in society at the expense of those factors holding it together. The evidence on which these lectures were based seems to me to suggest that behind the political and religious disagreements, at times admittedly very sharp, there was a massive consensus, based upon the widespread acceptance of aristocratic values and aristocratic leadership.

If this description strikes some readers as crude, and I do not deny that any attempt to exhibit the character of a century must be at best a mere approximation, disguising much more complex realities, to others it will seem painfully apparent. It will not, after all, have escaped the attention

---

[2] Review in *The Spectator*, 3 March 1973, of *Parliamentary Reform, 1640–1832*.

of many people that the nobility did well for itself in Hanoverian England. Since the Glorious Revolution is widely accepted as the work of the aristocracy, it is scarcely surprising that they should have proved the main beneficiaries. Nevertheless, this is not uncontroversial. Marxist historians see the decisive and irreversible shift in power as taking place in the 1640s: they therefore tend to downgrade the revolution of 1688 as a mere aristocratic skirmish or *coup d'état*, and to identify the main characteristic of Hanoverian England as the development of a bourgeois regime.

This view I take to be untenable. There is little or no evidence that after 1660 the bourgeoisie was in effective control of the national fortunes (which is far from saying that they had no influence or that those who were in control were indifferent to bourgeois interests). The dominance of the landed aristocracy, based upon 1688 and exemplified in Burley, Bowood, Chatsworth and Kedleston, increased in most areas during the eighteenth century. One of its most potent weapons in defence of its own privileged position was a powerful affirmation of the liberal and open nature of English society, and though this was, in my view, in many respects a myth, there was enough truth to make it a myth of widespread appeal. When ordinary eighteenth-century Englishmen boasted of their liberties in comparison with other nations, modern historians are apt to pity their innocence and remind them of the Waltham Black Act, the gallows, the debtors' prison, the special juries and the press gang. But from other parts of eighteenth-century Europe, there was envy. Habeas Corpus might, at times of crisis, be suspended, but it was there to suspend; Parliament might be manipulated and unrepresentative, but at least there was a Parliament.

Consequently, though there is much evidence that merchants and financiers, teachers and journalists, lawyers and architects, shop-keepers and industrialists prospered in Hanoverian England, the questions to be explained seem to me to be almost the opposite of Marxist historiography – not how did they come to control government, but why did they not challenge aristocratic domination until towards the end of the century? The remarkable thing is not their assertiveness but, from our point of view, their strange submissiveness, their acquiescence in aristocratic rule. The essential problem is not how a capitalist development grew up inside a bourgeois regime, which is what one would expect, but the paradox of a developing capitalism within the framework of a non-capitalist order. Much of the debate which has taken place recently on the attitude of the lower orders of Hanoverian society towards their betters – often in rather simple terms of deference or defiance – seems to me interesting but peripheral. It is surely the attitude of the middling orders which is more crucial and, in many ways, harder to explain.

To the four lectures as given in Belfast, I have added two more chapters, on religion and education and on marriage, together with a short conclusion. There is always some difficulty in preparing lectures for subsequent publication. I have removed some topical allusions and toned down some exuberances, but I hope that readers will forgive me for not eradicating all traces of their spoken origin. I did not wish to obliterate completely all evidence of so agreeable an occasion.

I

RECRUITMENT

The relationship between aristocracy and monarchy is the main theme of European political history in the century before the French Revolution. It is most apparent in France where the ability of the privileged orders, entrenched in the various *parlements*, to retard royal reform helped to bring the monarchy to its knees. Arthur Young, a keen observer of the early days of the Revolution, believed that the consequence of that upheaval would be a great extension of aristocratic influence. But the relationship was of crucial importance in many other countries. In Sweden, the absolutism of Charles XII was replaced by aristocratic supremacy until Gustav III, in his *coup d'état* of 1772, regained power by playing off the privileged against the non-privileged orders. Frederick IV of Denmark warned his successor in 1730 against aristocratic pretensions and the most dramatic episode in Danish eighteenth-century history, the rise and fall of Struensee, was essentially a confrontation between reforming monarchy and resistant nobility. In Russia, Prussia and Austria, the power of the nobility was a serious check upon the monarchy. Though Catherine the Great is still sometimes placed in the textbook category of enlightened despot, her reign has also been described as 'the golden age of the Russian nobility'.[1] Frederick the Great, often presented as the epitome of enlightened despotism, was careful not to challenge aristocratic power directly. Joseph II in the Habsburg dominions was less careful and the result was that he finished in 1790 a broken and defeated man: 'He had to face the fact', wrote Ernst Wangermann, 'that the continuing functioning of his monarchy, enlightened or otherwise, fundamentally depended upon the

---

[1] M. Raeff, *Origins of the Russian intelligentsia*, 10. See also, P. Dukes, *Catherine the Great and the Russian nobility* and R. E. Jones, *The emancipation of the Russian nobility, 1762–85*. A revisionist view which does not, I think, inhibit my general argument is I. de Madariaga, *Russia in the age of Catherine the Great*.

cooperation of the privileged classes.'[2] The Polish magnates, with the assistance of the *szlachta*, were strong enough to paralyse their elected monarchs and to bring their country to partition and destruction.

It would, of course, be foolish to present the relationship between monarchy and nobility solely in terms of confrontation. Monarchs were the first of their nobility and lived surrounded by noblemen, often on terms of personal friendship. Most of them were well aware that the institution of monarchy would not long survive the collapse of respect for the nobility. Frederick the Great made it the very first object of his policy, as stated in the *Political Testament* of 1752, to preserve his noble class. Yet the inexorable demands of the state forced even the least radical of rulers sometimes to challenge the privileges of the noble order, particularly their exemption from most forms of direct taxation and their monopoly of high office. Maria Theresa, by no means an advanced thinker, was obliged by her determination to recover Silesia to wage persistent war on the constitutional and financial privileges of her nobility. Nothing less than an army of 150,000 men would do and this demanded the implementation of the *contributio*, if necessary overriding the powers of the estates: 'In order to put all this on a firm and lasting foundation', she wrote, 'I found myself forced to depart from the old, traditional constitution, with the detrimental qualities which it had acquired.'[3] Gustav III of Sweden was one of the most fastidious of aristocrats, yet he was obliged in the end to attack them, with consequences to himself which were fatal.

In most European countries, with a scattered and illiterate peasantry and a small, if growing, middle-class element, only the nobility were capable of offering effective political resistance to the crown. Adroit aristocratic politicians broadened their appeal by claiming that they represented, not a mere class or sectional interest, but the first line of defence of the liberties and privileges of all subjects against royal despotism. Nowhere, perhaps, was this card played with more skill than by the *parlements* of France, which prevented the French monarchy from tapping the potential support of the professional and middling classes and mobilising their enlightened and egalitarian views in support of a reforming crown.

There was no lack of theory to justify aristocratic pretensions. The

---

[2] *The Austrian achievement*, 51.
[3] *Testament* of 1750, Section IV. A convenient translation is printed in C. A. Macartney, *The Habsburg and Hohenzollern dynasties in the seventeenth and eighteenth centuries*, Part 1, Document 12, 94–132.

most eminent of French political writers, the Baron Montesquieu, insisted on the supreme importance of the nobility as part of a *pouvoir intermédiaire*, which would prevent monarchy from degenerating into despotism by upholding the fundamental laws of the kingdom. Sir William Blackstone, whose *Commentaries on the Laws of England* proved so successful in the 1760s, concurred in awarding the nobility a central role in the constitution: the House of Lords formed a body 'to support the rights of both the crown and the people by forming a barrier to withstand the encroachments of both'.[4] The Russian prince, M. M. Shcherbatov, urging the claims of the *dvorianstvo* at the Legislative Commission of 1768, described them as 'the most enlightened about the true advantage of the fatherland', arguing that they alone were capable of a disinterested view of public affairs.[5] Lord George Augustus Cavendish, an equally impartial observer from Chatsworth, shunned elaborate theory and confided to Horace Walpole that he 'liked an aristocracy and thought it right that great families with great connections should govern'.[6]

The politics of eighteenth-century England are not often discussed in this context or in these terms. It is still commonly assumed that the Glorious Revolution set her on a path which diverged from that of the rest of Europe.[7] An example may be found in L. G. Pine, *The story of the peerage*: 'It is certain that in England the land-owning class fought and won a battle with the crown whereby they reduced the monarch to a passive role. In France, on the other hand, the crown overcame the nobility.'[8] This is a rather extreme version but the same tendency can be traced in more sophisticated and scholarly books. Professor A. R. Myers remarked of the eighteenth century that '*outside Great Britain*, the membership of Diets or Parliaments came to be dominated by aristocratic sentiments and values'.[9] It was a curious exception to make. Once we rid ourselves of the notion that mid-eighteenth-century Europe saw the high-water mark of royal despotism and acknowledge the

---

[4] Book 1, Chapter 2.
[5] Quoted Dukes, *Catherine the Great*, 55. Shcherbatov's views are most fully expounded in his *On the corruption of morals in Russia*, a translation of which was published by A. Lenton in 1969. For comment, see M. Raeff, 'State and nobility in the ideology of M. M. Shcherbatov', *American Slavic and East European Review*, XIX (1960).
[6] H. Walpole, *Last Journals*, II, 488.
[7] For interesting comment on the separate treatment of English intellectual development, see R. Porter, 'The Enlightenment in England', in *The Enlightenment in national context*, ed. R. Porter and M. Teich.   [8] Page 187.
[9] My italics. *Parliaments and estates in Europe to 1789*, 156.

underlying strength of the aristocracy, there will be little difficulty in fitting into the continental picture an England ruled by the Russells and the Cavendishes, the Pelhams and the Pouletts, the Berties and the Montagus.[10]

It is true that the revolutionary settlement after 1688 tipped the balance of the constitution against the monarchy but it was far from deciding, once and for all, the exact position of the crown. Within that settlement remained plenty of room for legitimate disagreement about the prerogatives of the monarch and both William and Anne fought strenuous rearguard actions. If the struggle was more muted under the first two Georges, it was in part because the identification of the Tories with Jacobitism, however unfair it may have been,[11] reduced the Hanoverian monarchs' room for manoeuvre. The Peerage Bill of 1719 was an effort to limit the powers of the crown in the way Swedish aristocrats were doing at precisely the same time and Russian aristocrats were to attempt a decade later.[12] The struggle between aristocracy and monarch was resumed in earnest at the accession of George III, when the collapse of the Jacobite cause had immeasurably strengthened the crown's position. The new king's confrontation with the Old Corps Whigs in the 1760s was certainly interpreted by many as his attempt to escape from an unwelcome aristocratic embrace.[13] Gustav III's coup in 1772 did not pass unnoticed by the adversaries of George III and their

---

[10] A newer note is struck by W. Doyle, *The old European order, 1660–1800*, 81. 'Perhaps more surprising, in a period traditionally described as one of "absolutism" and of the curbing of noble pretensions, is the extent to which nobles decided how power should be deployed. They did this by dominating estates and diets, both at local and national level. The powers wielded by these bodies varied enormously, but they existed in some form almost everywhere.' Even in Russia, where after the decline of the *zemsky sobor* there were no representative institutions, the nobility retained vast influence.

[11] For two remarkable and scholarly glosses on the phrase in parentheses, see E. Cruickshanks, *Political untouchables: the Tories and the '45* and Linda Colley's riposte in *In defiance of oligarchy; the Tory party 1714–60*.

[12] The fullest account of the Peerage Bill is J. F. Naylor, ed., *The British aristocracy and the Peerage Bill of 1719*. Though introduced primarily as a party measure, the encouragement it would have given to aristocratic exclusiveness was soon perceived and exploited by Walpole in his opposition to it. The Swedish constitution of 1720 severely limited the right of the crown to grant titles of nobility. An attempt to limit the Tsardom was made in 1730 by Prince Dmitry Golitsyn and his associates, and further attempts were made in 1740 and 1762. In each case, in England, Sweden and Russia, the position of the crown was temporarily weakened by a disputed succession.

[13] The royal cause was put thus: 'though a subject had connections with all the greatest families in England . . . he can have no natural pretension to be minister. That appointment is personal to the king.' The Duke of Devonshire's retort, on behalf of the Old Corps was, that 'if a King of England employs those people for his ministers that the nation have a good opinion of, he will make a great figure, but if he chose them merely through personal favour, it will never do'. Quoted J. Brewer, *Party ideology and popular politics at the accession of George III*, 116, 119.

apprehensions of a royalist counter-stroke were increased by the thought of what an army, flushed with victory in America, might do:

> What sort of spirit would have displayed itself had the colonies . . . been reduced to unconditional submission, and what measures would have been dealt out to the opposition had the royal army returned triumphant! Prerogative that spoke in so high a tone to a House of Commons that had bound its hands, would soon have issued *lettres de cachet de part le roi*.[14]

Such were Horace Walpole's nightmares. Perhaps the most striking clash came in the early 1780s when the Rockinghams, that most aristocratic of parties, determined to give 'a good stout blow at the influence of the crown', while George III and his supporters were resolved to resist the pretensions of what was later called 'the grand and leading party of the aristocracy'.[15]

There has however been very little systematic treatment of the English nobility in the eighteenth century. Disraeli, it is true, flung out an intriguing hint when he claimed to see the triumph of a Venetian oligarchy and remarked on that process of 'political mystification . . . during which a people without power or education had been induced to believe themselves the freest and most enlightened nation in the world'.[16] But Disraeli's initiative was never followed up.[17] This is, in part, because piety persuaded many historians to devote their energies to tracing the development of the constitution. When this impetus began to be exhausted, it was followed by a devotion to party history. This is an important and necessary task and has had its notable achievements. By the time interest in party history showed signs of flagging, the dispossessed, the excluded had come into their own, and attention was focussed on poachers, smugglers, rioters, unmarried mothers, anonymous letter-writers, wreckers and body-snatchers. By a kind of historiographical fluke, the nobility – which, whether one likes them or not, did exercise some influence on events – has managed to avoid analysis.

[14] Walpole, *Last Journals*, II, 413.
[15] The Rockinghams' spokesman in 1782 was Charles Fox: *Memorials and correspondence of Charles James Fox*, ed. Lord John Russell, I, 316. For the essentially aristocratic nature of Fox's political views, see J. R. Dinwiddy, 'Charles James Fox and the people', *History*, LV (1970), 342–59. The description of the Fox/North coalition is from *Quarterly Review* (1830), 311, echoing Dundas' description of it as 'an insolent aristocratic band'.
[16] *Sybil*, Chapter 3.
[17] I do not mean to be disrespectful to A. S. Turberville, whose three volumes on the House of Lords were an impressive pioneering venture, but they were largely narrative in character and uneven in quality. The first volume, based on Turberville's early research, was by far the best; the last volume was published posthumously. The volumes of the *History of Parliament*, as has often been pointed out, are something of a misnomer since they concentrate exclusively on the Commons.

It is the more surprising that little has been attempted on the eighteenth-century English nobility since, as I said earlier, it was in many ways very successful. It is an oddity that the peerage has been subjected to scrutiny for the fifteenth and the seventeenth centuries, when its achievements were not remarkable, and ignored for the eighteenth century.[18] Even those modern historians who have been most critical of the Hanoverian regime in certain respects have usually found something to admire. It removed or neutralised three of the great problems that had convulsed seventeenth-century England. First, it arrived at an illogical and unheroic degree of religious toleration which the Dissenters could put up with and which the Anglicans could just about stomach. Second, through the Act of Union of 1707, it achieved a settlement with Scotland which, though far from popular on either side, did much to release the energies of the British people in the course of the century. Third, as we have noted, it had gone a long way to resolving the problem of the role of the monarchy and, though this still caused difficulties and Hanoverian kings threatened abdication, it no longer caused civil war. In foreign affairs, it frustrated the attempt by Louis XIV to establish a European hegemony and by 1763 had acquired a colonial empire such as the world had never seen. In addition, if additions are called for, English aristocrats presided over the beginnings of that industrial development which was to transform the world. When one reflects upon the achievements of the British ruling class in the twentieth century, one is inclined to be less censorious towards the Duke of Newcastle, Lord Rockingham and Lord North. And after 1815, when the writing was on the wall for the old order, it fought a skilful and effective rearguard action, offering concession and compromise, defusing potentially revolutionary situations, and retaining some of its influence deep into the twentieth century.

To what extent the English aristocracy in the eighteenth century can be regarded as a separate bloc is a matter which the subsequent analyses are designed to test. It is a point of some substance. The view has often been expressed that the links between the aristocracy and the gentry, and the share in power accorded to the mercantile and commercial groups, produced a social mobility, even a social harmony, which goes far to explain the peaceful constitutional development and the economic vitality of the period. Voltaire set an early example of praise for the

---

[18] For the earlier period, see K. B. McFarlane, *The nobility of later mediaeval England* and A. Tuck, *The crown and the nobility, 1272–1461*. For the seventeenth century, see L. Stone, *The crisis of the aristocracy, 1558–1641*.

absence of barriers in English society, the freedom with which different social groups mixed, and the readiness of the sons of the peerage to engage in trade and manufacture.[19] W. E. H. Lecky, in the nineteenth century, turned it into a main theme of British history. In continental countries, he declared, the nobility had a tendency to become isolated, enervated, frivolous and idle. 'But in England the interests of the nobles as a class have been carefully and indissolubly interwoven with those of the people . . . The intermarriage of peers and commoners has always been legal and common . . . No other [peerage] has shown itself so free from the spirit of monopoly.'[20] Modern historians have found much in this with which to agree. T. H. Hollingsworth suggested that there was a liberalisation in the peerage in the 1720s amounting to a 'social revolution', which may have been the necessary condition for the subsequent industrial revolution.[21] Harold Perkin agreed that the greater degree of social mobility in Britain may have been a critical factor in promoting industrial development: the 'open' nature of the English aristocracy distinguished it 'from all other contemporary societies except Holland'. He even referred to eighteenth-century Britain as a classless society.[22] It is certainly true that no legal barriers to the acquisition of landed property existed in Britain,[23] in contrast to some continental countries, nor was there a formal law of derogation whereby nobles who engaged in trade would lose their rank. But other historians have sounded a warning note. Habakkuk insisted that the degree of mobility and interchange in Hanoverian Britain may easily be exaggerated: 'it was, in fact, extremely rare for a younger son of a peer to go into trade', while the strictness of the law of entail in Britain meant that the land market was limited and opportunities for the purchase of landed estates rather infrequent.[24] G. E. Mingay cautioned that, although the gentry and the peerage had much in common, the homogeneity of the landed elite could easily be overstated: 'between the main body of the peerage and the great majority of the gentry there yawned always a measurable social gulf'.[25]

If it is difficult to form a balanced estimate of social mobility in

---

[19] *Lettres philosophiques*, first published in London in 1733 under the title *Letters concerning the English nation*.

[20] W. E. H. Lecky, *A history of England in the eighteenth century* (1878), I, 172, 184.

[21] 'The demography of the British peerage', *Population Studies*, XVIII (1964/5), 10. For comment, see below, pp. 79–82.

[22] *The origins of modern English society, 1780–1880*, 17, 37.

[23] Save for legislation against Catholic recusants.

[24] H. J. Habakkuk, writing in A. Goodwin, ed., *The European nobility in the eighteenth century*, 19, 16.

[25] G. E. Mingay, *The gentry: the rise and fall of a ruling class*, 4.

England, it is scarcely easier for continental countries. Direct comparisons are difficult because of differences of definition and structure. Nor, for that matter, was Europe an entity: the differences and disparities even within particular countries were enormous. But what work has been done suggests that the traditional picture of continental exclusiveness may need to be modified. Of France it has been said that, in the eighteenth century, money rather than birth was becoming the key to society: 'the plutocracy was infiltrating into the aristocracy'.[26] Whereas there are few examples of the direct purchase of peerages in eighteenth-century England, the purchase of office carrying noble status was a commonplace in France: Necker, in 1785, calculated that there were more than three thousand offices granting hereditary nobility. Voltaire and Beaumarchais both purchased patents of nobility: Hume and R. B. Sheridan could not, and it was extremely unlikely that they would be given one. Moreover, the French nobility, far from shunning commercial activity as contamination, engaged in large-scale financial and industrial enterprises on their own account: most of heavy industry was owned by the French nobility.[27] Almost without exception, the trend of recent scholarship has been to emphasise the liberal character of pre-Revolutionary France. Professor Doyle has referred to eighteenth-century France as an 'open elite', and to the relatively easy access to the nobility, the large number of new nobles, and the well-established patterns of intermarriage between French nobility and commoners.[28] G. V. Taylor has drawn attention to the great contribution made by the French nobility to commercial and industrial development.[29] Forster has demonstrated the increasing respect felt by the nobility towards 'bourgeois virtues' and Chaussinand-Nogaret has argued that, particularly after 1760, bourgeois standards were increasingly dominant.[30] Colin Lucas strongly denied that nobles and bourgeois were at enmity and insisted that they formed part of the same social elite.[31]

[26] J. McManners, writing in Goodwin, ed., *The European nobility*, 26.

[27] Doyle, *The old European order*, 79.

[28] *Origins of the French Revolution*, 31; *The old European order*, 85.

[29] 'Types of capitalism in eighteenth-century France', *English Historical Review*, LXXIX (1964), 478–97.

[30] R. Forster, *The nobility of Toulouse in the eighteenth century*; G. Chaussinand-Nogaret, *La Noblesse au XVIIIe siècle*; *idem*, 'Aux origines de la Révolution: noblesse et bourgeoisie', in *Annales; économies, sociétés, civilisations*, 30, 2–3 (1975), 265–78.

[31] 'Nobles, bourgeois and the origins of the French Revolution', *Past and Present*, 60 (1973), 84–126. The argument is reinforced by E. Barber, *The bourgeoisie in eighteenth century France*, 100–2 and by F. L. Ford, *Robe and sword*, 144, 208.

A certain readjustment of our view of the other continental nobilities may also perhaps be overdue. Of the Swedish nobility, Michael Roberts observed that it was a numerous class, 'constantly receiving quite large accessions of fresh blood'.[32] Compared with the English peerage, the Swedish nobility must have seemed extraordinarily diverse: 'it was as though Pope and Priestley, James Watt and Gibbon, Adam Smith and Nicholas Hawksmoor had all sat on the same benches with Lord Carrington, Lord Rodney and the first Lord Liverpool'.[33] In 1756 a corporal in the Swedish army was elevated to the nobility: admittedly it was his reward for betraying a royalist conspiracy, but one cannot help suspecting that in Hanoverian England he would have been promoted sergeant. In the Habsburg dominions, too, we are told that ennoblements were fairly common: Maria Theresa sold titles at a fixed tariff, 250 florins for a marquisate.[34] Dittersdorf, the musician, purchased a title, and a patent of nobility was granted to a Jew more than one hundred years before Jews were allowed entry even into the Lower House of the British Parliament.[35] Olwen Hufton reports that it was easy for non-nobles to 'slip' into the Spanish and Italian nobility. Even in Prussia, sometimes regarded as totally rigid in its social structure before the reform period of the 1800s, there was social ascendancy through the ranks of the army. Though Frederick himself was, as we have seen, extremely anxious to preserve the noble order and in theory non-nobles were not permitted to buy *rittergüter* – landed estates – in practice, society could not be frozen. The bourgeoisie gained greatly in prosperity, particularly after the Seven Years War, many of them could outbid the poorer *junkers*, and officials could be persuaded to turn a blind eye to technical breaches of the law.[36] The comparison of liberal and responsible English noblemen with haughty and exclusive continentals looks facile.

As a group for study, the English peerage has two advantages. First, it is capable of precise legal definition through membership of the House of

---

[32] In Goodwin, ed., *The European nobility*, 143–5. Roberts added that, between 1719 and 1792, 725 individuals were ennobled in Sweden. The comparable figure for the English peerage is 121, with another 136 creations in the Irish peerage. The difference in populations should be borne in mind. Ford, *Robe and sword*, 133 puts the number of Swedish nobles in 1626 at 1547.

[33] For Carrington, see p. 23 below.

[34] *Cambridge Economic History*, v, 565.

[35] The Jew was Sonnenfels, a university professor. Though he was a convert, his wife remained a practising Jew.

[36] H. C. Johnson, *Frederick the Great and his officials*, 244–9.

Lords:[37] this distinguishes it from other social groups, such as country gentlemen, landed aristocracy, merchants or the middling ranks of society, which are not susceptible to exact definition. Second, it is small enough to be manageable, yet large enough to promise significant statistical returns.

The first thing to note is the smallness of the total membership. No more than 1,003 persons held peerages during the whole of the eighteenth century. By a lucky coincidence this is, if I remember rightly, the same as the total of Don Giovanni's conquests in Spain. The complete peerage of England, over all that period, was considerably less than the pupils at most comprehensive schools and distinctly less than the attendance at Darlington football club on a wet Saturday in February. There are three reasons for this. By common law, noble status in England applied only to the peer himself; younger sons and daughters were technically commoners, as were elder sons until they inherited the title. This distinguishes the English peerage sharply from most continental peerages and compounds the difficulties of comparison. Second, until the later part of the century, the creation of new peerages was severely limited. Even in the last two decades, when creations were more plentiful, it is doubtful whether they kept up with the increase of population. Third, nearly one hundred peers held their titles for fifty years or more. Outstanding in this respect were the Fitzroys, Dukes of Grafton, two of whom held the title for no less than one hundred and twenty years. Lord Fitzwilliam was a peer for seventy-seven years, starting his political career under the auspices of the 1st Duke of Newcastle and living to see the Reform Bill become law in 1832.[38]

The sample taken for analysis both under-estimates and exaggerates the size of the political elite. It represents, of course, no more than a fragment of the governing class. To this nucleus, we must add Scottish and Irish peers, and the relatives, advisers and associates of the peerage. We must also include the substantial gentry, some of whom possessed property far exceeding that of the poorer peers and many of whom would have been regarded as nobility by continental standards. Sir George Savile, 8th Baronet of Thornhill, Yorkshire, and Rufford,

[37] I.e., I have included surviving English peerages granted before 1707 and British peerages granted subsequently. My core group excludes Irish and Scottish peers, unless they also held English or British peerages. I do not include bishops or Scottish representative peers, though they held membership of the Lords.

[38] E. A. Smith, *Whig principles and party politics: Earl Fitzwilliam and the Whig Party 1748–1833*. For a discussion of the increasing use of special remainders to preserve peerages, see my Raleigh Lecture for 1982, 'The isthmus repaired: the resurgence of the English aristocracy, 1660–1760', *Proceedings of the British Academy*, LXVIII (1982), 431–53.

Nottinghamshire, Sir Edward Knatchbull, 4th Baronet of Mersham Hatch, Kent, Sir James Dashwood, 2nd Baronet of Kirtlington Park, Oxford, Sir John Hynde Cotton, 3rd Baronet of Madingley Hall, Cambridgeshire, Sir John Pakington, 4th Baronet of Westwood, Worcestershire, were not men to stand abashed in the presence of peers. In addition, any estimate of the ruling class must include the great commercial families of the city of London and the ruling oligarchies in important provincial centres like Norwich, Bristol, Newcastle, York, Bury St Edmunds, Liverpool and Hull. And although eighteenth-century government has been frequently and rightly described as a system based upon property, and having as its primary objective the preservation of property, Professor Geoffrey Holmes has reminded us that property was very widely, if unequally, distributed: influence of some sort extended far down the social pyramid, and was much prized.[39]

On the other hand, the total of 1,003 is swollen by persons some of whom were peers in name only. The forty-nine peeresses in their own right were of some social but little political significance.[40] The sixty or more peers who adhered to the Catholic religion lived almost as a group apart, excluded from public office, educating their children abroad, and marrying among themselves. Among the remaining paper peers, we must include several who were lunatics: the Shirley family had the misfortune to produce in the 3rd Earl Ferrers one avowed lunatic, and in his nephew the 4th Earl one who should probably have been so regarded.[41] Certain peers who were down on their luck were almost incapable of sustaining the rank. The last Baron Eure had been journeyman to a woollen draper at £20 p.a. before inheriting the title in 1672; the 7th Baron Hunsdon was said to have been apprenticed to a

[39] 'Property could be an estate of 40,000 acres, but it could also be a forty-shilling freehold, a clerkship in the Exchequer, a parish constableship, and so on.' Holmes was commenting on H. T. Dickinson's paper on 'Whiggism in the eighteenth century', in J. Cannon, ed., *The Whig ascendancy: colloquies on Hanoverian England*, 45.

[40] The peeresses included a clutch of royal mistresses. Lady Portsmouth and the Duchess of Cleveland were mistresses to Charles II and Lady Dorchester to James II. The Duchess of Kendal was mistress to George I and Lady Yarmouth mistress to George II. The Countess of Darlington, erstwhile Baroness von Kielmansegge and known colloquially for her formidable charms as the Elephant and Castle was the half-sister of George I; Lady Walsingham was his illegitimate daughter by the Duchess of Kendal. The husband of William III's mistress, Lady Orkney, was given his Scottish peerage for gallantry on the field of battle. Susan, Lady Belasyse, is said by Burnet to have been given her peerage by Charles II for resisting the advances of his brother James which, one might have thought, was not unreasonably difficult.

[41] Lawrence Shirley, who inherited the title in 1745, was a man of ungovernable temper. His wife obtained a separation on grounds of cruelty in 1758 and two years later he shot his steward. Despite a plea of 'occasional insanity of mind', he was found guilty of murder and hanged at Tyburn in May 1760.
　　To discriminate between lunacy and mere eccentricity is not easy, particularly in a period

weaver, and Theophilus Hastings, whose right to the earldom of Huntingdon was not established until fifteen years after his death, was the son of a shoemaker from Leicestershire.[42] Another group of peers who are included for purposes of statistical completeness are those who held the title very briefly. The 13th Earl of Suffolk has the record in this melancholy competition: the posthumous son of Lord North's Secretary of State, he held the title in 1779 for two fragile days. The 8th Baron St John died an infant when two and a half years old; the 5th Baron Lovelace inherited the title as a young boy, but died two weeks later in America; his contemporary the 3rd Earl of Coventry died aged ten at Eton, having held the title for one year and a half; Fulke Greville, Lord Brooke, died in 1711 at University College, Oxford, four months after inheriting. The 2nd Lord Bath shot himself in 1701 a fortnight after inheriting the title from his father and was buried at the same funeral service. At the other end of the scale are those persons who, having aspired to a peerage for many years, lived but a few months to enjoy it. Of these, the most famous is George Bubb Dodington, transmogrified into Baron Melcombe in 1761: 'his coronet seems only calculated to adorn his tomb', wrote Horace Mann, and the forecast proved right a year later.[43] Dodington was luckier than Sir William Courtenay, created Viscount in May 1762 and enjoying his new rank for a mere ten days. Altogether, twelve of the peers held their rank for less than one year and twenty-three for less than two years.

Let us begin with the comparatively simple task of establishing the exact numbers of the English peerage in the eighteenth century. A certain amount turns on definition. We have omitted royal peerages, except for

celebrated for odd behaviour. Among the clearer cases of lunacy were, it seems, the 4th Earl of Bradford, consequent upon a fall from horseback, the 5th Baron Leigh and the 3rd Earl of Portsmouth. The 2nd Duke of Cleveland, son of Charles II by Barbara Villiers, seems merely to have been of dull intelligence. The 3rd Earl Granville was intermittently deranged: in later life he went through a Fleet marriage with Molly Paddock, proprietress of a London brothel. The 8th Duke of Somerset developed a fear of smallpox which became totally obsessive. Vicary Gibbs, editor of the *The complete peerage of England, Scotland, Ireland* . . ., had a more robust way of classifying what Sidney Smith termed 'the nicer gradations of lunacy'. Of the 2nd Duke of Cleveland, he observed briskly: 'he was of weak intellect and voted with the Whigs', while of the 3rd Lord Portsmouth, he remarked 'so long as he was sane, he took no part in politics'.

[42] *Admissions to St John's College, Cambridge*, ed. R. F. Scott, III, 125. Other shabby peerage families included the Riches, Earls of Warwick, who were said to be too poor to educate their children, and the Bromleys of Cambs., whose ruin was brought about partly by electioneering. Henry Bromley, 1st Baron Montfort, having paid Lady Yarmouth for his peerage (*The House of Commons, 1715–54*, ed. R. R. Sedgwick, I, 492–3), fell into debt and shot himself in 1755 with appalling presence of mind. His grandson, the 3rd Baron, married at the age of twenty Betty, daughter of the keeper of a sponging-house at Islington, where he was confined for debt.

[43] Mann to Walpole, 25 April 1761, *Correspondence* (Yale edition), XXI, 500.

those granted to illegitimate children: Charles II's son by Nell Gwynn was created Duke of St Albans and the Beauclerks continued to hold that peerage throughout the century. We have omitted Jacobite creations after 1688 and we have struck off peers such as the 1st Viscount Bolingbroke while they were under attainder. Eighteen eldest sons of peers sat in the House of Lords in the eighteenth century, having been summoned in their father's baronies: these have, of course, been included. There are also a number of delicate decisions to be made where peerages were in dispute. We have included the 7th Baron Gerard, though he was a Jesuit priest and did not claim the title: however, there is no doubt of his legal right. Similarly, the 2nd Baron Griffin, whose peerage had been the last to be made by James II in December 1688, did not assume the title, but his son the 3rd Baron did, and was not denied it. On the other hand, the barony of Reede was dubious from the beginning: the only eighteenth-century baron neither claimed the title nor lived in England, and has been excluded.

For 1300, at a time when the peerage was, because of the growth of Parliament as an institution, acquiring more formal definition, the numbers have been estimated at 136.[44] During the reign of Richard II, the first letters patent were issued, which was to become the standard way of creating peers. But in the course of the fourteenth century the peerage declined in numbers, and McFarlane's estimate for 1400 was about 102. The following century saw a further decline, rates of creation not keeping pace with extinctions. By 1475, in the reign of Edward IV, the total had fallen to seventy-one. Henry VII was extremely sparing in his creations and, by the end of his reign in 1509, the peerage was at the lowest point ever reached, totalling about forty-four. Since some of these were minors and could not sit in the House of Lords, in that institution the spiritual peers – bishops, abbots and priors – were in a majority. Henry VIII's comparatively generous creations were offset by the remarkable restraint shown by Elizabeth: in the last thirty years of her reign she ennobled only one person. In 1603, the total was fifty-five or so. The early Stuarts, partly because of their impecuniosity and partly because of the backlog of claims which had built up, created on a lavish scale. James I ennobled no fewer than sixty-two persons and, by the outbreak of the Civil War, the peerage had more than doubled from Elizabeth's day, standing at about 138.[45] These creations, coupled with

[44] McFarlane, *The nobility of later mediaeval England*, 172–6.
[45] Estimate in *Gentleman's Magazine*, LIV (II), 896–7, quoting T. Walkley, *Catalogue of Dukes, etc.*, and confirmed by Turberville.

the exclusion of the abbots at the time of the Reformation, turned the House of Lords into an overwhelmingly secular body.[46] After the Restoration, there was a slow increase and by the accession of William and Mary the numbers had reached 153. At the start of the eighteenth century, they stood at 173.

The inflation of honours under the early Stuarts was clearly exceptional and the more normal policy of caution was maintained throughout the greater part of the eighteenth century. George II was particularly anxious not to dilute the ranks of the peerage: Sir Robert Walpole complained that he was 'as reluctant to bestow honours as money, and was more set against making peers than against any measure I could propose'.[47] Since George remained on the throne for thirty-three years, he was able to preside over a slight decrease in the total numbers. Not until the 1780s did the rate of creations begin to increase, and by 1800 the grand total had risen to 267 (see Table 1).

Several historians have testified that, in the period with which they are familiar, the majority of the peerages were of comparatively recent creation. McFarlane noted the very rapid rate of extinction among the later medieval peerage. Of seventeen earldoms in 1400, fourteen had been created in the previous seventy-five years. For 1300 he had traced 136 families which had received summons to the Lords in Parliament: by the year 1500, only sixteen of these were represented by a male, and of those several had not made good their claims to a peerage. Families like the Berkeleys of Gloucestershire whose peerage remained in existence from the twelfth to the twentieth centuries are extremely rare. Helen Miller, in her work on the Tudor peerage, noted that half the peerage in 1547 had been ennobled since 1485.[48] Turberville repeated the same message in his analysis of the peerage at the accession of William and Mary: the extent to which it was of Stuart creation was, he suggested, 'very remarkable'.

Though there were fluctuations, this state of affairs remained true throughout the subsequent century. In 1700, for instance, there were 163 male peers. Sixty-three of these (38%) held peerages which had been in existence less than twenty years: 82% had been created within the previous one hundred years. Despite the considerable number of

---

[46] The bishops were technically Lords of Parliament, not peers. They were not entitled to trial by the House of Lords and although they could hear impeachments, they retired before the verdict. See, e.g., *HMC. Carlisle*, 201–2 whether the bishops should be present for the trial of the Jacobite lords in 1746.

[47] Lord Hervey, *Memoirs of the reign of George II*, ed. J. W. Croker, III, 50.

[48] 'The early Tudor peerage, 1485–1547', M.A. thesis, London University (1950).

Table 1. *Number of peers on 1 January by decades*

1700	1710	1720	1730	1740	1750	1760	1770	1780	1790	1800
173	167	190	189	183	187	181	197	189	220	267

creations from 1784 onwards, the situation had not changed dramatically by 1800. The percentage of peerages created within the previous twenty years had risen from 38% to 43% but the percentage created within the previous one hundred years had actually fallen slightly, from 82% to 79%. The number of peerages dating from more than two hundred years remained small. In 1700 it was 7.9%: by 1800 it had fallen to 6.2%.[49]

The turnover of peerage families helps to create an impression that new men were continuously thrusting their way up into the ranks of the aristocracy and, in the course of time, this has hardened into one of the most cherished beliefs in English history. It has been given a semblance of support by the constant wail from established peers that men of vulgar and unworthy origins were being elevated. These protestations ought not to be taken at their face value. In every century we come across pitiful laments that the peerage is not what it was and that the very fabric of society is being rent asunder by injudicious creations. One of the complaints against Piers Gaveston, the favourite of Edward II, was that he was too slight a man to merit the earldom of Cornwall, conferred upon him in 1307.[50] The creation of Michael de la Pole as Earl of Suffolk in 1385 was much resented in Richard II's reign.[51] The lavish creations of the early Stuarts gave fresh vigour to the protests. Lionel Cranfield, Earl of Middlesex, was baited for his low origins by Lord Digby, and the Earl of Arundel in 1621 reminded Lord Spencer of Wormleighton that the earl's ancestors had been serving king and country at a time when the baron's forebears were tending sheep.[52] The charge of conniving at upstart promotions was levelled against George Villiers, 1st Duke of Buckingham,[53] and at the end of the century Lord Ailesbury declared

---

[49] Stone, *The crisis of the aristocracy*, uses a different method of analysis, counting generations. This seemed to me to involve difficulties of definition. Consequently I cannot offer direct comparison on this point with his work, though there is no reason to believe there is any clash of evidence.

[50] J. C. Davies, *The baronial opposition to Edward II: its character and policy*, 81–3.

[51] A. Tuck, *Richard II and the English nobility*, 77.

[52] *Cal. State Papers Dom., 1619–23*, 254, 257.

[53] Impeachment proceedings, see J. Rushworth, *Historical Collections*, 334–7.

that the peerage was so sadly degenerated that he was tempted to renounce his title and live as a private gentleman.[54]

The chorus continued unabated throughout the eighteenth century. In 1713 the elevation of Robert Benson as Baron Bingley provoked much sarcasm: 'every year', declared Lord Berkeley of Stratton, the House of Lords receives 'some great blow'.[55] Forty years later, the promotion of absurd candidates to the peerage was one of the favourite themes of Horace Walpole's correspondence; the fact that his own family had received its peerage as late as 1723 adding, no doubt, zest to his indignation. In 1762 the latest 'cargo of peers' evoked the usual scornful comment. His most scathing remarks were reserved for creations in the Irish peerage. In the batch created late in 1756 he could find nothing but 'brewers and poulterers': Lady Townshend had remarked, he reported to Mann, that she fully expected every day to receive a bill from her fishmonger signed Lord Mount-Shrimp. George Selwyn joined in in 1768, dismissing the Irish peers as 'riff-raff'. In 1776 Walpole described the admittedly large creation as 'mushrooms . . . half of whom will not be gentlemen under a generation or two . . . their very number makes them a mob'. Ten years later, he was at a loss to know why the government did not put paid at once to the problem of Irish terrorists by making them all peers.[56]

At the end of the century, fresh debate was triggered off by the elevation of Robert Smith, a banker, first to an Irish peerage and then, in 1797, to a British barony as Lord Carrington. The author of *Reflections on the late augmentations of the English peerage* brooded on the promotion of persons 'totally unknown to the general historian', and warned that to degrade the peerage was the first step to its total destruction. A correspondent in the *Gentleman's Magazine* of 1814 traced many of the evils of the day to Pitt's wholesale creations: 'society was turned upside down and the mud came uppermost'.[57] The *Quarterly Review* in 1830 agreed that the consequence of such abundant creations had been that 'all the long-accustomed respect for the higher classes suddenly diminished and in a few years became nearly extinct'. The ground was well prepared for Disraeli's celebrated description in *Sybil* of Pitt's creation of a plebeian aristocracy: 'he made peers of second-rate squires and fat

[54] *Memoirs of Thomas Bruce, Marquis of Ailesbury* (Roxburghe Club, 1890), 304.
[55] *The Wentworth Papers, 1705–39*, ed. J. J. Cartwright, 347.
[56] Walpole to Mann, 30 April 1762, *Corr.*, XXII, 31; to Mann, 29 Nov. 1756, *Corr.*, XXI, 24; Selwyn to Carlisle, 26 Feb. 1768, *HMC. Carlisle*, 246; Walpole to Mann, 16 July 1776, *Corr.*, XXIV, 227; to Lady Upper Ossory, 22 July 1786, *Corr.*, XXXIII, 520.
[57] 'A.F.A.' in *Gentleman's Magazine*, LXXXIV (i), 32.

graziers. He caught them in the alleys of Lombard Street and clutched them from the counting-houses of Cornhill.'[58] It remained only for these opinions to find their way into history books, and in 1874 John Richard Green duly obliged with a description in his *Short history of the English people* of the way in which Pitt had 'revolutionized the Upper House' by pouring into it members of the middle and commercial classes.[59]

We must be a little careful how we assess all this. Disraeli was writing as a novelist, while J. R. Green is not an historian noted for frigid accuracy. There is no reason whatever to believe that Pitt cherished any animosity towards the nobility as a class or wished to inaugurate profound political and social changes. The idiocy of those who award honours and the unworthiness of those who receive them has been a topic of great pleasure to the human race throughout history, and should not be regarded as uncontaminated evidence. There is, alas, no limit to envy and, even in our own lifetime, Sir Harold Wilson's honours list of 1976 provoked mirth.

A further reason for caution is that, at an early stage, the question of social mobility acquired a political dimension. Clarendon argued that the lavish provision of honours before 1640 was a major cause of the Civil War and though that explanation must, to modern historians, seem far too narrow, it remains true that much discussion in recent years has been in terms of a shift of power within the broad elite. Others took an opposite view, that social mobility encouraged stability. After the Glorious Revolution, defenders of the old order were apt to dwell upon the ease of promotion for men of real merit. This tendency became particularly noticeable as soon as the French Revolution had raised the very attractive slogan of the career open to talents. A correspondent of the *Gentleman's Magazine* for 1798 offered battle to 'the *enlightened* disciples of the infamous Tom Paine' and submitted a list of peers from 'moderate and some few in obscure situations' to demonstrate 'the proud pre-eminence of the British Government, where the highest honours are in reach of talents and honest industry'.[60] When Collingwood was raised to the peerage after the Battle of Trafalgar, Lord Eldon wrote that it would fall to his lot to welcome his fellow class-mate

---

[58] Book 1, Chapter 3.

[59] For the argument expressed at its most extreme, see Rosebery's *Pitt*, 276–7: 'His sympathies, his views, his policy were all with the middle classes . . . By a strange accident, he became the leader of the nobility. But he scorned them, and snubbed them, and flooded their blue blood with a plentiful adulteration of an inferior element.'

[60] 'Acis', in *Gentleman's Magazine*, LXVIII (II), 1035.

from Newcastle to a place 'to which neither of us could expect to be elevated': it was, he believed, a memorable instance 'of the blessings to be derived from the country of our birth and the constitution under which we live'.[61] These claims have been endorsed by many historians. Namier certainly exaggerated both the link between landed wealth and trade and between the gentry and nobility when he wrote of the 'social amalgamation' between nobility or the landed gentry and the big bourgeoisie.[62] Sir Anthony Wagner pushed the argument to its logical conclusion, suggesting that the 'absence of barriers between groups and classes' may have allowed great changes to take place 'with a minimum of violent upheaval'.[63]

A modern work of great merit which brings together these hints and nudges and weaves them into a major historical theme is Harold Perkin's *The origins of modern English society*. In Perkin's view, the rise of new men is 'the most distinctive feature of English history' and it is used to explain both political stability and economic expansion. This is elaborating a claim made in the early nineteenth century by Patrick Colquhoun and others that 'the rapid strides which this nation has made . . . towards wealth and power may fairly be imputed to the form of government'.[64]

The origins of modern English society is a book for which I have much respect and from which I have learned a great deal. It tackled an important theme and opened up large areas for discussion. I am not sure, however, that Perkin was always well served by his secondary authorities. In particular, he was inclined to exaggerate the differences between Hanoverian England and continental Europe.

One suggestion that we can dismiss fairly quickly without, I hope, being thought peremptory is that Hanoverian England was a classless society. Admittedly, Professor Perkin put it conditionally: 'if', he remarked, 'as one modern sociologist has put it, a classless society is one with a unified elite . . . then eighteenth-century England was a classless society'.[65] It seems to me that the modern sociologist in question was using words even more loosely than most modern sociologists. It is a self-evident proposition that a genuinely classless society will have a unified

---

[61] H. Twiss, *Life of Lord Chancellor Eldon*, II, 118; quoted J. Derry, 'Governing temperament under Pitt and Liverpool', in Cannon, ed., *The Whig ascendancy*, 145.

[62] *England in the age of the American Revolution*, 13.

[63] *Pedigree and progress: essays in the genealogical interpretation of history*, 115.

[64] Perkin, *Origins*, 57; Colquhoun, *Treatise on the wealth, power and resources of the British Empire in every quarter of the world*, first published 1814.

[65] Professor Perkin's reference is to Raymond Aron, 'Social structure and the ruling class', *British Journal of Sociology*, I (1950), 1–16.

elite, because it will have a unified everything, and perhaps a better way of putting it is that it would have no elite at all. But it does not follow that the reverse is true – that a society with a unified elite must necessarily be classless. The only meaning I can attach to the phrase 'classless society' is one where there is rough political, economic, social and educational parity between citizens. If it is being suggested that, because there were many fine gradations of rank in Hanoverian England, we cannot detect any significant political or economic differences between a Dorset ditcher in 1743 and Lord Chesterfield, then modern sociology is not particularly illuminating. To use the same term, 'a classless society', to embrace two concepts – a regime in which political and economic power is the preserve of a select group, from which the mass of citizens is excluded, *and* a regime in which political and economic power is diffused as widely as possible – is to stretch two words beyond mercy.

But Perkin's main thesis was that England was an 'open aristocracy', and that this was almost unique in eighteenth-century Europe: 'elsewhere the barriers between bourgeoisie and nobility were to all intents impenetrable . . . only in England was there an easy, continuous and accepted interchange between the two'. I would like, for the moment, to reserve judgement on this 'open aristocracy', especially when a few pages later it, almost by sleight of hand, turned into an 'open *dynamic* aristocracy', and was produced as part of the explanation of England's industrial revolution.[66]

In relation to the origins of the industrial revolution, Perkin's argument seems indistinct and rather extravagant. It is not easy to see how the elevation to the peerage of George Bubb Dodington, Spencer Compton, Horace Walpole, Sir Thomas Robinson, Henry Bromley, Lord Vere Beauclerk and Welbore Ellis contributed to that self-sustaining economic growth which, we are told, is the necessary precondition for industrial development, nor is it a formula which has been much employed by the developing countries in their own search for wealth and power. We are not, after all, dealing with the elevation of captains of industry, shipowners, forge-masters, textile manufacturers and the like but with persons who, for the most part, owed their peerages to years of tactful service at court, to sound voting in the House of Commons, or to the possession of borough interests. If the argument is that their elevation somehow cleared the way for others to rise from the ranks of the bourgeoisie into the gentry, we are moving from an area

[66] Perkin, *Origins*, 56, 61, 63.

which is at least to some extent quantifiable, to one which can hardly be so. Perkin pointed to the great rise of individual families into the gentry in the early seventeenth century, and added that 'the nobility was almost trebled to accommodate them'. This does not make it much easier to explain the industrial revolution. If vast peerage creations could have triggered it off, we should be looking for it in the 1630s and 1640s and George Villiers, Duke of Buckingham, may, by a strange metamorphosis, be the man we should hail as the founder of British industrial prowess. It would hardly be possible to find a period in modern British history, save for the reign of Elizabeth, when the rate of peerage creation was slower than the first three-quarters of the eighteenth century, yet, contrariwise, this was followed by an industrial revolution. If the argument is recast to point to the comparative ease with which the humble climbed into the ranks of the bourgeoisie, it seems much more plausible, but has little to do with an 'open aristocracy'.

The impression of recent and lowly origins, on which much of Perkin's argument depended, is substantially modified if we investigate peerage creations in rather more detail. Let us first examine the position in 1700. We have seen that, of the 163 peers, sixty-three held titles which were less than twenty years old. This seems a very vigorous blood transfusion. But of the sixty-three, twenty-eight were merely promotions to a higher rank and a further three had been called up in their fathers' baronies. Five more were foreign nobility – Schomberg, son of the Huguenot general who left France after the Revocation of the Edict of Nantes, and four Dutchmen, Albemarle, Grantham, Portland and Rochford. Five more were sons of peers and nine more were grandsons of peers. Lord Willoughby de Parham was granted succession to his cousin in 1680 and is only technically a new creation. This reduces our list to twelve. Perhaps these are the industrial entrepreneurs we are looking for? Dover was the brother of a peer and Herbert the nephew of a peer. Waldegrave had very sensibly married an illegitimate daughter of James II; Derwentwater's son was married to an illegitimate daughter of Charles II; John Churchill, though he had other claims to fame, had a sister Arabella who had been mistress to James II and was the mother of James, Duke of Berwick. This leaves seven good men and true. Christopher Vane created Lord Barnard in 1698 was the son of Sir Henry Vane, the famous regicide, of Raby Castle, Durham, and was married to the daughter of the Duke of Newcastle; George Legge, created Lord Dartmouth, had ancestors in the Irish peerage. Godolphin and Haversham were two political peerages: Godolphin was the son of a knight and his mother was the daughter of a knight; Haversham was married to the daughter of an earl. Lord Stawell, created in 1683, was the son of a Knight of the Bath, the great-grandson of a peer and his mother was the daughter of a knight. There are only two left on which to base our industrial revolution – Somers and Jeffreys – who turn out, inevitably, to be lawyers. Somers was the son of an attorney from Worcestershire; Jeffreys, of Bloody Assizes fame, was the grandson of a knight. What is going on is not so much replenishment as re-cycling. We are dealing with a stage army.

The need for caution is again borne out by an analysis of the peers alive on 1 January 1800, at a time when, as we have seen, there was public criticism of the vulgar antecedents of their lordships. Of the grand total of 257 peers, 113 held peerages which had been granted since 1780. This is spectacular. But twenty-five of these were promotions within the ranks of the English peerage itself, the original title having been held since before 1780.[67] A further seven were promotions from the Scottish peerage.[68] Seventeen were promotions from the Irish peerage, the Irish title having been granted before 1780.[69] Two more new peers had been called up in their father's baronies.[70] Of the remaining sixty-two creations, fifty-five were persons who already had connections with nobility.[71] The significant question is how many of the 113 creations

[67] Abergavenny, Amherst, Bath, Beaulieu, Beverley, Buckingham, Bute, Camden, Digby, Dinevor, Dorchester, Fortescue, Grosvenor, Hertford, Lansdowne, Leicester, Mount Edgecumbe, Mansfield, Montagu, Salisbury, Stafford, Talbot, Townshend, Uxbridge and Warrington. Four of these, viz. Amherst, Dinevor, Mansfield and Montagu, were not technically promotions: the new rank was the same as the old, but a special remainder permitted the peerage to continue in another line. Warrington was an adjustment more than a promotion: he had been Earl of Stamford but upon inheriting large Cheshire estates, asked for and received the more appropriate title of Earl of Warrington. Montagu went down in rank from Duke to Baron, with a special remainder.

[68] Douglas of Lochleven, Douglas of Amesbury, Hamilton, Norwich, Stewart of Garlies, Strange and Stuart of Castle Stuart.

[69] Brodrick, Bulkeley, Carleton, Clive, Dawnay, Fife, Fisherwick, Gage of Firle, Lyttelton, Macartney, Mulgrave, Rawdon, Saltersford, Tyrone, Upper Ossory, Verulam and Wellesley. Gage of Firle had been granted an English barony in 1780 and was given another barony in 1790 as Gage of High Meadow with special remainder to his nephew.

[70] Robert Hobart, son of the Earl of Buckinghamshire, was called up in 1798 in his father's barony of Hobart; and George Granville Leveson-Gower, son of the Marquis of Stafford, was called up in his father's barony of Gower the following year.

[71] Auckland, Bagot, Bayning, Berwick, Bolton, Boringdon, Bradford, Bridport, Brudenell, Calthorpe, Camelford, Camperdown, Carteret, Cawdor, Curzon, Delaval, Dorchester, Douglas of Douglas, Drummond, Dundas, Eliot, Fitzgibbon, Glastonbury, Grenville, Grey de Wilton, Gwydir, Harewood, Hawkesbury, Heathfield, Hood, Howard de Walden, Lilford, Lonsdale, Loughborough, Mackenzie of Kintail, Malmesbury, Mendip, Minto, Nelson, Newark, Northwick, Porchester, Ribblesdale, Rodney, Rolle, Rous, Sackville, Selsey, Sherborne, Somers, Southampton, Suffield, Sydney, Walsingham, Wodehouse of Kimberley.

were of persons who apparently had no previous connection with the peerage, and the answer is seven.[72] These seven repay further attention. Four of them were lawyers – Ashburton, Eldon, Grantley and Kenyon: the years of preliminary legal study were not attractive to most aristocratic young men, yet the need for specialist legal advice and support in the House of Lords made governments eager to encourage and promote legal talent.[73] The remaining three persons, though without direct peerage connections, were nevertheless men of substantial property and position. Sir Francis Basset, ennobled in 1796 as Baron de Dunstanville, came from a distinguished Cornish family. He, his father and grandfather had all been MPs; his wife was heiress to a Somerset estate and his brother-in-law had been an MP; his mother was both daughter and sister of an MP and baronet. Though there were no very close peerage connections, he was related to the Herberts, Earls of Pembroke, and there were other family connections with the Clanricardes, the Lansdownes and the Whartons. James Boswell, who visited Basset in 1792, remarked on the 'large and splendid' house at Tehidy, adding that Basset had had 'three grand-uncles killed in battle for Charles I'.[74] Though Basset's antique title attracted some sarcasm, he was far from being an upstart. Nor was

Of the above, thirteen were grandsons of peers, six were nephews of peers, six married daughters of peers, six married granddaughters of peers, three were sons of peers, two were brothers of peers and two were great-grandsons of peers. The remainder fall into various categories, the chief being relations by marriage.

[72] Ashburton, Basset, Carrington, Eldon, Grantley, Kenyon and Yarborough.

[73] John Dunning (Ashburton) was the son of a Devon attorney and married in 1780 into the banking family of Baring. John Scott (Eldon) had probably the most humble origins of the seven, being the son of a prosperous Newcastle hostman or coal-fitter: he had the common sense to elope at the age of twenty-one with the heiress of a banker, the celebrated Bessy Surtees. We should not however exaggerate the lowliness of Eldon's origins, since H. Twiss says that Eldon's father left his sons between £24,000 and £25,000 (*Life of Lord Chancellor Eldon*, I, 102). Fletcher Norton (Grantley) was of Yorkshire gentry: his ancestors had suffered in Tudor times as recusants and rebels, but one had been sheriff of the county (1568/9) and had married the daughter of Lord Latimer; through his marriage in 1741 to Grace, daughter of Sir William Chapple, Fletcher Norton acquired a connection with the Pitts, Earls of Londonderry. Kenyon was of gentry stock.

It may appear surprising that none of the seven were naval officers, since the navy was always regarded as much more free from aristocratic influence than the army. There were, of course, many naval officers ennobled for their services, including Anson, Bridport, Camperdown, Hawke, Hood, Nelson, Rodney and St Vincent. But, on investigation, each of them had peerage connections that could scarcely have failed to further his career. Nelson was great-great-nephew of Sir Robert Walpole, 1st Earl of Orford (and a fellow Norfolkman); Alexander Hood's marriage in 1761 connected him with the peerage families of Chatham, Lyttelton, Londonderry and Camelford; St Vincent (Jervis) was related to the Macclesfields through both his wife and his mother, and other Macclesfield family connections included Anson and Lord Heathfield; Hawke was related to the Lords Blaney (Irish peers) and Duncan (Camperdown) to the Earls of Thanet.

[74] *The House of Commons, 1754–90*, ed. L. B. Namier and J. Brooke, II, 62–4.

Charles Anderson-Pelham, created Lord Yarborough in 1794. Reputed be one of the richest commoners in England, he had served twenty-six years in Parliament; his wife was the daughter of an MP, who was himself the grandson of a French marquis. Through his mother, Anderson-Pelham was related to the Barons Poulet. This leaves Robert Smith, Lord Carrington, as the remaining example of a 'self-made' man.

The case of Lord Carrington should be looked at in a little more detail, since, as we have seen, his elevation to the peerage was much commented on at the time and has been frequently cited by historians since. The pedigree by J. H. Round observes that the family was entirely of plebeian origins.[75] This can mean a variety of things. Smith was himself a wealthy banker, partner in Smith, Payne and Co. But the emergence of the Smith family was neither sudden nor recent. His great-grandfather's elder brother had been sheriff of Leicestershire in 1718. His grandfather had built up an important electoral interest in Nottingham by 1747 and his father sat as an MP from 1774 until his death in 1788. Robert Smith's elder brother represented Nottingham from 1778–9 and, on his early death, Robert Smith held the seat, keeping it until his elevation to the British peerage in 1797. Another brother, Samuel, was an MP from 1778 until 1832 consecutively. Robert Smith's uncle, Sir George Smith, had been awarded a baronetcy in 1757, and in 1747 had married into the family of the Howes, Irish peers and among the largest landowners in Nottinghamshire; his wife was cousin and ward to Lady Pembroke, who managed the Howe electoral interest at Nottingham in the 1740s. The son of that marriage married in 1778 the niece of Lord Scarsdale, daughter of the future Lord Curzon. The supreme example in the eighteenth century of a *nouveau riche* peer turns out to be remarkably well connected.[76] The eyebrows raised at his elevation suggest not a new class entering the peerage, but the extreme fastidiousness which still prevailed.

This analysis of the new creations from 1780 to 1800 indicates that there is no reason to believe that they were significantly different in social origins from those of previous decades. It is true that there was a considerable increase but it must be doubtful whether this did more than keep up with the increase in the total population in the period. It remains remarkably difficult to find new peers who had not already some connection with the nobility.

[75] *Peerage and pedigree*, II, 213–20.
[76] For an analysis of Pitt's creations as a whole, reaching similar conclusions, see Gerda C. Richards, 'The creation of peers recommended by the younger Pitt', *American Historical Review*, XXXIV (1928/9), 47–54.

An analysis of the whole of the eighteenth century confirms the position just described. The grand total of peerage creations was 229.[77] Of these no fewer than 206 had previous peerage connections and only twenty-three were without them. The peerage connections of the 206 are as follows:

Sons of peers	40
Grandsons of peers	26
Transferred from Irish peerage	29
Married to daughters of peers	23
Nephews of peers	15
Transferred from Scottish peerage	12
Great-grandsons of peer	9
Cousins of peers	6
Brothers-in-law of peers	6
Married to granddaughters of peers	6
Brothers-in-law to daughters of peers	5
Great-nephews of peers	3
Great-great-grandsons of peers	2
Great-great-nephew of peer	1
Brothers of peers	3
Grandson of foreign nobleman	1
Miscellaneous	19

The small number of twenty-three non-peerage creations must, of course, cast doubt on how 'open' the English peerage really was and how easy it was for persons from other orders of society to infiltrate.[78] Eleven of the twenty-three were lawyers.[79] A twelfth, Nathaniel Ryder, was given a barony in 1776 as Lord Harrowby in part because his father, Sir Dudley Ryder, a former Attorney-General and Lord Chief Justice of King's Bench, had been granted a peerage in 1756 but had died before he could kiss hands for it. Of the remaining eleven, Cadogan and Ligonier

---

[77] This figure excludes promotions within the English peerage and new grants with special remainders (such as the Duke of Newcastle's fresh grant of a dukedom in 1756 so that his nephew could inherit) since the recipients were already peers. It should be noted that this calculation is not strictly comparable with the one above since the basis of calculation is different.

[78] The twenty-three in chronological order were as follows: Cowper, Bathurst, Cadogan, Macclesfield, Onslow, Oxford, Romney, King, Raymond, Talbot, Bath, Montfort, Grantham, Ligonier, Harrowby, Thurlow, Ashburton, Grantley, Kenyon, Basset, Eldon, Yarborough, Carrington.

[79] Cowper, Bathurst, Macclesfield, King, Raymond, Talbot, Thurlow, Ashburton, Grantley, Kenyon and Eldon.

were rewarded for outstanding military services.[80] Oxford and Bath were politicians of the first rank. Onslow and Grantham appear to have been given peerages as part of a reshuffle of offices.[81] Romney and Montfort are said to have bought their peerages.[82] The remaining three peers, Basset, Yarborough and Carrington, have been discussed above.

It may be wise to repeat the warning given earlier that although these twenty-three men are classified as not having peerage connections, it by no means follows that they were without substantial property, influential relatives and powerful friends. A few examples must suffice. Sir Robert Marsham, 1st Baron Romney, though descended from a London alderman, was a baronet and an MP; his father and grandfather had both been baronets, and he was related through his uncle Sir John Marsham to the Earls of Downe. Sir Richard Onslow was an MP, baronet and had been Speaker of the House of Commons; his father had been a baronet and his mother's father was a baronet; his father and two uncles had been MPs and his grandfather had been a member of Cromwell's House of Lords; an ancestor, Richard Onslow, had been Speaker of the House of Commons from 1566–7. The 1st Lord Bathurst's father was a knight, an MP and had been Governor of both the Royal Africa Company and the East India Company; Bathurst's mother was the daughter of a knight and an uncle was dean of Wells and president of Trinity College, Oxford. Robert Harley's family in Herefordshire went back at least to an early fourteenth-century knight, Robert de Harley; his father had been a Knight of the Bath; through his grandfather Sir Robert Harley's wife Brilliana there was a connection with the de Veres, Earls of Oxford; the family was wealthy enough to have suffered very heavy losses on behalf of the parliamentary cause during the Civil War.[83]

Though peers of non-aristocratic origin are hard to find at any time in the eighteenth century, there is some evidence to suggest that there were more of them in earlier decades than in Pitt's period. Table 2 gives peers of non-aristocratic origin as a proportion of total creations, by decades.

[80] Cadogan's barony followed his success in dealing with the Jacobite rising of 1715 but he was also a political ally of the Duke of Marlborough; Ligonier was of French origins and his mother and father were of noble rank.

[81] Onslow lost the Chancellorship of the Exchequer in 1715 and Sir Thomas Robinson lost the Mastership of the Great Wardrobe in 1761.

[82] Sir Robert Marsham was said to have paid £5,000 for the barony of Romney in 1716 and Henry Bromley was reported to have paid the Countess of Yarmouth (George II's mistress) for her help in 1741 in acquiring the barony of Montfort.

[83] The Herefordshire losses in 1646 were put at £13,000. See A. MacInnes, *Robert Harley, Puritan politician*.

Table 2. *Peers of non-aristocratic origins as a percentage of total creations*

Decade	Total creations	No. of non-DPCs[a]	Percentage of non-DPCs to total
1700–09	12	1	8.3
1710–19	38	6	15.7
1720–29	16	1	6.25
1730–39	6	2	33.3
1740–49	18	2	11.1
1750–59	8	—	—
1760–69	24	2	8.3
1770–79	13	2	15.3
1780–89	40	3	7.5
1790–99	54	4	7.4
Total	229	23	10.04

The evidence is perhaps clearer if presented in twenty-year periods:

1700–19	50	7	14.0
1720–39	22	3	13.6
1740–59	26	2	7.6
1760–79	37	4	10.8
1780–99	94	7	7.4

[a] By 'non-DPCs' is meant peers without previous direct peerage connections.

This demonstrates not only the rather sparing creation of peerages in general during the middle years of the century but that it seems to have been most difficult then for an aspirant without strong peerage connections to gain his objective. As in many other fields, the time of closest oligarchy appears to be in the later years of George II's reign. But it also suggests that the last twenty years, far from being a time when men of modest birth were penetrating the peerage, was still very austere in its attitude. The comparatively high number of creations of peers without previous connections in the decade 1710–19 is probably less concerned with the financial and commercial developments of that period than with the intensity of party warfare and, in particular, the struggle for control of the House of Lords.

A recent article by Professor McCahill, while accepting that there was o significant change in the social origins of Pitt's peers, draws attention other aspects which are in danger of being overlooked.[84] First, he ointed out that there was a great increase in the number of Scots and rish being given peerages and that the effect was to begin creating, for the first time, a unified British peerage. There is certainly much truth in his suggestion, though it came about less as a matter of policy than as the mechanical result of other decisions.

As far as the Scots were concerned, their position was much affected y a series of decisions subsequent to the Act of Union of 1707.[85] First it vas resolved in 1709 that Scottish peers holding British titles could not ote in the election of the Scottish representative peers. Subsequently, in 711, it was resolved by the House of Lords that they were not eligible to it in that House. Consequently, for most of the eighteenth century, cottish peers with British titles could neither vote nor take their seats: nglish peers with Scottish titles, on the other hand, possessed both rivileges. A state of affairs so mortifying to the Scottish peers was bound be questioned but a revolt in 1712 collapsed and the anomaly was not ectified until 1782, when the 8th Duke of Hamilton successfully ppealed against the ruling. In the intervening seventy years, govern-ents achieved some slight modification of the position by giving British peerages to a few eldest sons of Scottish peers: hence the Earl of innoull's heir, Lord Dupplin, was given a British barony of Hay in December 1711.[86] The decision in favour of Hamilton, reversing the revious position, had two immediate results. It depressed the reputation f the sixteen Scottish representative peers and, at the next general lection in 1784, there was some reluctance to stand.[87] Second, it led to a rowing demand for British peerages from Scots, whether they held cottish peerages or not. Between 1782 and 1800, seven more Scottish

M. W. McCahill, 'Peerage creations and the changing character of the British nobility, 1750–1830', *English Historical Review*, XCVI (1981), 259–84.

See G. S. Holmes, 'The Hamilton affair of 1711–12', *English Historical Review*, LXXVII (1962), 257–282.

Two more heirs to Scottish dukedoms of Montrose and Roxburgh were given peerages in 1722 as Earls Graham and Kerr, and in 1776 the heirs to the earldoms of Marchmont and Bute were given baronies as Hume and Cardiff respectively. The Duke of Argyll's son was given a barony in 1766 as Lord Sundridge, but the Campbells had held an English peerage as Earls of Greenwich since 1705, before the Act of Union.

See M. W. McCahill, 'The Scottish peerage and the House of Lords in the late eighteenth century', *Scottish Historical Review*, 51 (1972), 177.

peers were given British titles, and a further nine Scottish commoners were elevated.[88]

The Act of Union with Ireland in 1801 also had a marked effect upon the number of Irishmen given British peerages. First, the political manoeuvring needed to steer the Act of Union through Parliament resulted in the promise of British peerages to several influential Irish politicians;[89] second, the closing of the independent Irish peerage meant that candidates for ennoblement could aspire only to the British peerage. Decades of fobbing off claimants with an Irish peerage came to an end. Henceforth, Clive's successors as military heroes and Sir Sampson Gideon's as persons of dubious origins would have to go straight to Westminster. A further factor in the promotion of Scots and Irish was the prolonged period of warfare, in which many distinguished themselves at sea or on the field of battle.

The time has now come to consider some reservations and objections to the general argument which has been advanced.

The first is methodological. The reader may be uneasy at the category of 'peerage connections' and complain that the inclusion of great-grandsons and great-nephews of peers will overload the category, is unreasonably tenuous, and distorts the findings in favour of noble exclusiveness. Of course one reaches a point when 'connections' become too remote to be regarded as relevant and, in the last analysis, this must be a matter for editorial judgement. But it should be remembered that we are dealing with a century in which patronage and influence counted for a vast amount, even at humble levels. Very distant relationships were pressed into service, as every wealthy peer knew to his cost. Family pride was such that members were usually well aware of distinguished connections, particularly when there was the prospect that they might be turned to advantage. Let us give an example. Charles Talbot, a lawyer, was created Lord Talbot in 1733. Though he was related to the Talbots, Dukes of Shrewsbury, I have not classified him as a peerage connection since the common ancestor was as far back as the time of Henry VIII.[90] In this case, my judgement has been austere. Nevertheless, in practice, even

---

[88] Queensbury, Gordon, Abercorn, Atholl, Galloway, Moray and Morton were given British peerages as Douglas of Amesbury, Norwich, Hamilton, Strange, Stewart of Garlies, Stuart of Castle Stuart and Douglas of Lochleven respectively. Another Scot, James Duff, who held an Irish peerage, was given a British barony of Fife. Two other Scots, who would have been Scottish peers but for attainders, were given British baronies as Perth and Seaforth. Six new creations were Lord Heathfield, Dundas, Douglas of Douglas, Cawdor, Camperdown and Minto.

[89] Carysfort, Drogheda, Ely, Ormonde.

[90] G. E. Cockayne, *The Complete Peerage* (subsequently referred to as *GEC*), XI, 731.

that tenuous relationship was of importance. The 1st Duke of Shrewsbury corresponded with his kinsman, Charles Talbot's father, who
became bishop of Oxford.[91] Bishop Talbot's first preferment – often the
most critical of all – was to a living in Berkshire in the gift of the Duke of
Shrewsbury.[92]

Similarly, the category 'miscellaneous' which I have employed may
appear peculiarly unconvincing and the last refuge of a harassed
historian. It does not, however, imply a very remote relationship, but a
network of relationships too complicated to be easily categorised. Let me
take, this time, some examples from the Irish peerage, which I want to
discuss a little later. Thomas Pakenham, created 1st Baron Longford in
1756, was married to the great-great-niece of the last Earl of Longford,
who died in 1704. The modern reader might be forgiven if, with some
impatience, he protested that this was too remote to be of any
consequence at all. On the contrary, it obtained Longford his peerage in
1756 and later, in 1785, one for his wife also: on the latter occasion, her
son pointed out to the king that she was the direct descendant of the last
earl.[93] Sir John Brownlow, raised to the peerage as Viscount Tyrconnel in
1718, is classed as 'miscellaneous', but there is little doubt that he moved
in aristocratic circles. His first wife, who was also his cousin, had one sister
Jane married to the Duke of Ancaster, another Elizabeth married to the
Earl of Exeter, and a third Alice married to Lord Guilford. Another
'miscellaneous' is Charles Bingham, created Baron Lucan in 1776. He
was the great-great-grandson of Charles II by his mistress, Lucy Walters.
On his mother's side he was related to the Earls of Clancarty and
Clanricarde, and to the Sarsfields, Jacobite Earls of Lucan. His mother's
first cousin was created Lord Dartrey in 1770 and advanced to Viscount
Cremorne in 1785. Dartrey's first wife was a daughter of the Earl of
Pomfret. Bingham's aunt by marriage was the sister of the 1st Baron
Knapton, who had married a granddaughter of the 6th Earl of Abercorn
in the Scottish peerage, and whose son was promoted Viscount de Vesci
in 1776. Finally, through his paternal grandfather, Bingham had
connections with the Pakenhams and the Longford peerage.

A different objection might be, particularly in the light of comments
on the absurdity of the Irish peerage, that it was there that men of humble
and modest antecedents might expect to be pulled in. We have already
had some unkind and sarcastic references to the Irish peerage and I do not

[91] T. C. Nicholson, and A. S. Turberville, *Charles Talbot, Duke of Shrewsbury*, 154–6, 204.
[92] *Dictionary of National Biography, sub* William Talbot.
[93] *The correspondence of King George III*, ed. J. W. Fortescue, v, No. 3272.

wish to embarrass my hosts by multiplying them unduly. Wraxall has an offensive story that when Sir Richard Philipps was refused permission in 1776 to make a carriage-way through St James's Park to his front door, he was offered an Irish peerage by Lord North instead, to soften the blow.[94] But, difficult though it is to credit, the Irish were not popular in eighteenth-century England, and we must not believe all we are told about them. It is certainly true that, in the scale of charges said to have been understood in George II's reign, an Irish peerage came substantially cheaper. There were examples of the creation of persons from non-aristocratic backgrounds: the promotion in the same year of Sir Sampson Gideon, whose father had been a practising Jew, and Nicholas Lawless, who had been engaged in woollen manufacture, caused considerable comment.[95] Another exhaustive analysis of origins would probably, at this stage, be more than unwelcome. Suffice it to say that of the 198 persons created Irish peers in the course of the century, at least 160 already had peerage connections. The 160 are classified as follows:

Married to daughters of peers	33
Grandsons of peers	28
Sons of peers	12
Brothers-in-law to peers	12
Nephews of peers	10
Brothers of peers	7
Married to granddaughters of peers	7
Great-grandsons of peers	7
Cousins of peers	6
Married to great-granddaughters of peers	3
Great-nephew of peer	1
Great-great-nephew of peer	1
Great-great-grandson of peer	1
Married to peeress	1
Already an English peer	1
Miscellaneous	30

---

94 N. W. Wraxall, *The historical and posthumous memoirs, 1772–84*, ed. H. B. Wheatley, 1, 67–8. He was created Baron Milford.
95 In 1789. Gideon's father was a government financier and Gideon himself was given a baronetcy at the age of thirteen. He subsequently sat for Cambridgeshire. Wraxall described him as one of the richest but also most benevolent men of the time. He married a daughter of Sir John Eardley Wilmot, Chief Justice of Common Pleas, changed his name to Eardley, and took the title, Baron Eardley. Lawless became Lord Cloncurry.

Of the thirty-eight persons not closely connected to the aristocracy, eleven were lawyers or had a legal background;[96] three were army officers and one a naval officer;[97] three had been in the employ of the East India Company;[98] three had been diplomats;[99] the remaining seventeen include Cloncurry, Eardley and Carrington (see pp. 23, 30 above), Carbery was said to have been ennobled by George I on account of his remarkable looks, and several were ennobled for general political services.[100]

Finally, we should look again at the possibility that there was a much wider 'open aristocracy', consisting of both peerage and gentry, into which new families were being recruited in considerable numbers. Our first difficulty is that this is not quantifiable in the way that the peerage is. It is possible, however, to make some estimate of the 'titular aristocracy', more often known as the social elite, and, although this will by no means represent the total numbers in the 'open aristocracy', it might bear a constant relationship. To the English and Irish peers already discussed, we would add the Scottish peers. Since there were no creations in the Scottish peerage after the Act of Union, the numbers declined steadily, from 135 in 1700, to eighty-six in 1750, and to sixty-eight by the end of the century. We should also include the baronets of all three kingdoms: my calculation suggests that the total declined from about 860 in 1700 to 621 by 1770. A third, and more questionable, component of the social elite is the category of knights. Though the figures are tedious to calculate, there is no doubt that there was a very marked decline in total

[96] Sunderlin was registered at the Inns of Court but I do not know whether he ever practised as a barrister; Bantry's fortune came to him through his grandfather, a highly successful lawyer. The other nine lawyers were Avonmore, Barrington, Bowes, Carleton, Jocelyn, Kilwarden, Lifford, Midleton and Tracton.
[97] Blakeney, Sheffield, Tyrawley, Shuldham.
[98] Caledon, Pigot, Teighmouth.
[99] St Helens; Whitworth; Sydney had been minister at the Danish court from 1763 to 1765 and received his peerage in 1768.
[100] The seventeen were: Blundell, Carbery, Carrington, Clonbrock, Cloncurry, Conynham, Eardley, Farnham, Fermanagh, Ferrard, Headley, Longueville, Micklethwaite, Ongley, Rancliffe, Russborough and Waltham. As with the English peerage, membership of the House of Commons, either at Westminster or Dublin, seems to have been of considerable assistance. Of the thirty-eight non-DPCs, only six had not served as MPs (Tyrawley and Shuldham were military men, Whitworth and St Helens were diplomats; Teighmouth had spent nearly thirty years abroad on the service of the East India Company and Bantry was ennobled in 1797 for his part in resisting the French invasion). Of the remaining thirty-two, two were both English and Irish MPs, thirteen were English and seventeen were Irish.

Table 3. *The composition of the social elite*

	1700	1710	1720	1730	1740	1750	1760	1770	1780	1790	1800
English peers	173	167	190	189	183	187	181	197	189	220	267
Irish peers	88	90	96	103	100	102	118	129	145	155	169
Scottish peers	135	134	109	106	100	86	82	81	78	75	68
Baronets	860	839	809	735	711	651	624	621	635	659	699
Knights	290	180	180	150	70	70	70	110	90	130	160
Total	1,546	1,410	1,384	1,283	1,164	1,096	1,075	1,138	1,137	1,239	1,363

numbers from the seventeenth century to the mid-eighteenth century (see Table 3).[101]

There is little evidence here to suggest that the social elite was expanding vigorously in the eighteenth century and finding room for large numbers of newcomers. On the contrary, it indicates a considerable narrowing of the commanding social heights. Even the modest expansion towards the end of the century in no way kept up with the rapid increase of population.[102] This does not make it any easier to explain the industrial revolution and Professor Kenyon's paradox remains intact. But it suggests that assertions of the uniquely liberal character of eighteenth-century English society should be treated with some reserve.

[101] The numbers are not absolute since, to avoid double counting, duplicates have been omitted – i.e. baronets who are also peers are included as peers only. The figures for knights are an approximation, derived from W. A. Shaw, *The knights of England*, 2 vols. The great decrease in the number of knights and the change in their status makes it peculiarly difficult to compare the social elite of the seventeenth century with that of the eighteenth. Whereas the House of Commons in 1661 contained ninety-eight knights, that of 1761 contained only fifteen. In 1661 there were eighty-eight baronets in the House; in 1761, sixty-two. (I have excluded Scottish seats in 1761 to make a comparison with 1661 possible.) In the eighteenth century knighthoods were given mainly to lawyers, sheriffs, Lord Mayors and admirals.

[102] The population of the British Isles is given in P. Deane and W. A. Cole, *British economic growth, 1688–1959* (2nd edition), 6 as follows:

1701	9.4 millions
1751	10.5 millions
1801	15.9 millions

As a proportion of the total population, the social elite declined from 0.000164% in 1701 to 0.000104% in 1751 and 0.0000857% in 1801.

2

EDUCATION AND RELIGION

Within the confines of this study, it is hardly possible to treat either
education or religion in other than a mechanistic fashion. We are less
concerned with the strictly pedagogic achievement of eighteenth-
century education than with its contribution to aristocratic hegemony.
In the same way, I do not comment on the quality of religious experience
among the upper classes but confine myself to the public and political
role of religion. The reader should therefore bear in mind that there is a
vital element – perhaps the vital element – missing from the discussion.

In the support the education of the English upper classes gave to their
political supremacy, we may identify four aspects. First, their education
was intended to fit them for their leading role in society and for their
responsibilities in government. One of the arguments which eventually
carried the day in favour of a public school rather than a private
education was the claim that it was a more appropriate preparation for
that public life which was the destiny and duty of the upper classes.
Neither the election hustings nor the eighteenth-century House of
Commons was a place for faint hearts. Second, the increasingly
standardised education encouraged a common attitude and a common
sense of purpose. At Eton, Westminster and Winchester, boys read
almost exclusively in Latin authors and when they proceeded to
university often did little more than read them again. This overwhelmingly classical curriculum was deplored by advanced thinkers. But many
members of the upper classes drew from it not only vast personal
pleasure, but also a pervasive code of values. Chief of these was the duty
of service and a conviction of the rightness of patrician rule. Classicism
shaped the context of their lives intellectually and physically. They
adorned their houses with pilasters and porticoes, they filled their rooms
with urns and busts and their gardens with temples, statues and satyrs.
Their minds were stocked with classical images and examples. When
they needed pseudonyms for a newspaper controversy, they described

34

themselves without embarrassment as Cato, Tribune, Lucius or Atticus: when Henry Sampson Woodfall and the author of *The Letters of Junius* wished to correspond through the *Public Advertiser* by means of a secret code, they hit upon Latin tags. The virtues they admired were the classical virtues of order, symmetry, balance and restraint and their favourite author was Horace, advocating moderation, detachment and love of the countryside. In Polybius they read that a balanced and mixed constitution – just such a one as Britain had had since the Glorious Revolution – was a formula for stability, and within that formula the nobility was allotted the crucial balancing role. By Aristotle they were assured that 'the more nobly born are more fully citizens than the non-noble, good birth being held in esteem in every country; and the off-spring of the better sort are likely to be better men, for good birth is excellence of stock'. People do not often challenge assumptions which are so flattering and convenient to themselves.[1] Third, their stay at school and university created a network of acquaintance which reinforced close family ties. For most of the eighteenth century there were no more than a hundred or so peers of much influence and though they competed with each other with gusto and often hated each other unashamedly, they did so within the confines of a common inheritance and a common interest. The dreadful events of the 1640s were a constant warning what could happen if the upper classes split, and though party animosities still ran deep, they rarely threatened the survival of the regime. The French might believe in 1784 that the English were on the verge of civil war and revolution, but nobody else did. Lastly, the virtual monopoly of higher education which the upper classes possessed – and safeguarded – gave apparent validity to their rule. To the claims of blue blood, they could add superior education: it was, in the eighteenth century, a formidable combination. They were right to mistrust Dissenting Academies as threats to their position, and their determination to exclude Dissenters from Oxford and Cambridge suggests a recognition of the important part which educational privilege played in maintaining aristocratic supremacy.

---

[1] *Politics*, III, 13. The best introductions to the classical influence are R. R. Bolgar, *The classical heritage and its beneficiaries* (1954) and R. M. Ogilvie, *Latin and Greek: A history of the influence of the classics on English life from 1600 to 1918* (1964). The latter is particularly related to the theme of this chapter, though, in my view, the author was persuaded by reliance on Christopher Hill (which is acknowledged) to predate the political supremacy of the middle classes. This creates some difficulty in explaining why a commercial and financial elite should be wedded to a classical education which seems scarcely appropriate to their needs. Professor Ogilvie's views on the dominance of a classical curriculum in the eighteenth century fit more naturally into my own explanation of the aristocratic character of that period.

The education of the lower orders is outside my terms of reference, though it has a direct bearing on political relationships. It would be foolish to deny that many noblemen, and particularly their widows, founded small schools on their estates. However, the scale was limited, the education fairly rudimentary, and the supervision strict. At the school founded by Anne, Countess of Salisbury, the girls of Hatfield were taught knitting, sewing and the catechism, while parents were warned that if they took their daughters away without the Countess's approbation, neither themselves nor their offspring would 'for the future partake of her Ladyship's bounty in any kind whatsoever'.[2] In a tiny market town, nestling at the gates of the great estate, that was no idle threat. Other noblemen must have shared the views of Soame Jenyns, who anticipated Oscar Wilde's Lady Bracknell: 'Ignorance is a cordial administered by the gracious hand of Providence; of which [the poor] ought never to be deprived by an ill-judged and improper education.'[3] When, in the 1790s, the upper classes discovered that humble people were reading Tom Paine in large numbers, they were right to be alarmed.

Jonathan Swift, writing in 1728, was sceptical of the education given to aristocratic youths:

From frequently reflecting upon the course and method of educating Youth in this and a neighbouring kingdom . . . I am come to this determination, that Education is always the worse in proportion to the wealth of and grandeur of the parents; nor do I doubt in the least, that if the whole world were now under the dominion of one monarch . . . the only son and heir of that monarch would be the worst educated mortal that ever was born since the creation.[4]

One cannot test such an opinion and Swift was, after all, offering captious irony rather than a solemn estimate. But it may be doubted. Most eighteenth-century commentators attached great importance to education. 'Of all the men we meet with', wrote Locke, 'nine parts out of ten are what they are, good or evil, useful or not, by their education. 'Tis that which makes the great difference in Mankind.'[5] Locke's concept of the mind, at birth, as a *tabula rasa* necessarily gave decisive significance to the role of the teacher and, if anything, eighteenth-

[2] Lord David Cecil, *The Cecils of Hatfield House*, 183.
[3] *Free enquiry into the nature and origin of Evil* (1757), 34.
[4] *An essay on modern education*. A convenient text is *Satires and personal writings*, ed. W. A. Eddy (reprinted 1951), 75.   [5] *Some thoughts concerning education*, Par. 1.

century thinkers tended to exaggerate the importance of education.[6]

Aristocratic parents, in particular, were unlikely to be negligent in such matters. Most of them were well aware of the responsibilities their heirs would face and the hazards that would surround them. They did not have to look far for examples of the damage that could be done to a family inheritance by a feckless and spendthrift young man. The heir to a great estate, employing hundreds of servants and tradesmen and on whom dozens of tenants might depend, had heavy duties, regardless of any he might choose to accept in the service of his country. Heirs were not often unencumbered with good advice, and though the son and godson of Lord Chesterfield may have been unlucky in the minuteness of their instruction, they were by no means exceptional.

Throughout much of the century there was a running debate between the advocates of a private and a public education.[7] Locke himself, a respected authority, had no doubt on the subject. He had spent six years at Westminster school during the regime of the redoubtable Dr Busby, and at a time when the headmaster's ferocity was untempered by age. He does not appear to have enjoyed it. To the argument that a public school was a better preparation for life, he retorted: 'how any one's being put into a mixed herd of unruly boys . . . fits him for civil conversation or business, I do not see'. The harshness of pedagogic discipline and the brutality of many of the boys made him despair for the character of anyone exposed to them: 'you have a strange value for words . . . to hazard your son's innocence and virtue for a little Greek and Latin . . . The faults of a private education [are] infinitely to be preferred.' His terse advice was: 'spare no care nor cost' to get a good tutor.[8]

Locke's view had strong support. Richard Steele drew a terrifying portrait of one of Eton's flogging headmasters: 'so very dreadful had he made himself to me that although it is above twenty years since I felt his heavy hand, yet still once a month, at least, I dream of him'.[9] Lord

---

[6] See J. A. Passmore, 'The malleability of man in eighteenth-century thought', *Aspects of the eighteenth century*, ed. E. R. Wasserman. Its supremacy had not then been challenged by advances in genetics stressing the pre-natal inheritance, nor by the advent of psycho-analysis which, by discounting the rational element in man, casts doubt on the value of disciplined training.

[7] There is a good discussion of the issue in Chapter 7 of G. C. Brauer, *The education of a gentleman: theories of gentlemanly education in England, 1660–1775*. For a contemporary comment, see Eustace Budgell in *The Spectator*, No. 313 of 28 Feb. 1712.

[8] *Thoughts* (1902 edition), ed. R. H. Quick, 48, 46, 68.

[9] *The Spectator*, No. 168 of 12 Sept. 1711. Steele purported to be quoting a correspondent. The headmaster has been identified as Dr Charles Roderick. But Roderick is said to have been mild and retiring and it is possible that there is a confusion with his predecessor, John Rosewell, who was rumoured to have flogged a boy to death. 'Above twenty years' would strictly take the reminiscence back into Rosewell's time and it appears to be an example of character assassination by accident.

Chatham, hardly a born victim, confided to Shelburne that he had 'scarce observed a boy who was not cowed for life at Eton; that a public school might suit a boy of turbulent forward disposition, but would not do where there was any gentleness'.[10] Lord Chesterfield sent his son Philip to Westminster, but warned him against 'illiberal manners and brutal behaviour'. 'Are you sufficiently upon your guard', the poor youth was catechised, 'against awkward attitudes . . . and disgusting habits; such as scratching yourself, putting your fingers in your mouth, nose and ears?'[11]

There were, in addition, objections to public schools peculiar to the nobility. A good deal of disdain was felt towards schoolmasters as pedagogic martinets of humble birth and the continuation of the practice of flogging in Latin verbs made aristocratic parents reluctant to entrust their sons to them. Defoe put the argument with vigour in *The compleat English gentleman*:

Shall *my son* be sent to school to sit *bare-headed* and say a lesson to such a sorry, diminutive rascal as that, be brow beaten and hectored and threatened with his authority and stand in fear of his hand! *My son*! That a few years after he will be glad to cringe to, cap in hand, for a dinner . . . *My son* is a *Gentleman*, he shan't be under such a scoundrel as that.[12]

Among the other dangers facing noble boys was that of forming unfortunate friendships which might prove, in Richard Hurd's melodramatic phrase, 'if not the bane, yet the dishonour and incumbrance of their future lives'.[13]

The counter-arguments, however, were weighty. If attendance at Eton or Westminster might foster low acquaintance with boys, an upbringing at home might encourage familiarity with domestic servants.[14] It was easy enough for Locke to urge the employment of a virtuous, learned and reliable tutor, but could such paragons be found? Appearances were sometimes deceptive. Lord Chesterfield, who can scarcely be accused of neglecting education, selected for his godson a cleric 'of unexceptionable character and very great learning . . . the best

[10] Lord Fitzmaurice, *Life of William Earl of Shelburne* (1875 edition), I, 72. The mother in Johnson's *Rambler*, No. 109 made the same point when she 'would not suffer so fine a child to be ruined' by loutishness.

[11] *Letters*, ed. B. Dobrée, IV, Nos. 1687 and 1694.   [12] Ed. K. D. Bülbring, 7.

[13] *Dialogues on the use of foreign travel, considered as a part of an English gentleman's education between Lord Shaftesbury and Mr Locke* (2nd edition, 1764), 145–6. The remark is given to Locke.

[14] See Lady Harley to Sir Edward Harley, 19 Jan. 1671, *HMC. Portland*, III, 319. 'My judgement is not for the boys being kept at home, for it is not possible to keep them from associating with servants and getting a strange clownish speech and behaviour . . . besides I think learning alone makes them have a greater aversion to their books, having nothing of emulation to spur them on.'

and most eloquent preacher in England'.[15] This was the unfortunate Dr Dodd, subsequently hanged at Tyburn for forgery.[16] Defoe had such a low opinion of tutors as a group that he called them 'murderers of a child's morals'.[17] Those tutors who were well-intentioned and competent were in a delicate position, facing the possibility that the child would appeal to his parents against any act of correction, and knowing that his own position in the household was probably not high. 'As the case now stands', wrote Steele in 1713, 'those of the first quality pay their tutors but little above half so much as they do their footmen.'[18]

The strongest argument in favour of the public schools was that, whatever their defects, they were less sheltered than a private education. Boys would face up to competition and learn to take the rough with the smooth. Defoe was one of the most persuasive advocates of the public schools, insisting that their pupils had proved to be 'the glory of their country', while those privately educated were no more than 'the mere outsides of gentlemen, useless in their generation, retreated from the state'.[19]

The debate continued throughout the century, with Hurd, Sheridan, Chapman, Knox, Stockdale and Cowper picking up the arguments propounded by Burnet, Locke, Steele, Defoe and Budgell.[20] William Cowper rendered the discussion into heroic couplets without much advancing the argument.[21]

The majority of commentators have assumed that the proponents of private education were more persuasive. Brauer's summary was that aristocrats 'found private upbringing more to their taste' and Hans

---

[15] *Letters*, VI, Nos. 2366 and 2367.

[16] Dodd was then starting a very small and select private school for wealthy boys. In 1777 he forged a bond worth £4,000 against his erstwhile pupil, then the 5th Earl of Chesterfield. He had apparently been living beyond his means for some years previously.

[17] *The compleat English gentleman*, quoted W. A. L. Vincent, *The grammar schools: their continuing tradition, 1660–1714*, 198.

[18] *The Guardian*, No. 94.   [19] *The compleat English gentleman*, 8.

[20] R. Hurd, *Dialogues on the uses of foreign travel*; Thomas Sheridan, *A plan of education for the young nobility and gentry of Great Britain* (1769); George Chapman, *A treatise on education* (1773); Vicesimus Knox, *Liberal education* (1781); Percival Stockdale, *An examination of the important question, whether education at a great school or by private tuition is preferable* (1781).

[21] *Tirocinium, or a review of schools*, (1784):
   Would you your son should be a sot or dunce,
   Lascivious, headstrong, or all these at once;
   Train him in public with a mob of boys,
   Childish in mischief only and in noise,
   Else of a mannish growth, and five in ten
   In infidelity and lewdness men.
   There shall he learn, ere sixteen winters old,
   That authors are most useful pawned or sold.
Cowper was presumably drawing upon his experiences as a boy at Westminster.

Table 4. *School education of the peerage*

	Period I	Period II	Period III	Period IV	Total
Eton	19	46	53	92	210
Westminster	15	31	78	40	164
Winchester	7	4	13	7	31
Harrow	1	1	2	17	21
St Pauls	5	—	—	1	6
Rugby	—	6	—	—	6
Other British schools	15	8	17	8	48[a]
Abroad	12	9	5	5	31[b]
No evidence	185	130	76	46	437[c]
Total	259	235	244	216	954

[a] This category breaks down as follows:

English grammar schools	17
Charterhouse	2
Private schools	27
Warrington Academy	1
Dalkeith	1

Potential lawyers, such as Kenyon, Dunning and Eldon, often went to their local grammar schools.
[b] Includes eleven sons of Catholic peers who attended Douai and two who attended St Omer; and peers of foreign extraction, such as Schomberg, Ligonier and William Henry Nassau van Zuylestein, 1st Earl of Rochford.
[c] Includes some peers who died before school age.

wrote that 'the more discerning parents of the titled aristocracy and of the gentry' chose private tuition.[22] In a controversy as vigorous and well-balanced as this, it takes a confident historian to decide where true discernment lay. But what one can say is that, whatever the results of the theoretical discussion, the practice of the aristocracy increasingly favoured public schools, until by the end of the century there was a remarkable cohesion in the educational experience of the peerage.

Table 4 gives the school education of the 954 male peers. They are divided into four roughly equal groups according to the dates of birth:

[22] Brauer, *The education of a gentleman*, 226; N. Hans, *New trends in education in the eighteenth century*, 29. Vincent, *The grammar schools*, 191–6, follows Hans. F. Musgrove, 'Middle class families and schools, 1780–1880', *Sociological Review*, VII (1959), 171–2, wrote that 'the declining eighteenth century reputation of the public and grammar schools . . . gave rise to the extension of the domestic alternative'. His argument was based largely upon literary evidence.

Table 5. *Numbers at Eton, Westminster, Winchester and Harrow*

Period I	42 out of 259	=	16.2%
Period II	82 out of 235	=	34.9%
Period III	143 out of 244	=	58.6%
Period IV	156 out of 216	=	72.2%

Period I   Peers born before and including 1680
Period II   Peers born between 1681 and 1710 inclusive
Period III Peers born between 1711 and 1740 inclusive
Period IV Peers born after 1740

We can now abstract the numbers in each period attending the four great public schools of Eton, Westminster, Winchester and Harrow, and present them as a percentage of the peers in that period (see Table 5). This cohesiveness of the school experience of the peerage was increased by the extent to which the two great schools dominated: in Periods III and IV more than half the peers had attended Eton or Westminster.[23]

[23] This analysis is, of course, open to the methodological objection that it includes persons like the 1st Earl of Hardwicke who were not of noble family when they received their school education. We can check to what extent this factor invalidates the findings by subtracting from Table 4 all peers who were without peerage connections at the age of eleven. The revised Table 4 would then appear as follows:

	Period I	Period II	Period III	Period IV	Total
Eton	15	37	50	83	185
Westminster	13	27	71	38	149
Winchester	7	4	12	7	30
Harrow	1	1	2	16	20
St Pauls	5	—	—	1	6
Rugby	—	6	—	—	6
Other British schools	8	6	10	6	30
Abroad	12	9	4	5	30
No evidence	165	116	62	41	384
Total	226	206	211	197	840

Table 5 would then read:

Period I	36 out of 226	=	15.9%
Period II	69 out of 206	=	33.5%
Period III	135 out of 211	=	64.0%
Period IV	144 out of 197	=	73.1%

The element of distortion is therefore negligible.

Table 6. *Number of MPs 1715–90 attending*
public schools

	1715–54	1754–90
Westminster	167	301
Eton	162	331
Winchester	31	38
Merchant Taylors'	11	8
St Pauls	11	1
Rugby	9	9
Charterhouse	7	10
Harrow	4	35
Shrewsbury	3	6
Total	405	739

The general movement towards public education may also be demonstrated by another and overlapping section of the political elite, the MPs whose biographies are included in *The House of Commons, 1715–54* and *The House of Commons, 1754–90*. The earlier volumes provide biographies for 2,041 members; the later volumes for 1,964 members. The results are shown in Table 6.

If we represent the totals of the four schools previously taken – Eton, Westminster, Winchester and Harrow – as percentages of the total number of members in each period, we find that it increases from 18% to 36%. Some of the reasons which explain why this rise is less emphatic than that we have noted for the peers are of a technical character. The period under survey is shorter. The House of Commons survey includes Scottish members, few of whom attended English public schools. The two periods have 476 MPs in common, whose careers straddled the dividing date of 1754. But the main reason for the difference is that the House of Commons was much more likely to include a considerable number of self-made men, such as Robert Mackreth, who had started his career as a billard-marker in a coffee-house and whose education, if any, was not recorded.

How can we explain this increasing preference for a public-school education? The balance of pedagogic advice may even have been in the other direction. Though individual headmasters acquired reputations which gave their own schools an advantage for a while, there was no fundamental change in either the syllabus or the teaching methods that might have made schools more attractive.[24] Nor is it easy to suggest any economic factors that might have affected the balance between private and public schooling.[25] The most probable explanation is the growing importance of Parliament in the national life after the Revolution of 1688 and the extent to which Westminster was replacing St James's as the centre of power and influence. Unimpressed by Locke's arguments, the nobility seems to have come round to the opinion that the rough and tumble of a public school was the best preparation for public affairs. 'I have perceived a certain hardihood and manliness of character', wrote John Moore, 'in boys who have had a public education, superior to what appears in those of the same age educated privately.'[26] Some support for this interpretation may be gained from a further analysis. We have seen that the proportion of MPs between 1754 and 1790 attending the four great schools was 36%. But if we consider separately those members who were sons and grandsons of English peers and therefore the nearest thing we have to 'predestined Parliament men', the proportion rises to 68%.[27] If we then confine our analysis to peers' sons elected at or subsequent to the general election of 1761 (thereby omitting many who were at school in Anne's reign), the proportion rises again to 77%.[28]

If preparation for public life was the reason for this shift away from private education, it seems to have been justified by results. Westminster School early acquired a reputation as a nursery for statesmen. Westminster pupils who went on to distinguished parliamentary careers included Halifax, Peterborough, Nottingham, Sunderland, Carteret, Pulteney,

Edward Barnard was as successful in the 1750s and 1760s in establishing Eton's reputation as Richard Busby had been at Westminster a hundred years earlier. Winchester's reputation suffered from the charge of Jacobitism.

Fees and board were so much a matter for private negotiation that it is difficult to establish any average cost. C. Hollis, *Eton*, 129, estimates William Pitt's expenses in 1719 at £50–£60 p.a. J. Sargeant, *Annals of Westminster*, 159, puts board and tuition at between £25 and £35 p.a., but there is a reference in *Political and social letters of a lady of the eighteenth century, 1721–1771*, 46, ed. E. F. D. Osborn, to Dr Burton at Winchester in 1731 taking ten young noblemen at £200 p.a. each. More evidence of Eton fees is in Lord Ilchester, *Henry Fox*, I, 17–19. Payments to private tutors were even more variable.

A view of society and manners in France, Switzerland and Germany (1779), Letter XXXI, 291.

I have included grandsons of peers in direct line (e.g. G. A. North whose father was still technically a commoner when he was first returned in 1778), the sons of heirs apparent who died prematurely (e.g. the sons of the Marquis of Tavistock and the Marquis of Granby). I have excluded sons whose father's peerage was a new creation and came after the son's eleventh birthday (e.g. John Byng, the unlucky Admiral, a member of Parliament until his execution in 1757, but whose father was not created Viscount Torrington until Byng was 17). The figures were: Eton 70; Westminster 48; Winchester 6; Harrow 11; total 135; others 64.

I.e. the second analysis deals with members 1761–90. This omits, for example, William Finch, second son of the 2nd Earl of Nottingham, who had been born in 1691, was first returned in 1727 and continued to serve until 1761.

Chesterfield, Newcastle, Henry Pelham, Shippen, Grantham, Herve and Hynde Cotton, to be followed, later in the century, by Mansfield Rockingham, Bedford, Grafton, Portland and Richmond. Nor wa Eton outclassed when it could boast Stanhope, Walpole, Bolingbroke Sir William Wyndham, Henry Fox, Chatham, George Grenville, Bute North and Charles Fox. If to be first minister of the crown was an objec of ambition, education at Eton or Westminster was a sound investment Of the twenty-six first ministers between the advent of the House o Hanover and the passing of the Great Reform Act, only four had beer privately educated: Eton provided ten and Westminster seven, witl Harrow making a late run to secure two places in the shape of Spence Perceval and Viscount Goderich.

Schooling at Eton and Westminster provided more than a fai knowledge of classical literature and the chance to shrug off undu diffidence. The social contacts were often of abiding value. One must no be sentimental. Most school friendships, then as now, did not survive Nor can we rule out the possibility of enmities originating at school. But among the peerage, a common school education, reinforced by ties o blood and interest, helped to create an identity of outlook. One whe exploited his school contacts to the full was the Duke of Newcastle always on the look-out for assurance. Lord Shelburne, after noting tha the Westminsters were 'always the ruling party at Christ Church', wen on to complain that Newcastle surrounded himself with Westminste men. Of Lord George Germain, he wrote that his 'Westminste connection secured him constant access to the Duke'.[29] It was reporte during Newcastle's campaign for the chancellorship of the University o Cambridge that 'the Westminster people, and particularly a clerk in th Duke of Bedford's office, whose name I have forgot, but I know he is Westminster, have been very active also'.[30] The old school tie may hav been a nineteenth-century invention but the sentiment was no unknown in earlier decades.

When we turn to university education, the first task is to establish, wit reasonable accuracy, the number of students at Oxford and Cambridg in the eighteenth century. Fortunately the matriculation registers fo both universities survive and though, at an earlier period, they are not satisfactory guide to total numbers, since many students were admitte

---

[29] Lord Fitzmaurice, *Life of William Earl Shelburne*, 1, 18, 344, 349.
[30] D. A. Winstanley, *The University of Cambridge in the eighteenth century*, 44.

Table 7. *Matriculations at Oxford and Cambridge in the eighteenth century*

Decade	No. at Oxford	No. at Cambridge	Total
1700–09	3,008	2,036	5,044
1710–19	3,062	1,871	4,933
1720–29	2,972	1,939	4,911
1730–39	2,723	1,436	4,159
1740–49	2,223	1,433	3,656
1750–59	1,820	1,392	3,212
1760–69	2,064	1,128	3,192
1770–79	2,335	1,370	3,705
1780–89	2,531	1,707	4,238
1790–99	2,452	1,615	4,067
Total	25,190	15,927	41,117

to colleges but did not matriculate, by the eighteenth century the discrepancy is small. The evidence suggests a total of about 16,000 undergraduates at Cambridge and just over 25,000 for Oxford.

Of greater interest however is an analysis showing matriculations decade by decade.[31] This is given in Table 7.

These figures reveal a very substantial fall in numbers from 1700 to mid-century, followed by a partial recovery at both universities towards the end of the period. The fall began earlier at Cambridge than at Oxford and was sharper. Coupled with evidence that the proportion of wealthy and privileged students was tending to rise,[32] the falling admissions figures suggest a growing measure of social exclusiveness. The sons of grocers and plasterers still found their way to university but the road was harder.

[31] The figures are taken from the Matriculation Registers in the Bodleian and Cambridge University Libraries. Annual figures for Cambridge are given by W. W. Rouse-Ball and J. A. Venn in *Admissions to Trinity College*, I, Introduction, 10–11 and are very accurate. The Oxford figures given in their accompanying graph are however five-year averages. I have excluded the category of 'privileged persons'. They were not scholars, but servants, tradesmen and workmen, employed by the university and entitled to certain rights. See *Register of the University of Oxford*, ed. A. Clark, II, 1, 381–6.

[32] Hans, *New trends in education*, 44–6 shows that Fellow Commoners at Cambridge increased from about 10% in the first half of the century to 18% by the end. His sample for Oxford suggested that the proportion of *graduates* claiming armigerous ancestry rose from 5% to 30%, while the

The evidence reminds us how tiny the universities were by modern standards. In some years of the eighteenth century, the number of students matriculating at Cambridge fell below one hundred, with some three to four hundred in residence.[33] The total number of students at Oxford and Cambridge for the whole of the eighteenth century was roughly comparable to the number in residence in the University of London in any one year of the 1970s. In these circumstances it was easy enough for noblemen and Fellow Commoners who were up together to know each other.

The effect of this decline on some colleges was dramatic. There were, of course, fluctuations in reputation. Balliol, Oxford, suffered from the imputation of Jacobitism.[34] At Pembroke, Cambridge, the entry in the early years of the eighteenth century was only ten or so, and declined still further, until in the 1760s only four freshers a year were being admitted.[35] At St John's, the largest of the Cambridge colleges, admissions during Anne's reign averaged fifty a year: they dropped steadily to reach a low of thirty-one during the 1760s, before climbing to over forty in the last decades. Trinity College, Cambridge, had admitted just over fifty undergraduates p.a. in the late 1630s and 1640s and again after the Restoration, but, by Anne's reign, the intake had almost halved and it continued to fall until the 1760s, with an average of twenty-three. The year 1765 saw only ten admissions – lower than even the abnormally low intake of thirteen in 1643, the first year of the Civil War. Christ's College, Cambridge, was down to some six admissions in mid-century.[36] At Caius, Cambridge, the average fell from twelve or thirteen in Anne's reign to seven during mid-century: one hundred years earlier, in the decade following the Restoration, the college had been admitting twenty-two a year.[37]

Against this background of declining overall numbers, we can place

proportion of graduates of plebeian origins fell from 35% to 11%. Confirmation of this trend comes from *Admissions to the College of St John the Evangelist in the University of Cambridge*, ed. Sir R. F. Scott, showing that at St John's the proportion of Fellow Commoners rose from 5% in the first decade of the eighteenth century to 17.2% for 1781–90. For the last decade it was 14.6%.

[33] In the years 1718, 1734, 1735, 1765 and 1769. Rouse-Ball and Venn, *Admissions to Trinity College*, I, 10–12. At Oxford, the lowest figures were for 1756 with 161 matriculations, followed by 1755 (167), 1758 (173), 1766 (175) and 1765 (178). There were, of course, by modern standards, a disproportionate number of dons.

[34] H. W. C. Davis, *Balliol*, 170.

[35] A. Attwater, *Pembroke College, Cambridge*, 89, 101.

[36] D. A. Winstanley, *Unreformed Cambridge*, 185–6.

[37] *Biographical history of Gonville and Caius College, 1349–1897*, ed. J. A. Venn.

Table 8. *Attendance at Oxford and Cambridge of peers, 1700–99*[38]

	No. at Oxford	No. at Cambridge	Total	No. of peers in group	Percentage at O. or C.
Period I	54	38	92	259	35.52
Period II	75	37	112	235	47.65
Period III	69	52	121	244	49.59
Period IV	77	47	124	216	57.40
Total	275	174	449	954	

our analysis of the university education of the peerage. Table 8 is divided into four roughly equal groups, according to date of birth:

Period I   Born before and including 1680
Period II   Born 1681 to 1710 inclusive
Period III   Born 1711 to 1740 inclusive
Period IV   Born 1741 and subsequently

The evidence of a shift towards university education on the part of the peerage can be presented in another way by comparing the position at ive points of time in the course of the century, as in Table 9.

We have established that an increasing proportion of the English peerage was educated at Oxford or Cambridge and this at a time when, for much of the period, admissions generally to the two universities were falling. The aristocratic influence in university life was probably greater than at any other period. Coupled with the evidence of the increasing

[8] This table is also open to methodological objection. For purposes of completeness, it includes seven peers who, dying before the age of fifteen, did not have the chance to attend or not attend university. It also includes sixty-four Catholic peers who were not allowed to attend. In addition, there are eighty-eight other peers who, according to my records, had no peerage connections at the age of fifteen. A more realistic impression of the position relating to the *effective* English peerage is given by subtracting these 159 peers. The revised Table 8 then reads as follows:

	No. at Oxford	No. at Cambridge	Total	No. of peers in group	Percentage at O. or C.
Period I	50	32	82	208	39.4
Period II	66	31	97	192	50.5
Period III	63	44	107	203	52.7
Period IV	71	42	113	192	58.8

Table 9. *University education of peerage in 1701, 1710, 1750, 1790 and 1799 (on 1 January)*

	No. at Oxford	No. at Cambridge	Others	No. of peers not at university	Total	Percentage at university
1701	34	18	0	110	162	32.09
1710	38	19	1	103	161	36.02
1750	53	35	2	90	180	50.00
1790	67	57	7	80	211	62.08
1799	87	66	9	93	255	63.52

Table 10. *Peerage attendance at Oxford colleges*

College	Period I[a]	Period II	Period III	Period IV	Total
Christ Church	31	40	25	51	147
Magdalen	4	3	5	5	17
Trinity	6	4	4	2	16
University	—	5	5	5	15
New	3	5	5	—	13
Oriel	—	3	4	5	12
Queen's	1	2	4	2	9
St John's	2	3	4	—	9
Balliol	—	4	3	—	7
Exeter	1	3	—	1	5
Brasenose	—	—	2	3	5
Wadham	1	2	—	—	3
Merton	—	—	1	2	3
St Mary Hall	—	—	3	—	3
Pembroke	1	—	1	—	2
Hertford	—	—	2	—	2
Jesus	1	—	—	1	2
St Edmund Hall	2	—	—	—	2
Corpus	—	1	—	—	1
Lincoln	1	—	—	—	1
Worcester	—	—	1	—	1
Total	54	75	69	77	275

[a] For division of periods, see Table 8.

Table 11. *Peerage attendance at Cambridge colleges*

College	Period I[a]	Period II	Period III	Period IV	Total
Trinity	10	4	7	12	33
St John's	3	6	6	17	32
King's	6	4	8	5	23
Clare	1	8	9	2	20
Christ's	4	2	3	—	9
Jesus	2	2	3	1	8
Magdalene	5	2	—	—	7
Trinity Hall	—	2	3	2	7
Corpus	—	1	4	2	7
Peterhouse	2	1	3	—	6
Queens'	—	2	2	2	6
Emmanuel	1	2	—	2	5
Pembroke	1	—	2	1	4
Sidney	1	1	1	1	4
Caius	1	—	1	—	2
St Catharine's	1	—	—	—	1
Total	38	37	52	47	174

[a] For division of periods, see Table 8.

popularity of the public schools, it suggests that something like a standard education was emerging among the aristocracy, and it was a public one. I have already suggested that a common educational experience was an important prop to the regime. This argument is powerfully reinforced if we examine the attendance of the peerage by college (see Tables 10 and 11). The favoured colleges were few in number and their domination increased towards the end of the eighteenth century.

As these tables show, Christ Church received more than half the peers attending Oxford and in the fourth period the proportion rose to more than two-thirds. No college at Cambridge succeeded in establishing a comparable supremacy, though Trinity and St John's combined accounted for 62% in the fourth period.

The inclusion in the sample of men who were ennobled after their university career produces the usual distortion and it would be simple to

Table 12. *Attendance of peers and peers' sons at Oxford*

College	1700–19	1720–39	1740–59	1760–79	1780–99	Total
Christ Church	37	21	21	40	75	194
University	2	7	1	4	1	15
Trinity	—	2	3	4	4	13
Oriel	—	—	3	3	6	12
New	7	1	3	—	—	11
Balliol	5	5	—	—	—	10
Magdalen	1	3	5	1	—	10
Queen's	—	5	2	—	1	8
St John's	—	5	—	—	—	5
Hertford	—	—	3	2	—	5
St Mary Hall	—	—	3	1	1	5
Brasenose	—	1	—	2	2	5
Merton	2	1	—	—	1	4
Exeter	—	2	—	1	1	4
Wadham	2	1	—	—	—	3
Hart Hall	2	—	1	—	—	3
St Alban's	—	—	—	1	—	1
Corpus	—	1	—	—	—	1
Worcester	—	—	—	—	—	—
Total	58	55	45	59	92	309

Table 13. *Attendance of peers and peers' sons at Cambridge*

College	1700–19	1720–39	1740–59	1760–79	1780–99	Total
Trinity	8	6	3	22	26	65
St John's	4	4	5	13	22	48
King's	6	4	1	4	1	16
Clare	5	2	4	1	3	15
Corpus	—	3	6	1	—	10
Jesus	—	1	2	—	3	6
Christ's	2	2	—	—	1	5
Trinity Hall	2	1	—	1	1	5
Queens'	—	2	2	1	—	5
Emmanuel	1	—	1	1	1	4
Peterhouse	—	—	3	—	1	4

Table 13. (cont.)

College	1700–19	1720–39	1740–59	1760–79	1780–99	Total
Pembroke	1	—	—	1	2	4
Magdalene	1	—	—	1	—	2
Sidney	—	1	—	—	—	1
Caius	—	—	—	—	—	—
Downing	—	—	—	—	—	—
St Catharine's	—	—	—	—	—	—
Total	30	26	27	46	61	190

Table 14. *Consolidated list of attendance of peers and peers' sons at Oxford and Cambridge*[39]

	1700–19	1720–39	1740–59	1760–79	1780–99	Total
Oxford	58	55	45	59	92	309
Cambridge	30	26	27	46	61	190
Total	88	81	72	105	153	499

subtract these. But a better representation of the pattern of peerage attendance may be obtained by a different analysis, taking persons who, *at matriculation*, were English peers or the sons of English peers, as in Tables 12 and 13. Table 14 shows the result of a conflation of the two analyses.

In these tables, the tendency towards college exclusiveness is even more apparent. At Oxford, Christ Church achieved an overall dominance in the century of 62%, rising in the last two decades to nearly 80%. At Cambridge, Trinity and St John's together accounted for 60%, rising in

The large number of creations from 1780 onwards creates a statistical complication but does not invalidate the trend. Of the 150 peers' sons attending 1780–99, twenty-three had fathers ennobled within that period – i.e. 15%. But of course the same is true of other periods. The proportion in the period 1700–19 was also 15%, and over the century as a whole it was 13%. There is consequently no particular reason to make any adjustment to take into account the increases in peerage creations towards the end of the century.

Table 15. *Attendance of peers and peers' sons against total matriculations* ▪ *Oxford and Cambridge*

	No. of peers and peers' sons	Total no. of matriculations	Percentage of noble students
1700–19	88	9,977	0.882
1720–39	81	9,070	0.893
1740–59	72	6,868	1.048
1760–79	105	6,897	1.522
1780–99	153	8,305	1.842

the last two decades to nearly 80%. There is little doubt which were th▪ socially prestigious colleges.

We can now plot peers and peers' sons at Oxford and Cambridg▪ against the total matriculations in order to see whether the proportion ▪ aristocratic students was rising or falling (Table 15).

As a proportion of the total student body, the nobility more tha▪ doubled in the course of the century.[40]

These conclusions, that the two universities were increasing▪ favoured by the nobility, are at variance with those offered by Lawrenc▪ Stone in the opening essay of *The university in society*. Taking peer▪ baronets and knights as forming the elite, he suggested that 'throughou▪ the late seventeenth and eighteenth centuries a smaller and small▪ proportion of the children of the social elite was attending Oxfor▪ University'.[41] Stone's findings were summarised in a broadcast revie▪ by Professor Trevor-Roper as indicating that the universities were, ▪ the eighteenth century, 'deserted by the nobility'.[42]

---

[40] Since this appeared to be a developing trend, I extended the analysis to cover 1800–19, with t▪ following result: Oxford, 116, Cambridge, 86, Total, 202. Plotted against total matriculations 10,350, this gives a further increase to 1.95%. During this period, Christ Church, Oxfor▪ maintained a share of 76.7% of admissions of peers' sons and, at Cambridge, Trinity and St John▪ combined accounted for 74.5%.

These analyses are confined to the sons of English peers and therefore greatly understate the re▪ aristocratic element. I have omitted the sons of Irish and Scottish peers, who attended increasing numbers, illegitimate sons of English peers, and sons whose father was ennobl▪ during their university careers. In addition, of course, there were cousins, nephews and the lik▪

[41] 'The size and composition of the Oxford student body, 1580–1910', 47.

[42] *The Listener*, 4 Dec. 1975, 756–8.

It must at once be conceded that Professor Stone's investigation was larger and more ambitious than my own. Nevertheless, I am not sure that his conclusions are necessarily correct nor that they are the most convincing part of his article. There are a number of difficulties, some of a technical character.

At first sight, the argument looks sound. Stone tells us that in 1686, eighteen students from the social elite were admitted to Oxford, and with a total elite estimated at about 1,560 fathers, the student/father ratio was 1.2. By 1785/6, when only seven students were admitted out of a total elite of about 1,100 fathers, the ratio had fallen to 0.6. But closer examination provokes doubt. The earlier figure, it transpires, is an estimate only. The second figure is an error, according to the evidence offered by Stone himself in his Table 2, which is in conflict with his Table 5. The annual average for 1785/6 should be eleven, not seven, and the student/father ratio will then be 1.0.[43] This would be a very narrow margin on which to base general conclusions. But there is a third difficulty. The figures for admission of the social elite to Oxford vary so much from year to year that it is most unwise to rely upon a sample. Professor Stone took 1785/6 with an average of eleven admissions. But had he taken 1784/5 the admissions would have been, not eleven, but sixteen, and the student/father ratio would have risen to 1.45. Had he taken 1798/9, the average admissions would have been nineteen, the ratio 1.7, and his argument would have to put in reverse, viz., that the proportion of the social elite attending Oxford *rose* during the eighteenth century.[44]

There are, I think, two broad reasons for this apparent conflict of evidence. The first is that the falling-off in attendance at Oxford by the social elite, which Professor Stone detected, is largely a seventeenth-century phenomenon. It is noticeable that, although he quotes a good deal of literary evidence which shows that many persons considered the universities effete, most of the examples are drawn from the earlier century. Second, the concept of a social elite is, as I have suggested, an elusive one and the attempt to quantify it fraught with uncommon difficulty. In particular, the dramatic decline in the eighteenth century in the number of knights, to say nothing of the decline in their status,

---

[43] According to my own records, eleven is the correct figure.

[44] Stone seems to have taken 1785/6 under the impression that it was 'an all-time low' (*The university in society*, 47). This is a further error. The titular elite for 1748/9 averaged six, and for 1752/3 averaged four and a half.

unbalances the figures and renders comparisons between Stuart England and Hanoverian England extremely hazardous.[45]

The increased desire of the peerage to have their sons educated publicly, which the previous analyses have suggested, may seem to indicate a more liberal, or even egalitarian, attitude. We have seen it argued that it was to the advantage of noble youths to leave their country houses and mix in the world. Nevertheless, it is an interpretation which should not be driven too hard. There is scanty evidence that the sons of the aristocracy were anxious to abandon the privileges of their order. The arrangements for both school and university often provided them with a private suite of rooms, they took with them their own servants, and it was not in the nature of things that prudent schoolmasters or dons should be too severe with young persons who, in the course of time, might command very considerable patronage. The difficulties of controlling the sons of noblemen may be gauged by a letter in 1699 from the Revd Robert Uvedale, master of a private school at Enfield. The fourteen-year-old Lord Winchester, son of the Duke of Bolton, was in hot pursuit of a daughter of Lady Falkland: 'he declines all business, and refuses to be governed, absenting himself from school, and by no persuasion will be

---

[45] The decline in the number of knights was part of a process since the mid-seventeenth century. In 1700 they still formed about 19% of the titular elite, but by 1740 were no more than 6%. The creations of Knights Bachelor 1600–29 totalled about 2,930; between 1660 and 1689 it was 1,100; between 1730 and 1759 a mere 114.

The number of sons of titled fathers entering the two universities can be plotted against total admissions to estimate what proportion of undergraduates came from the privileged group. The result is as follows:

	Oxford elite	Cambridge elite	Combined elite	Total admissions	Percentage of elite
1700–09	171	96	267	5,044	5.29
1710–19	130	94	224	4,933	4.54
1720–29	139	79	218	4,911	4.44
1730–39	130	72	202	4,159	4.86
1740–49	91	66	157	3,656	4.29
1750–59	68	91	159	3,212	4.95
1760–69	115	57	172	3,192	5.39
1770–79	100	88	188	3,705	5.07
1780–89	118	109	227	4,238	5.36
1790–99	161	120	281	4,067	6.91

In other words, a rather moderate fall by mid-century was followed by a substantial increase towards the end of the century.

prevailed upon to follow his studies, but takes what liberty he thinks fit upon all occasions'. His headmaster refused to accept responsibility for him for one hour more.[46]

Teachers were not unaware of the publicity value of their noble charges. At Eton the practice grew up of placing noble boys at the head of each class list and from 1766 onwards their names were printed in red.[47] Winchester, not to be outdone, placed peers at the head of the whole school.[48] The Duchess of Northumberland noted in her diary: 'Number of boys at Eton, July 23 1755 was 466, of which Noblemen 41.'[49]

At university, the privileges of rank were so great as to reinforce rather than diminish the concept of hierarchy. There are many references to the miserable position of sizars and servitors, getting through college by performing menial tasks for their fellow undergraduates. William Shenstone, the poet, recorded that he could not even visit publicly an acquaintance at Oxford who was a servitor.[50] But for the better off, university life was not too demanding. Credit was easily obtained, especially for the well-connected, and complaints of over-spending and indebtedness are frequent in the correspondence of fathers with their sons at college. Rooms were far more luxurious than in the crowded Stuart days. The universities shared to the full the growing comfort and diversity of Hanoverian social life, with coffee-rooms and taverns, entertainments and theatricals, riding to hounds, and a variety of dining and political clubs. Since noblemen were entitled to a degree without even the formality of a token examination, they were under no great incentive to furious study, provided that they could pacify their fathers. They often came to university in their early teens and departed after a few terms. Henry, 3rd Duke of Beaufort was thirteen when admitted to University College, Oxford in 1720, and Anthony Ashley Cooper, heir to the Earl of Shaftesbury, was the same age when he entered New College in 1724. The Duke of Buckingham arrived at Queen's College, Oxford in 1732 at the age of sixteen, but stayed only one year: 'he did not like them, as 'tis given out', remarked Thomas Hearne.[51] When Lord Sidney Beauclerk, descendant of Charles II by Nell Gwynn, expressed a desire to take an MA in 1727, the university gave him a special congregation.

Under these circumstances, it is rather creditable that a number of

[46] HMC. 11th Report, App. VII, 151.   [47] Hollis, Eton, 138, 146.
[48] See GEC, VI, 269, Note c.   [49] The Diaries of a Duchess, ed. J. Greig, 8.
[50] Quoted in A. D. Godley, Oxford in the eighteenth century, 119.
[51] Remarks and collections of Thomas Hearne, ed. H. E. Salter, XI, 88, 235.

aristocratic undergraduates worked hard and read widely. North
command of the classics was enough to give him solace during h
blindness when his children read to him. Charles Fox, despite an absurdl
indulgent childhood, entered Hertford College, Oxford at the age c
fifteen and read with such zest that he was able, in later life, to produce a
almost unique testimony – a letter from his tutor advising him not t
overdo things. On his deathbed he comforted himself with reading
from the *Aeneid*. William Grenville, earnest son of an earnest fathei
showed uncommon diligence at Christ Church, Oxford in the 1770s.[5]
William Pitt arrived at Pembroke College, Cambridge at the age c
fourteen, accompanied by a characteristically priggish note from h
father,[53] devoted himself to his books, became an ornament of th
university, and stood for election as burgess at the age of twenty-on
Castlereagh, though he did not take a degree, had the reputation at S
John's, Cambridge as a reading man.[54] These were no doubt the brighte
and best of their generations. But even Lord Edward Bentinck, not
fierce intellect, attended Blackstone's lectures while at Christ Churcl
Oxford in 1762, though he borrowed his brother's lecture notes.[55]

Against these shining examples must be set a rather large number o
noble youths whose undergraduate careers were not distinguished. 'Yo
are now but nineteen', Lord Chesterfield told his son, 'an age at whicl
most of your countrymen are illiberally getting drunk in port at th
University.'[56] Lady Leicester, great-aunt to Thomas William Coke, wa
so convinced that universities were schools of vice that she offered hin
£500 p.a. at the age of seventeen to embark on the Grand Tour at once.[5]
The 1st Duke of Chandos sent his eldest son, John Brydges, to Ballic
College, Oxford in 1719, where his conduct was so extravagant that h
was removed after eighteen months, leaving college debts of more tha
£300. As a consequence, the Duke decided to send his second sor
Henry, to St John's, Cambridge, where the result was, if anything
worse. The first meeting between father and son revealed an embarrass

---

[52] There is no biography of Grenville but an excellent sketch by Peter Jupp is included in *The prin*
ministers, ed. H. Van Thal, I, 252–70.

[53] 'Too young for the irregularities of a man, I trust, he will not, on the other hand, prov
troublesome by the puerile sallies of a boy . . . Such as he is, I am happy to place him
Pembroke.' The letter is printed in full in Rosebery's *Pitt*, 7–8.

[54] J. W. Derry, *Castlereagh*, 28.

[55] Lord Edward to W. H. C. Bentinck, 18 Nov. 1762, Nottingham University, Portland MS, Pw
515.   [56] *Letters*, v, No. 1886a.

[57] A. M. W. Stirling, *Coke of Norfolk and his friends* (1912 edition), 56. The result was ratho
successful. Less happy was the experience of Viscount Montagu of Cowdray, specificall
prohibited by a codicil to his father's will from attending an English university: he went
Germany and was drowned in a foolhardy attempt to shoot the falls on the Rhine.

ᴵg lack of progress. In history, Henry had apparently mastered two ᴵages on Ethelwulf in six months. He was despatched to Leiden ᴵrthwith where his conduct did not much improve.[58]

The Oxford career of the 5th Duke of Hamilton (Duke of Brandon in ᴵe English peerage) was short and spectacular. He arrived in the summer ᴵf 1718 at the age of fifteen with his 'governor' and decided to rent ᴵoms at the Angel, presumably lest the discipline of Christ Church ᴵrove irksome. A year later Canon Stratford reported that he had ᴵehaved himself very rudely to the Dean . . . He says when he came to ᴵe "Angel" . . . he sent to give the Dean notice that he was in town and ᴵxpected the Dean should have visited him first.' The duke's rank ᴵpparently supplied any deficiency of respect and the vice-chancellor ᴵave him a doctorate, largely to spite the dean. The duke then departed ᴵmid a litter of unpaid bills.[59]

John, Lord Boyle, another Christ Church man to be in trouble with ᴵis father, wrote of his stay in the 1720s that 'that college caused two ᴵears of my life to glide away in a very agreeable manner and as much to ᴵny profit and improvement as my idle temper would permit'.[60]

The experiences of John, 1st Earl of Bristol must stand for those of ᴵany eighteenth-century peers, though they were expressed with a ᴵeevishness all his own. Tom Hervey, his third son, went to Christ ᴵhurch, Oxford under the guidance of the dean, George Smallridge, ᴵho was also bishop of Bristol, with the confidence that his 'natural and ᴵcquired foundations' would enable him to become a substantial man. ᴵis behaviour was soon giving cause for concern: he had taken to ᴵambling and not writing home. After repeated protestations of ᴵnmediate reform, which will not be totally unfamiliar to present-day ᴵutors, he began absenting himself and had to be threatened with ᴵemoval. Henry, the fifth son, then took up at Christ Church where Tom ᴵad left off and during his first year was assured by Lord Bristol that he ᴵad given 'more anxiety and disquiet than all my other children put ᴵogether', which, if true, was no mean achievement. Henry was ᴵeproached with the comments of his dean, the bishop:

ᴵhe younger is very idle, and is not by anything which either his tutor or I can ᴵay to him to be prevailed with to apply himself to his studies, so that there is no ᴵrospect of his improving that very small stock of learning which he brought

ᴵ C. H. C. Baker and M. I. Baker, *The life and circumstances of James Brydges, first Duke of Chandos*, 236–47.
ᴵ Stratford to Harley, 7 June 1719, *HMC. Portland*, VII, 252.
ᴵ *Orrery Papers*, ed. Countess of Cork and Orrery, I, 43.

from school: when I talk with him, he seems to be convinced of his error, an very readily promises to do better, but those promises are soon forgot.

Charles, the sixth son, was sent to Queens' College, Cambridge, by wa of a change, and possibly because it was nearer to Ickworth and thu easier to exercise control. The experiment was not successful. Afte several years Bristol complained that he was 'to my great surprise rathe less improved of late . . . than he was before'. To Charles' tutor, th Revd William Sedgwick, Bristol wrote menacingly: 'I wish you coul help me to disculpate you entirely on this occasion being otherwis tempted by the great concern this disappointment has thrown me into t suspect your part in this misfortune may not appear quite so blameless a it ought.' Charles never reached the highest offices of the church no became an ornament of his country, as his father had intended, and had t be content with a rather obscure family living. But the Revd Willian Sedgwick flourished and spent his last thirty years as President o Queens'.[61]

Privileges of the Fellow Commoners at Cambridge and the Gentle men Commoners at Oxford were considerable. They dined at high tabl with the Fellows and had access to the Fellows' garden and the colleg cellars. At Lincoln College, Oxford, and no doubt elsewhere, it wa understood that Gentlemen Commoners were not expected to bow t the Fellows and they were provided with keys to the college library.[6] Not having to take examinations, they were under no obligation t attend lectures. There were few limitations on academic dress fo noblemen, though an Oxford regulation of 1750 declared that th privilege of wearing hats did not extend to lace ones. The design of nobleman's gown was a matter for aesthetes and exquisites. The portrai of the 7th Viscount Fitzwilliam, founder of the museum at Cambridge shows him in a very fetching red gown with gold brocade facing.[63] The problem of a gown for George Howard, son of Lord Carlisle, when h went up to Christ Church, Oxford, in 1790, was just the thing to engag George Selwyn's interest. To Lady Carlisle, he wrote:[64] 'I hope that yo approve of my choice of what the colour of his gown is to be. I think

---

[61] *Hervey letter books*, II, Nos. 549, 550; III, No. 924.

[62] A. Clark, *Lincoln*, 145. For further evidence on the position of Gentlemen Commoners at Lincoln see V. H. H. Green, *The commonwealth of Lincoln College, 1427–1977*.

[63] The portrait by William Hoare of Derby hangs in the entrance to the left of the door. Fitzwilliam was admitted to Trinity Hall in 1761 at the age of sixteen.

[64] *HMC. Carlisle*, 689. Lord Stafford, Lady Carlisle's father, had been at Christ Church from 1740 Selwyn's own, much interrupted, Oxford career was between 1739 and 1744, when he withdrew to avoid expulsion.

ight blue *celeste*, which Lord Stafford had, would be detestable, and
carlet is too glaring. No, it must be a good deep green.' Another
ommentator, looking back on Cambridge in the later eighteenth
entury, remarked of the Fellow Commoners: 'their robes, which are
ow uniformly purple, at that time were of various colours, according to
he taste of their wearers, purple, white, green, and rose-colour were all
o be seen at the same time'.[65]

This impression of a none too strenuous existence is confirmed from
many sources. N. Amhurst, author of *Terrae-Filius, or the secret history of
the University of Oxford*, wrote in 1726:

here are many within and without the walls of our universities, who know and
vill acknowledge . . . that the education of a person of distinction at Oxford,
istead of being as it ought, the most strictly taken care of, is of all the most
eglected; a nobleman may bring anything from college but learning; but there
generally effectual care taken that his G— shall not want temptations
o entice him from studying too hard. A Gentleman Commoner, if he be a man
f fortune, is soon told, that it is not expected from one of his form to mind
xercises.[66]

At the end of the century, the *Gentleman's Magazine* denounced
Gentlemen Commoners and Fellow Commoners: 'they take the lead in
very disgraceful frolic of juvenile debauchery'.[67] That the dons had a
ood deal to put up with may be inferred from the remark in *Advice to a
oung man of fortune and rank upon his entrance to the University* that *even* the
ellows were entitled to 'decent respect'. One of the reasons for the
uccess of Christ Church, Oxford, in the later eighteenth century was the
vonderful tact shown by Dean Jackson in handling 'that most
nmanageable class of undergraduates, noblemen'.[68]

Religious belief which, in the seventeenth century, had done so much to
ndermine the political and social order, was harnessed in the eighteenth
entury to the cause of stability. Though few would have put it with such
rutal candour, many Hanoverian aristocrats would probably have
greed with the sentiments expressed by Napoleon Bonaparte to his
Council of State: 'I don't see in religion the mystery of the incarnation
ut the mystery of the social order. It ties up to heaven an idea of equality
vhich prevents the rich from being massacred by the poor.'

That coolness of tone and mistrust of enthusiasm, sometimes called
atitudinarianism, so characteristic of Hanoverian upper-class Christian-

[5] H. Gunning, *Reminiscences of the university, town and county of Cambridge from the year 1780*, I, 28.
[5] Page 43.   [67] Jan. 1798, LXVIII, I, 15.
[8] C. E. Mallet, *A history of the University of Oxford*, III, 170–1, quoting George Cox.

ity, proved to be a very appealing point of consensus and helped to bind the religious wounds of the past. One of the most remarkable features of the late seventeenth and early eighteenth centuries was the speed with which the Puritan ideal collapsed, to be replaced by a comfortable orthodoxy by no means hostile to hierarchy or aristocracy. Though particularly in its early manifestations, Methodism showed some hostility towards the wealthy and well-bred, so that it neither made nor perhaps desired much progress among the ruling elite, two considerations modified any subversive effects it might have had. First, it grew comparatively slowly and as late as the 1790s the total number of Methodists was reckoned at no more than 90,000. Second, for fifty years John Wesley imposed upon the new movement a conservative and loyal character. Only during the later years of his life, and partly in response to American and French developments, did Dissent develop a more critical and aggressive posture. Nor, among the upper classes, was there much freethinking of the kind fashionable in advanced circles in France or Germany. Indeed, one of the many reasons for the widespread mistrust of Viscount Bolingbroke was that he was thought to be unsafe on religious questions.[69]

To the emergent aristocratic regime, moderate Anglicanism proved highly acceptable. Supported by the attractive influence of place and favour, it established a powerful hold among the upper classes. Peers who had had Presbyterian or Puritan sympathy, like Lord Haversham or the 1st Duke of Bedford, seemed old-fashioned survivors and there were few new recruits to Protestant Dissent in the course of the century.[70] Even more important was the steady diminution in the number of Catholic peers. Lawrence Stone's assessment of the position in 1641 is that one-fifth of the 121 peers were Catholic, another one-fifth were Puritan in

---

[69] It was in answer to the publication in 1754 of Bolingbroke's *Collected works* that Edmund Burke produced his first pamphlet, *A vindication of natural society in a letter to Lord ———*, pointing out that 'civil government borrows a strength from ecclesiastical, and artificial laws receive sanction from artificial revelations'. The pamphlet was not a total success. Burke's irony was mistaken by many, and his illustration of the inequality of society was done with such force that it overbalanced the argument: 'The whole business of the poor is to administer to the idleness, folly and luxury of the rich; and that of the rich, in return, is to find the best methods of confirming the slavery and increasing the burdens of the poor . . . A constitution of things this, strange and ridiculous beyond expression. We scarcely believe a thing when we are told it, which we actually see before our eyes every day without being in the least surprised . . . In a misery of this sort, admitting some few lenities, and those too but a few, nine parts in ten of the whole race of mankind drudge through life.' For Bolingbroke's view, see H. T. Dickinson, *Bolingbroke*, 298–301.

[70] Haversham's father had been a Cromwellian and Haversham moved from staunch Whiggism to High Tory in Anne's reign. Bedford was the father of Lord Russell, executed in 1683.

ympathy, and, allowing for youth, age and indifference, less than one-half of the nobility were deeply committed to the Church of England.[71] Up to 1688 the support given by Charles II and James II sustained the Catholic position: indeed, several peers like Sunderland and Salisbury misread the signs and embraced Catholicism just before James fled. But after the Glorious Revolution there was a debilitating attrition in Catholic numbers. In 1703 there were still nineteen Catholic peers, though they were excluded from public office and political life. Attainders for Jacobitism accounted for the Radcliffes, Earls of Derwentwater and the Widdringtons, five Catholic peerages became extinct,[72] and seven more peers renounced their faith.[73] As a proportion of the peerage as a whole, the Catholic group shrank from 12% at the beginning of the eighteenth century to a mere 3% at the end.[74] Excluded from both court and Parliament, the remaining Catholic peers married among their own number, sent their sons abroad to be educated, and made little contribution to society. The result was that the deep religious antagonisms dividing the peerage and the nation in the seventeenth century were mitigated and an additional element of unity added to aristocratic supremacy.

The great network of ecclesiastical patronage belonging to the Hanoverian peerage, as well as ensuring that aristocratic sentiments were delivered from many pulpits, was a source of considerable political power. We should distinguish between the share of high ecclesiastical office which the peerage acquired and the influence it exercised through lay patronage.

Bishoprics such as Bristol, St Asaph, Rochester and Llandaff, at the lower end of remuneration, might not seem attractive to well-connected clergy. But the episcopal income could be augmented by benefices held *in commendam* and, in any case, clerics of noble descent did not expect to remain for long near the bottom of the ladder. Of the twenty-four

---

[71] *The crisis of the aristocracy*, 742.

[72] Carrington (1706), Dover (1708), Gerard (1733), Stafford (1762) and Langdale (1778). The last Earl Rivers, who succeeded in 1712, was a Catholic priest and on his death in 1737 the title became extinct.

[73] Cardigan (1709), Waldegrave (1720), Fauconberg (1737), Audley (1740), Montagu (1767) and Teynham (1781). The worst blow to the Catholic cause was the conversion of Lord Surrey, heir to the premier dukedom of Norfolk, before embarking in 1780 on an active political career. The Griffins, given a barony in December 1688 by James II, did not use the title. The third baron renounced Catholicism but the title became extinct on his death in 1742.

[74] The remaining Catholic peers in 1799 were Arundell of Wardour, Clifford of Chudleigh, Dormer, Petre, Shrewsbury and Stourton. The 1st Duke of Shrewsbury renounced Catholicism in 1679 and played a prominent part in public life for the next forty years, but was succeeded in the earldom by his cousin, a Catholic priest, who did not claim the title.

aristocratic bishops during the century, none began their careers in the poorest sees, and only six remained in their first diocese. John Harley died within a year of his appointment to Hereford in 1787. His successor James Cornwallis, stayed there for forty-three years, but he held in addition the deanship of the Chapel Royal at Windsor from 1791 to 1794, and the deanship of Durham (worth £1,500 p.a.) subsequently Frederick Keppel at Exeter from 1762 to 1768 was also, from 1766, dean of the Chapel Royal.[75] Aristocratic clerics who did particularly well for themselves were James Yorke, son of the Earl of Hardwicke, translated three times in seven years from St David's via Gloucester to Ely (1774, 1779, 1781), and Brownlow North, son of the Earl of Guilford and brother of the first minister, who managed three promotions (Lichfield £1,400 p.a., Worcester £3,000 p.a. and Winchester £5,000 p.a.) within the twelve years of North's administration. Of the twenty-four aristocratic bishops, twelve reached the Top Six bishoprics[76] – a success rate of 50% compared with 27% for non-aristocratic bishops. The deanship of the Chapel Royal at Windsor, one of the plums of the profession and at £900 p.a. worth more than several of the smaller bishoprics, was almost a preserve of the aristocracy. It was held from 1714 through to 1882 by a noble cleric.[77]

Of greater consequence however than merely illustrating aristocratic success is to establish the trend. In 1752 William Warburton, himself an aspiring bishop, wrote of the vacancy at Durham, caused by the death of Joseph Butler: 'Reckon upon it, that Durham goes to some noble ecclesiastic. 'Tis a morsel only for them. Our *grandees* have at last found their way back into the church. I only wonder they have been so long about it.'[78] Warburton was a good prophet. Durham duly went to the Hon. Richard Trevor, son of the 1st Baron Trevor. An analysis of the prelacy, distinguishing the position before 1740 from that afterwards, suggests that the trend was developing and, indeed, some

---

[75] The other three were James Beauclerk at Hereford from 1746, Charles Lyttelton at Carlisle from 1762 to 1768, and Henry Egerton at Hereford from 1723 to 1746.

[76] Canterbury, Durham, Winchester, York, London and Ely. I have included William Stuart who went to the primacy of Armagh in 1800.

[77] The sole exception was John Douglas who held it from 1788 to 1791 while bishop of Carlisle. N. Sykes, *Church and State in England in the eighteenth century* made the point that it must not be presumed that noble bishops were neglectful of their duties. James Beauclerk at Hereford, for example, was a respected and efficient bishop: see W. M. Marshall, 'The Administration of the Dioceses of Hereford and Oxford, 1660–1760', 244–5, Ph.D. thesis, Bristol University. See also a favourable assessment of Keppel at Exeter in A. Warne, *Church and society in 18th century Devon*, 26–7.

[78] *Letters from a late eminent prelate to one of his friends* (2nd edition, 1809), 118–19.

ontemporaries regarded it with gratification. Of the eighty-five bishops olding their sees in the eighteenth century and appointed before 1740, nly four were of aristocratic origins – a proportion of 4.7%. Of the venty-six appointed after 1740, twenty were noblemen, a proportion f 26%. The trend certainly continued into the nineteenth century. In 808, for example, noblemen held both archbishoprics, the bishoprics of)urham, Winchester and Ely (i.e. five of the Top Six), the bishoprics of ichfield, Peterborough, Exeter and Norwich (i.e. nine out of twenty-x). They also held the four Irish archbishoprics of Armagh, Dublin, :ashel and Tuam, and seven of the remaining eighteen Irish bishoprics. ımong additional perquisites, they shared the deanships of Durham and f Dublin.[79]

The nobility also exercised very direct influence over a substantial part f the church through its ownership of advowsons.[80] The antiquarian ¡rowne Willis published in the 1720s and 1730s a complete account of cclesiastical patronage, diocese by diocese, under the title *A survey of the :athedrals of England*. He went to considerable trouble to obtain his vidence and published amendments and additions. Of the 9,800 hurches listed, peers presented to some 1,200 – about 12% of the vhole.[81] Even this is not the grand total of aristocratic patronage. The)uke of Beaufort, for example, also presented to five prebendaries in the xeter diocese.[82] Lady Elizabeth Hastings is given as patron of Bardsey ll Saints, Collingham and Ledsham in the diocese of York, Lord ¡eorge Howard as patron of Rotherham in the same diocese, and the lon. Mrs Thynne as patron of Burton and Lillington in Dorset, part of ıe diocese of Sarum.[83]

⁹ A comparison of the social origins of English and French bishops was offered by N. Ravitch in the *Historical Journal*, VIII (1965), 309–25. There are some difficulties in using it, partly because the category 'genteel' employed seems vague and partly because bishops of 'uncertain' origin account for as much as 50% at certain periods. But greater preciseness is possible in the category 'Father was peer or close kin of a peer'. This Ravitch gives as rising from 5% in William III's reign to 28% in the second half of George III's reign: the increase in aristocratic domination of the Irish bench is more marked, rising from 0% in the reign of William, Anne and George I to 42% in the second half of George III's reign. Ravitch's conclusion was that English society was more open: that the French church represented a caste, the English an aristocracy. I think a conclusion of equal validity is that the English and Irish churches were becoming markedly less open. Ravitch's work was subsequently developed in a book entitled *Sword and mitre: government and episcopate in France and England in the age of aristocracy*.
⁰ The rights of lay patrons were fully restored on Charles II's return by 12 Charles II c. 17, Clause XXXI.
¹ In order to facilitate comparisons with other contemporary surveys, I have ignored chapels.
² See under 'Chumleigh', III, 156.
³ *Ibid.*, I, 185, 186, 187, 191; III, 130. A recent analysis is D. R. Hirschberg, 'The government and church patronage in England, 1660–1760', *Journal of British Studies*, XX, 1 (Fall 1980), 109–39. Hirschberg also puts the peerage share at 12%, with 9.6% in the hands of the crown, 26%

The largest patronage empires belonged to the dukes. The Duke o Norfolk was patron of no fewer than thirty-one livings, twenty-one o them in the diocese of Norwich.[84] Next came the Duke of Devonshir with twenty-nine and a half livings, fourteen in the diocese of Lichfiel and eleven in York. The Beauforts held twenty-seven and a half living: sixteen of which were in the dioceses of St David's or Llandaff. The Duk of Rutland held twenty-four, mainly in the diocese of Lincoln Newcastle held twenty-two, nine of them in the diocese of York Somerset and Bedford held twenty-one and twenty respectively. Th leading non-dukes were the Petres, like the Norfolks a Catholic family they held eighteen livings, and were followed by Lord Mansell wit seventeen (all in St David's or Llandaff). Abergavenny and Exeter als possessed seventeen livings. Altogether, forty-nine peerage families ha at least eight livings at their disposal.[85]

belonging to the church, and 6.7% to educational foundations, such as Oxford and Cambridg colleges. Table 1, 112 conveys a slightly false impression of certainty, however. Browne Willi collected his information over a considerable period. His first volume came out in 1727 an referred to material gathered from 1723 onwards; Volume II appeared in 1730 and Volume III i 1733. The survey therefore is roughly 1723 to 1730. The 1742 edition seems to be a reprint with different title page but does not really reflect the position at that date. It was apparently a pirat publication and denounced by Browne Willis as such.

[84] Norfolk was a Catholic. By the act of 3 James I c. 5 the advowsons of convicted recusants wer allotted to the Universities of Oxford and Cambridge, the former taking western and southern counties, the latter eastern and northern. It seems to have been widely evaded by the use o Protestant trustees and a further act, 1 William and Mary c. 26, charged archbishops and bishop with the task of investigating. A third act was 12 Anne c. 14. Soon after the Glorious Revolutio there was a legal action between the University of Cambridge and Lord Petre. It is summarised i *English Reports*, 83, 715–16. There are further references to the question including counsel' opinion in Essex CRO, Petre MSS, D/DP:L 73A and L 74. There seems to have been no genera attempt to enforce the legislation.

[85]

Norfolk	31	Salisbury	12
Devonshire	$29\frac{1}{2}$	Poulet	12
Beaufort	$27\frac{1}{2}$	Middleton	$11\frac{1}{2}$
Rutland	24	Nottingham	11
Newcastle	22	Bradford	11
Somerset	21	Craven	11
Bedford	20	Digby	11
Bolton	19	Rochford	11
Dorset	19	Rockingham	$10\frac{1}{2}$
Petre	18	Arundel	10
Kingston	$17\frac{1}{2}$	St John	10
Mansell	17	Bridgwater	10
Abergavenny	17	Weymouth	10
Exeter	17	Ashburnham	10
Montagu	17	Cornwallis	10
Lovell	16	Winchester	10
Townshend	16	Manchester	10
Ancaster	15	Cardigan	9
Kent	$14\frac{1}{2}$	Castleton	9

Patronage on this scale could be exploited in a variety of ways. At its simplest it could provide for relatives who otherwise would have to be privately supported. An unusual application was noted by the *Gentleman's Magazine* for 1738, under marriages:

Rev. Mr. Clavering (lately) to Miss Hawkins of Simsbury, Dorsetshire, sister to the late incumbent of that place, valued at £600 per ann., the presentation to which, being fallen to her by his death, she gave with herself and £1500 in specie to the said reverend gentleman.[86]

Lord Salisbury, having married his steward's niece, was under an obligation to provide for her relatives: her brother took Holy Orders and was presented to the family living at Hatfield. Lord William George Henry Somerset, son of the 5th Duke of Beaufort, found the family patronage distinctly useful after changing his military career for that of cleric. In the 1820s he appears to have held five livings in the Beaufort gift, at Stoke Gifford, Llangattock, Magor with Redwick, Llanfihangel with Crickhowell, and Tormarton with Acton Turville, augmented by a prebend at Bristol from 1822 to 1851:

It was stated by those who knew him that he never wrote a sermon; but there is a tradition that he preached twice in the Cathedral in the course of twenty-three years. On the other hand, he had all the skill of his family for driving a coach and four . . . and the stables he built at Tormarton were much more imposing than was the rectory.[87]

Patronage was also used to bring forward clerics who might be valuable political allies as pamphleteers or agents. Clergymen were highly regarded as canvassers at election time. They had usually a good working-knowledge of the district, professional excuses for visiting, experience in talking to people, and a formidable reputation for indefatigability in argument. A witness before a House of Commons select committee on bribery was not speaking merely for the nineteenth century when he declared:

I find clergymen not only the most persevering and unscrupulous canvassers, but also the best keepers of their promises in not continuing their custom or otherwise . . . A clergyman generally is a good political partisan; a voter cannot

Chandos	14½	Huntingdon	9
Pembroke	14	Leigh	8
Bristol	14	Oxford	8
Hobart	13	Scarborough	8
Yarmouth	13	Thanet	8
Marlborough	12		

[86] VIII, 276.   [87] Quoted J. A. Venn, *Alumni Cantabrigienses*.

get rid of him; he is not satisfied with the voter's saying 'I cannot vote for yo friend, because I prefer the political principles of the other gentleman.' He is n content with that, but he brings all his influence to bear to an immense extent.

Livings could also be used to pay off debts. Thomas Gilbert wrote t the 1st Earl Gower after the general election of 1754:

You will be pleased to observe by the Accounts p. 9 that Mr Simpson a lawyer unpaid for about £79 of his bills for business done after the election of 1747 . . As to what he and his son have done since, he does not intend to charge anythin but . . . hopes your Lordship and Lord Anson will give or procure son preferment in the Church for Mr Reynolds, his son-in-law.[89]

There was, of course, nothing to stop arrangements being made wit other patrons where convenient. In July 1726 Lord Bristol wrote to th bishop of Lincoln on behalf of the Revd Battely, of a Bury St Edmun family, asking for a prebend occupied by Dr Thomas Wise, who cou not last: 'If your Lordship would please to bestow the same on him, should take it as so particular a favour done to myself, that if on an future occasion a living in my gift should fall, to which your lordshi would recommend a friend or relation of your own, you shoul certainly command it.'[90]

Though there are methodological difficulties, it is not impossible t

---

[88] *Select committee of 1835*, 51. See also evidence on political sermons, 179.

[89] Leveson-Gower MSS, 25 Dec. 1754, quoted J. R. Wordie, *Estate management in eighteenth-centu England: the building of the Leveson-Gower fortune*, 231, Note 10. See also the note that barons we entitled to three chaplaincies and earls to five, each of whom could hold two livings *in absentia*. was therefore a very convenient way of qualifying and much sought after.

[90] *Hervey letter books*, III, No. 859. Dr Wise died on 24 July 1726. The bishop, a very experience cleric, did not fall for the suggestion and Wise was succeeded by William Musgrave.

It has sometimes been suggested that the archetypal eighteenth-century letter is one beginnin 'The Dean cannot last the night . . .'. One of the most premature appeals was made by Thom Wilson who wrote in 1737 asking for the succession to William Lamplugh, said to be dying of a ulcer on the kidney: he survived until 1776. See *Diaries of Thomas Wilson 1731–7 & 1750*, 21

Clerics were not as grateful, and certainly not as gracious, as one might have expected. August 1768, Thomas Secker, archbishop of Canterbury, slipped from his couch and broke h thigh. The clerical vultures unfolded their wings. Thomas Newton, bishop of Bristol, wrote once to Grafton, to beg the deanery of St Paul's. Though he got it in the general reshuffle, h thanks were qualified: 'there is so much propriety and justice in my plea, that it would really hav been an hardship and indignity to set me aside; but that will not lessen but rather heighten m obligations to Your Grace'. Another letter of modest rapture came from John Egerton, translate from Bangor to Lichfield on the same occasion:

Though the bishopric of Lichfield is very little, if at all, more in value than Bangor, yet th desire I have of being nearer those friends to whom I am under the greatest obligations woul determine me at once to be at the expense of a translation. I am anxious that my living at Ros which clears me two or three hundred p.a. should not be taken from me upon this occasion, the putting it in order has been a very considerable charge to me and the income of it, upo account of my family, will not be an inconsiderable object.

Newton to Grafton, 3 Aug. 1768 and 22 Aug. 1768; Egerton to Grafton, 13 Aug. 1768, Suffo RO, Grafton MSS, 423/344, 345, 346.

nake some comparison of the overall patronage position in the early years of Walpole's ministry with that one hundred years later. A aborious method is to check Browne Willis' survey with the information given by Samuel Lewis in his *Topographical Dictionary* (1831), which, for almost every parish, gives the name of the patron.[91] Though a number of new parishes had been created in the meantime,[92] we can meet the difficulty by comparing the nineteenth-century position only with those parishes described by Browne Willis. The nineteenth-century position will not therefore be complete, but a comparison can be attempted.

The evidence provided by Lewis suggests that, in the country as a whole, there was an increase of some 14% in the number of livings under aristocratic patronage. Browne Willis' evidence suggested some 1,200 livings in the hands of the peerage: by the early 1800s, the figure had risen to just under 1,400.[93]

Fortunately there is a second source which enables us to run a check upon these findings. *Patroni Ecclesiarum*, published in 1831, gives a list of patrons of advowsons, based upon returns made in 1818. Though there are differences in detail, to be explained by the different time-bases, the conclusion is much the same, that there was an increase of between 13% and 14%.

We can therefore provide a second list of the larger patrons to set against that given in Note 85, derived from Browne Willis. *Patroni Ecclesiarum* identifies sixty-four peers with eight or more livings at their disposal, making a total of 836½ livings.[94] The figures for the 1720s were forty-nine peers and a total of 698½ livings.

[91] Lewis gives the position at a number of different dates, so that an exact chronological comparison cannot be established.

[92] E.g. the parish of Stoke was sub-divided by Act of Parliament in 1801 and separate parishes established for Newcastle, Burslem, Bagnall, Whitmore and Norton.

[93] I put the figure approximately to remind the reader that exactitude is hardly possible. Apart from the difficulty mentioned in Note 91, there were very considerable place-name changes in the period under review which makes it impossible to guarantee that every living has been properly identified.

[94] List of patrons abstracted from *Patroni Ecclesiarum*:

Devonshire	37	Spencer	11
Lonsdale	31	Buccleuch	11
Rutland	29	Middleton	10
Fitzwilliam	29	Orford	10
Beaufort	28	Salisbury	10
Bedford	27	Monson	10
Egremont	26	Cardigan	10
Ilchester	20	Dorset	10
Bristol	19	Hardwicke	10
Abergavenny	18	Howe	9½

It must again be emphasised that these figures do not represent the full amount of aristocratic ecclesiastical patronage. Lord George Augustus Henry Cavendish, third son of the 4th Duke of Devonshire, is credited in *Patroni* with ten advowsons in his own right, but, since he was not at that time a peer, he is not included in our totals.[95] There were other forms of patronage which usually or invariably went to clerics. Lord Melbourne appointed the headmaster of Hertford Grammar School and Lord Hardwicke that of Buntingford Grammar School; Viscount Valletort nominated to St Maude Grammar School at Plympton, Devon.

A more detailed analysis reveals a good deal of reshuffling of the patronage empires and some spectacular collapses. The Norfolk holdings shrank from thirty-one to seventeen, but the Dukes of Devonshire had moved up from twenty-nine to thirty-seven, Lord Fitzwilliam had moved into third place, and Lonsdale, Rutland, Bedford and Bristol had made considerable gains. Among the large advowson clusters which had collapsed in the course of the century were those of the Dukes of Somerset, Chandos, Kent, Kingston and Ancaster, the Earls of Yarmouth and the Barons Mansell. The 6th Duke of Somerset ('the proud duke') had held some twenty-one advowsons. When the 7th Duke died in 1750, the estates were alienated from the title, which went to a fifth cousin once removed. In the 1820s the Dukes of Somerset held only two advowsons. Most of the others went via the heiress Elizabeth to the reconstituted dukedom of Northumberland or to the Egremont branch

Norfolk	17	Sondes	9
Pembroke	15	Bute	9
Willoughby de Eresby	15	Powis	9
Yarborough	15	Portland	9
Bridgwater	15	Oxford	9
Exeter	15	Scarborough	9
Brownlow	14	De Grey	9
Northumberland	13	Hastings	9
Craven	13	Digby	9
Buckingham	13	Stafford	8
Rivers	13	Bolton	8
Marlborough	12	Albemarle	8
Bath	12	Foley	8
Ashburnham	12	Guilford	8
Suffield	12	Newcastle	8
Shaftesbury	12	Bradford	8
Thanet	12	Coventry	8
Manvers	12	Willoughby de Broke	8
Rolle	11	Ailesbury	8
Cleveland	11	Aylesford	8
Cawdor	11	Winchelsea	8
Chesterfield	11	Coventry	8

[95] He was created Earl of Burlington in 1831.

t Petworth. James Brydges, 1st Duke of Chandos, had held fourteen and half advowsons, mainly in his native diocese of Hereford, but the amily fortunes collapsed after his death in 1744. Most of the advowsons were sold off with the estates and the dukedom itself became extinct in 1789. The Dukes of Kingston died out in 1773 and their holdings, mainly n the diocese of York, finished up as part of the Manvers empire.[96] The Kent holdings, after the death of the 1st Duke in 1740 went, via his granddaughter Jemima, to her eldest daughter, created Countess de Grey n 1816. The Dukes of Ancaster had held some fifteen advowsons in the 1720s. On the death of the 4th Duke in 1779 at the age of twenty-two, the Lincolnshire estates descended to his sister Priscilla, who married Peter Burrell, created Lord Gwydir in 1796. The Pastons had been in financial straits for decades before the extinction of the title in 1732: the 2nd Lord Yarmouth was said in 1708 to have 'vast debts . . . and scarce a servant to attend him'.[97] Most of their thirteen advowsons, all in the diocese of Norwich, went to non-peers, but some finished up as part of the Anson empire.[98] Another disintegrating cluster was that of the Barons Mansell, who had held seventeen advowsons in the dioceses of Llandaff and St David's. Their peerage became extinct in 1750 and most of the livings were alienated, save for Penrice and Briton Ferry, which went, by inheritance, to the Earls of Jersey.

The general increase in aristocratic holdings masks some significant local variations. Of the twenty-six dioceses, eighteen showed an increase, three remained the same, and five showed a decrease. The largest proportional increase was in the diocese of Bristol, and was mainly attributable to the emergence of two new peerage families, the Earls of Ilchester and Lords Rivers, together with a strengthening of the older Shaftesbury interest. In the diocese of Chester, the increase was due to the arrival of the Grosvenor interest and the expansion of the Lonsdale interest. In the diocese of Exeter, the most significant development was the establishment of the Rolle interest. In the large diocese of Lincoln, the building up of two powerful new interests, Monson and Yarborough, and the extension of two long-established interests, Bedford and Rutland, help to explain the growth. In Norwich, another large diocese, the increase was almost entirely due to the establishment of new interests,

[96] Charles Medows, nephew of the 2nd Duke, succeeded to the estates, was created Viscount Newark in 1796 and Earl Manvers in 1806.
[97] *Letters of Humphrey Prideaux*, Camden Society, NS, xv (1875), 200.
[98] Viscount Anson, created 1806, had acquired a Norfolk interest by marrying in 1794 at Holkham the daughter of Thomas William Coke, subsequently Earl of Leicester.

Calthorpe, Suffield, Wodehouse, Henniker, Stradbrooke, Huntingfield and Gosford.

To the general pattern of modest increase, there are two marked exceptions. The diocese of Hereford was one of the smaller ones, with 286 livings in the 1720s. Of the thirty-five livings then under peerage patronage, eight were in the hands of the Duke of Chandos; the collapse of that empire and the sale of the advowsons was enough to produce an overall decrease.[99] The second exception is of more than local interest. The dioceses of London, Rochester and Winchester registered overall losses. Winchester took in most of Surrey, Rochester comprised north-west Kent, and the diocese of London included Middlesex, Essex and south Hertfordshire.[100] In other words, the influence of the metropolis was beginning to affect the pattern. Three factors may explain this. The first is the possibility of competition for the purchase of advowsons from the London 'monied interest'. The second is that, with the spread of the suburbs, the metropolitan area was becoming less attractive to the peerage, socially and politically. The third underlines our basic argument. Very few of the new peers, building up ecclesiastical interests in the later eighteenth century, were men of commercial, financial or industrial wealth from the London area. The Crewes, Rolles and Anderson-Pelhams were old-established county families. The new recruits to the peerage were not, by and large, the possessors of the new wealth. Though the total of aristocratic ecclesiastical patronage continued to expand, in the London area it was pushed back or chose to withdraw into the shires. But the great growth of London was followed in turn by Birmingham, Manchester, Sheffield, Leeds, Liverpool and Bristol. Even in the dry statistics of advowson holdings we can discern those shifts which brought about the eventual decline of the aristocratic interest and the establishment of a different political and social order.

---

[99] Another Herefordshire peerage interest which collapsed was that of Coningsby, based upon Hampton Court. After passing to the Earls of Essex, the estate was sold in the early nineteenth century to Richard Arkwright, son of the entrepreneur. Though he was said to be talented, hard-working and the richest commoner in England, he was not offered a peerage and had to be content with a medal from the Horticultural Society for improvements in growing grapes.
[100] North Herts. was in the archdeaconry of Huntingdon, in the diocese of Lincoln.

3

MARRIAGE

The 2nd Viscount Bolingbroke, having lost money on the turf, cards and women, decided in 1767 'to marry a rich monster and retrieve his affairs'. First it was necessary to divorce his wife. Though the divorce bill went through, the 'rich monster' escaped and Bully spent some time in the 1770s on a proposal to enclose part of Sedgmoor, which would put £30,000 into his own pocket. That, like most of Bully's schemes, also failed and by 1777 he was driven back to his former suggestion: 'he is gone down to Bath in pursuit of a lady, who he proposes should retrieve his finances. Her name is Curtis: she is about thirty years of age, and has a fortune of forty-three thousand pounds.' But Miss Curtis found Bully's fading charms insufficient and two years later he declined into madness.[1] His son, George Richard St John, freed from parental control, compounded the disaster with an imprudent early marriage to the penniless daughter of his tutor, and when, after years of separation, she died, he married his German mistress. It required only the 5th Viscount in 1869 to marry the daughter of a Belgian schoolmaster and, on her death, the daughter of a blacksmith, for the ruin of the family to be complete. Their delectable house at Lydiard Tregoze in Wiltshire became a corporation museum.

Careful marriages, on the other hand, were of great importance in consolidating or increasing family fortunes. The Gowers, at the time of the Glorious Revolution were Staffordshire baronets.[2] Promoted to a barony in 1703, they attained an earldom in 1746, a marquisate in 1786

---

[1] Selwyn to Holland, 29 Aug. 1767, *Letters to Henry Fox, Lord Holland*, ed. Lord Ilchester, 280; Charles Townshend to George Selwyn, 9 Dec. 1777, *George Selwyn and his contemporaries*, ed. J. H. Jesse, III, 247. Bully's wife, Lady Diana Spencer, daughter of the Duke of Marlborough, was divorced in 1768 and married Topham Beauclerk, 'the hero of the Affair'. Bully even persuaded George Selwyn out of his habitual lethargy to chair the Commons' committee on the Sedgmoor Bill, but he was unable to save it, *HMC. Carlisle*, 301–11.

[2] The 4th baronet was married, however, to the daughter of the 1st Earl of Bath.

and emerged as Dukes of Sutherland in 1833. Their rise was based upon political acumen, sound marriages and luck. They received a large inheritance in 1711 when the twenty-year-old Earl of Bath died of smallpox, and another in 1734 on the death of the widow of the 2nd Duke of Albemarle. The third baron married in 1744 the daughter of an MP, who brought in £16,000. On her death within eighteen months, he married the daughter of the 1st Duke of Bridgwater. This marriage produced enormous dividends in 1803 when the third Duke died unmarried, leaving estates worth at least £75,000 p.a. The 4th Baron, in 1785, married Elizabeth, Countess of Sutherland in her own right, adding more than one million Scottish acres to the family holding.[3] Equally spectacular was the success of the Grosvenor family, who moved from baron (1761), earl (1784), marquis (1831) to become Dukes of Westminster in 1874. Here the key was a marriage in 1677 by Sir Thomas Grosvenor to Mary Davies, heiress of the manor of Ebury, which became Belgravia: the family fortunes floated on rising urban rents.[4] The shaky position of the Cecils, Earls of Salisbury, was restored by the marriage in 1683 to the daughter of Simon Bennet, who had amassed great London wealth, and reinforced in 1821 by the Gascoyne marriage, bringing in Liverpool property.[5] Perhaps the most remarkable personal rise was that of Hugh Smithson, grandson of a Yorkshire baronet, whose immediate ancestors had kept a haberdasher's shop in Cheapside. In 1740 he paid his addresses to Elizabeth, daughter of the 7th Duke of Somerset; his mother was the daughter and heiress of the last Earl of Northumberland, whose death in 1670 had brought the Percy line to a close. In the face of rather lukewarm opposition from the parents, Smithson carried the day. The death of his brother-in-law in 1744 from smallpox began his rapid rise. Smithson's wife was now sole heir. In 1749 Somerset was created Earl of Northumberland, with a special remainder to Smithson. On inheriting the title a year later, Smithson changed his name to Percy, was given the Garter in 1757, and in 1766 was created Duke of Northumberland. Horace Walpole, who could be relied upon to be spiteful, thought that the new Duke was inclined to overdo the Percy connection.[6]

[3] Wordie, *Estate management in eighteenth-century England.*
[4] G. E. Mingay, *English landed society in the eighteenth century*, 76–8.
[5] H. J. Habakkuk, 'The rise and fall of English landed families 1600–1800', *Transactions of the Royal Historical Society*, 5th series, 29 (1979), 193. The article gives other examples of lucky marriages.
[6] There is a good account of the Smithson courtship, with letters in G. Brenan, *A history of the House of Percy*, II, 424–53. The diaries of the Duchess of Northumberland were edited by J. Greig, *The Diaries of a Duchess.*

Sex and property are said to make an irresistible plot. Certainly the eighteenth century found it so. One of the crucial ingredients in the success of Edward Cave's *Gentleman's Magazine* was the monthly column of marriages, which gave the amount of dowry, real or invented, and any piquant garnishings that could be provided.[7] Marriage gossip was the staple fare of many eighteenth-century correspondences, often with considerable detail of the financial arrangements. Where much was at stake, nuptial performance was monitored. Horace Walpole was disappointed that he had 'no anecdotes of the wedding-night' to pass on after Lord Fitzwilliam's marriage in 1744 and when Lord Beauchamp in 1768 married a daughter of Viscount Windsor, an Irish peer, George Selwyn reported of the honeymoon that: 'Beauchamp is seen out so early in a morning that it does not look as if much business was doing.'[8]

Matrimonial alliances were of great moment to families. The terms were a matter of close and hard bargaining, often protracted over months, the amount of the dowry and the jointure being of particular importance. Lord Rockingham warned his heir that settlements could be tedious business: 'you may see by Lord Granby's affair, this is a work of time, his has taken up more than a whole year'.[9] When Lord Egmont was negotiating a marriage between his son and Catherine, daughter of the 5th Earl of Salisbury, the Cecils' lawyer spent a whole morning checking Egmont's rent-rolls and steward accounts 'and was very well pleased with them, for he never saw an estate that had fewer deductions'.[10]

The development of the entail or strict settlement in the later seventeenth century helped to block up one hole through which the family estates might drain and where it operated the heir had, in effect, only a life interest in the family property.[11] Another cause of anxiety was the possibility of an heir contracting an ill-advised marriage at an early age. Lord Tankerville, when he was eighteen, eloped with a butcher's

---

[7] 'A pensioner of *Chelsea* college, upwards of 80, to a widow, worth £3,000, near 90 years of age, who fell in love with him.' *Gentleman's Magazine*, XIV (1744), 619.

[8] Walpole to Hanbury-Williams, 26 June 1744, *Corr.*, XXX, 49–50; *HMC. Carlisle*, 238.

[9] Quoted R. Trumbach, *The rise of the egalitarian family: aristocratic kinship and domestic relations in eighteenth century England*, 74.

[10] *HMC. Egmont*, II, 327. See also the hard bargaining on pages 337–8.

[11] Entail is discussed more fully in Chapter 5. Though its prime purpose was to prevent alienation, it served also to protect the rights of younger children. The critical feature was the establishment of trustees to supervise the settlement. It was very common however to leave some property out of the settlement to afford some discretion in case of emergency. The entail could be broken only by special Act of Parliament.

daughter whom he had met at an assize ball in Newcastle.[12] It was to guard against this, and, in particular, to put a stop to the notorious Fleet marriages that the bill against Clandestine Marriages was introduced in 1753.

It provoked a storm of controversy. The intention was to regularise marriage by instituting the calling of banns, based upon a month's residence in the parish, and prohibiting the marriage of persons under the age of twenty-one without the consent of their father or guardian. Though in retrospect it appears a modest measure of administrative reform, eradicating undoubted abuses, the debates reveal a widespread mistrust of the nobility. The fact that it had originated in the Lords and at the suggestion of the Earl of Bath, who was both rich and unpopular, did not assist its reception in the Commons.

The bill was in fact the culmination of a struggle between Lords and Commons over the issue which went back at least eighty years. Repeatedly the House of Commons had refused to join with the Lords in tightening up the marriage laws. In 1677 the Lords sent down a bill with a preamble which rehearsed the dangers in which young children stood: 'their fathers, having no means to avoid such marriages, are often reconciled thereto rather than wholly desert their children'. The Commons were not moved. First an attempt was made to make off with the bill and then it was abandoned. A similar bill failed again in the Commons in 1685, though the House of Lords sent a reminder.[13] Another bill and another reminder went unheeded in 1689, and in 1691 the bill was dropped though the House of Lords sent three reminders. Another attempt in 1697 failed on prorogation and in December 1697 the Commons, presumably running short of evasive tactics, negatived the measure. The issue was again joined in 1711 and 1735. Its success in 1753 therefore is some indication of the enhanced influence which the Lords wielded over the Commons.[14]

Ryder, the Attorney-General, who introduced the measure, stressed the danger to property from Fleet marriages: 'what distress some of our best families have been brought into, what ruin some of their sons or

---

[12] *GEC*, XII, 1, 633, Note e gives details. The Bennet family failed to break the marriage and Miss Colville made rather a good countess, becoming a Lady of the Bedchamber to Queen Caroline and a favourite of George II.

[13] Most of these bills offered the same safeguards but there were disagreements about the age at which father's consent should become unnecessary. The 1753 bill, in proposing the age of twenty-one, gave greater command to the father than some of the previous versions which had suggested as low as sixteen for boys and fourteen for girls.

[14] *HMC. House of Lords MSS*: (1678–88), 276–9; (1689–90), 243–9, 267–73; (1690–1), 253–60; (1695–7), 547–8; (1697–9), 1–2; *HMC. 9th Report*, II, 90–1; *Commons Journals*, IX, 445.

aughters have been involved in, every gentleman may from his own
nowledge recollect'. Some of the opposition was personal, factious and
ynthetic. Henry Fox, who had eloped in 1744 with the daughter of the
)uke of Richmond, took it as a point of honour to defend runaway
natches, and was joined by Charles Townshend, at the beginning of his
hort but spectacular career, reacting no doubt against a heavy father.[15]
3ut Robert Nugent and George Haldane took a more general political
tance. Nugent expressed no surprise that the bill had originated in the
Lords: 'they will thereby gain a very considerable and a very particular
dvantage; for they will in a great measure secure all the rich heiresses in
he kingdom to those of their own body'. Haldane insisted that the bill
vas merely the first step in turning the nobility into a Venetian
·ligarchy. The property gained through marriage would be used to buy
1p seats in the Commons and the balance of the constitution would be
lestroyed: 'and as our nobility would always take care to have some of
hemselves at the head of our army and navy, it would be impossible for
he king or people to recover themselves out of their hands'. In the end,
he bill went through comfortably, though attempts to repeal it
ontinued for some time.[16]

  In the first chapter we saw at work the amiable English gift for
entimentalising their institutions, by contrasting the flexibility of the
:nglish social structure with the rigidity of that on the continent. A
imilar indulgence insisted on the openness of aristocratic marriage. It
vas no doubt good for the morale of English seamstresses, kitchen-maids
nd governesses to feel that at any moment they might be whisked off to

⁵ For Fox, see Lord Ilchester, *Henry Fox, first Lord Holland*, I, 184–97; Townshend's attitude is
  discussed in L. B. Namier and J. Brooke, *Charles Townshend*, 29–30. Horace Walpole thought it a
  statute which 'breathed the very spirit of aristocracy and insolent nobility'. It became law as 26
  George II, c. 33.
⁶ *Parliamentary history*, xv, 1–86. The bill produced a crop of pamphlets, novels and caricatures.
  Mrs Delany, who read Shebbeare's novel *The Marriage Act* against the bill disliked its tone: 'I
  don't understand the policy of making all the nobility appear odious.' *Autobiography and
  Correspondence of Mary Granville, Mrs Delany*, ed. Lady Llanover, 1st series, III, 329. There were
  two reasons why the bill was not totally effective. Aristocratic girls who eloped had damaged
  their marriage prospects so badly, even if the marriage was void, that parents were still likely to
  acquiesce in the end: indeed, the object of many pursuits was to ensure that a genuine marriage did
  take place. Second, Scotland remained a loophole and Gretna Green beckoned. Lord
  Westmorland's melodramatic dash to Gretna in 1782 was a snug compromise between romantic
  and prudent marriage, since he eloped with the daughter of a prominent banker.
    Trumbach, *The rise of the egalitarian family*, 101–9 tries to place the bill in the context of his
  general thesis of a move towards greater equality, but not without difficulty. He argues that the
  younger sons, sitting in the Commons, at last realised that it was very wrong to look to
  matrimony to establish their fortunes (pages 108–9). It may be so. But of the four younger sons
  who took part in the debate, three (Fox, Townshend and William Beckford) offered violent
  opposition. The fourth was Murray. It seems clear that the intention of the bill was to strengthen
  patriarchal authority.

a coronet. Cinderella has always been a popular fairy story. But Eliz
Haywood in 1743 warned female servants not to imagine that 'becaus
such matches have sometimes happened, it will be your fortune'.[17]

Defoe acknowledged this belief in the mingling of ranks when, in hi
The compleat English gentleman, he compiled a list 'where inferior ladie
are married to persons of rank and dignity'.[18] But we should be cautiou
about the status of these 'inferior' ladies before saluting new opportuni
ties for women. Camilla, the butcher's daughter, made her rightfu
appearance as the wife of Lord Tankerville. But in other respects it was
very odd list. Only eleven names are included and the marriages rang
over a period of some forty-five years. The 4th Duke of Hamilton shoul
be deleted. Disguised as 'Mrs Gerrard', his wife of 1698 sound
splendidly ordinary, but she was in fact the daughter of the 5th Baroi
Gerard by the daughter of the 1st Earl of Macclesfield. The Duke o
Wharton's marriage (a Fleet marriage at the age of sixteen) was to th
daughter of a Major-General. 'Mrs Child', married in 1682 to th
Marquis of Worcester, was the daughter of Sir Josiah Child, baronet an
chairman of the East India Company, and brought a portion of £25,00C
Mrs Howland, who married the Marquis of Tavistock in 1695 (he wa
fifteen, she thirteen and, it was said, worth £100,000), was th
granddaughter of Child: to mark the occasion, the marquis' grandfathe
the Duke of Bedford, was granted the barony of Howland, with a specia
remainder to the offspring of the married pair. Lord Islay's wife, Mi
Whitefield, was daughter of an MP and Paymaster of Marines. Argyl
his brother, had married in 1701 the daughter of John Brown
(Duncombe), Receiver-General of the Excise. The Earl of Bucha
married in 1697 the granddaughter of Sir Thomas Browne, the authoi
her father, Henry Fairfax, was a Berkshire landowner, educated at Chris
Church, Oxford. Lord Onslow married in 1708 the niece and heiress of
colonel, worth £70,000. The Earl of Exeter married in 1724 the daughte
of a merchant from London and Derby. Lastly, the 5th Duke c
Hamilton married, as his second wife in 1727, the daughter of Thoma
Strangeways of Dorset. He was one of the greatest landowners in th
West of England, had succeeded his father as MP for the county, and h
estates went, in the end, to found the earldom of Ilchester. Even draggin
in five Scottish peers, Defoe can scarcely offer a plausible list. Indeed, h
point may be reversed. If these brides were considered 'inferior ladies
the standards of Augustan society were fairly demanding.

[17] *A present for a servant maid, or a sure means of gaining love and esteem*, 46.
[18] Ed. K. D. Bülbring, 261.

Another list to be treated with some caution was provided by Lord Egmont in February 1745:

This has been a lucky season for low people's marrying, for I am told that since the Duke of Chandos' marriage with the innkeeper's maid near Slough, the Duke of Ancaster has married his kept mistress, and the Duke of Rutland will own his with his kept mistress, the Earl of Salisbury has married his steward's niece – Miss Keate, daughter to a barber and shewer of the tombs in Canterbury, and the Earl of Bristol his late wife's maid. And the Duke of Bridgwater his tutor's niece.

The marriages of Chandos and Salisbury were true enough. Five years later Ancaster married Mary, the daughter of Thomas Panton, a racehorse trainer at Newmarket. But Bridgwater, who had inherited in January 1745 at the age of seventeen, did not marry and died aged twenty. Nor did Rutland or Bristol remarry after the deaths of their former wives.[19]

In the course of the century, a number of genuine cases of humble marriages did something to keep hopes alive. Lord Melcombe and Lord Carteret of Hawnes both married mistresses of many years standing, the latter after forty-three years of cohabitation. The 4th Earl of Gainsborough did a Lady Chatterley in reverse and in 1728 married his gamekeeper's daughter.[20] The 3rd Lord Montfort, confined for debt in a sponging-house in 1793, married Betty Watts the daughter, presumably to make his stay more comfortable. Nancy Parsons, famous as the mistress of the 3rd Duke of Grafton while he was first minister, persuaded Lord Maynard at an impressionable age to make her a viscountess. Of the wife of the 3rd Earl Granville, who was of unsound mind, we know no more than that she was 'said to have been a French woman'. Mary Cole, the butcher's daughter from Gloucester, who married the 5th Earl of Berkeley, was comely, dignified and an excellent wife.[21]

What, if anything, do these picturesque examples signify? Most of the *mésalliances* were the product of the impetuosity of youth, the complaisance of age or the decay of faculties. They certainly do not mean that there was not a very powerful prejudice against marrying outside one's order. Samuel Pepys in October 1660 was witness to a discussion between Lord Sandwich and his wife on the prospects for their daughter

---

[19] HMC. *Egmont*, III, 307–8.   [20] He had held the title since the age of six.

[21] The Earl held the title since the age of nine. The date and place of the marriage was disputed and led to the Berkeley peerage case. For Mary Cole, see the biography by Hope Costley-White published in 1961.

Jemima: 'my lady saying that she would have a good merchant for her daughter Jem, he answered that he would rather see her with a pedlar' pack at her back, so she married a gentleman rather than that she should marry a citizen'. Though Sandwich's logic was curious, his authority carried the day and Jemima married the son of Sir George Carteret, one of Sandwich's colleagues at the Navy Board: their son was created 1st Baron Carteret.[22] Forty years later, on several occasions in *The Spectator* Addison deplored the reluctance of the upper classes to see their children in trade: 'Will Wimble is the case of many a younger brother of a great family, who had rather see their children starve like gentlemen, than thrive in a trade or profession that is beneath their quality.'[23] These attitudes died hard. Even professional men were looked at askance. When Lady Jane Evelyn in 1772 married the very distinguished physician Dr Lucas Pepys, Mrs Boscawen, her sister-in-law, was much put out: 'one cannot but think it an *unequal* match! . . . *Au reste*, I believe he is a gentleman by birth.' She had much difficulty in composing a suitable letter in reply to the news: 'I could not *rejoice with her*, for I did *not* rejoice (*au contraire*); and I did not congratulate upon what I could not approve . . . I had rather have wrote ten letters than that one answer.'[24] By the time Pepys had gained a baronetcy in 1784, Lady Jane had succeeded as Countess of Rothes in her own right, so presumably the match stayed unequal. By most people marital equality was regarded as part of the natural order of things. Chesterfield's advice to his godson was to marry a woman 'of a rank not indecently below your own'.[25] Henry Stebbing, taking part in the controversy over the Clandestine Marriages Act, insisted that 'the world *naturally* runs this way without the help of laws. The lower classes of men have it not in their *power* to marry above their rank, or very rarely. The rich and great have as rarely so little *pride* as to permit them to marry below theirs.'[26]

There are however considerable methodological difficulties in forming a systematic estimate of the degree of social flexibility in aristocratic marriages. The evidence to be obtained from the status of the fathers of wives does not always permit an exact assessment of their social position, particularly if the survey attempts to include the marriages of

[22] *Diary*, ed. R. C. Latham and W. Matthews, 1, 20 Oct. 1660. There is a long description of Jemima's wedding in the diary for 31 July 1665. Jemima's husband was killed with his father-in-law at the naval battle in Sole Bay in 1672.

[23] No. 108. See also No. 21.

[24] *Autobiography and correspondence of Mrs Delany*, 2nd series, 1, 463.   [25] *Letters*, No. 2618.

[26] *A dissertation on the power of states to deny civil protection to the marriages of minors* (1755), quoted Trumbach, *The rise of the egalitarian family*, 107–8.

ounger sons, and we have seen that anecdotal evidence is often more lurid than accurate. Though the analyses which have been made commonly take as their basic units cohorts according to dates of birth, it should be remembered that the marriages of a particular decadal cohort may well be scattered over forty years. It is therefore unwise to try to date changes of attitude or practice too precisely. Lastly, though it is a comparatively easy matter to trace the sons and daughters of peers, it is laborious to track down more distant peerage connections. Yet unless they are taken into account, a false impression may be given. It would hardly be sensible to record that the 9th Lord Westmorland did not make an endogamous marriage, since his bride was not the daughter of a peer, without adding that she was the daughter of Lord Montagu Bertie, fourth son of Robert, 1st Duke of Ancaster. If the analysis is then extended to include nieces, sisters and granddaughters of peers, one runs into areas of nice discrimination since, in marriage negotiations, a peerage connection in the family was an important asset, even if it was at some distance.

We are fortunate in having one important pioneering work on which to build. T. H. Hollingsworth followed his early study of British ducal families[27] with a more comprehensive survey of the British peerage as a whole.[28] Many of the questions he was concerned with are not strictly germane to my enquiry, and his analysis covered a much wider period, from 1550 to the twentieth century.

The general tendency of Hollingsworth's analysis was to trace a decline in endogamous marriages by the peerage over the whole period. There was no strong incentive to marry within the limited circle of the nobility as there was on the continent . . . the theory of noble blood which held sway on the continent was only feebly held in Britain.'[29] This puts the contrast too strongly. Though there was no formal law of dérogeance in England, there remained considerable social disdain for inappropriate marriages. But Hollingsworth's main claim was to identify three social 'revolutions', each marking a substantial decrease in peerage exclusiveness, the first around 1721, the second around 1880 and the third around 1929.

To this one must suggest three reservations. First, the terminology seems a little extravagant. Social revolutions I take to be momentous things and if one did take place about 1721 I do not think we would be

---

[27] 'A demographic study of the British ducal families', *Population Studies*, XI, (July 1957), 4–26.
[28] 'The demography of the British peerage', Supplement to *Population Studies*, XVIII (Nov. 1964), 1–168.   [29] *Ibid.*, 6.

hunting for it among peerage marriages. Second, Hollingsworth's use of his own statistics seems, at times, difficult to understand. His second social revolution occurs 'about 1880, certainly between 1870 and 1895' It must therefore arise from the difference in the marriage pattern of the cohort born 1850–74 from that of the 1875–99 cohort. But the decline for endogamous marriages of peers' sons, is only from 20.2% to 18.7% – no more than 1.5% – and for peers' daughters it is a mere 0.6%. If this decline is sufficiently important to be termed a revolution, why is there no comment on other changes in Hollingsworth's Table 1 which were much more substantial? The differences between cohorts born 1775–99 and 1800–24, for example, run at 3.2% and 2.3% respectively, and the *increase* in endogamous peers' marriages between 1550–74 and 1575–99 was no less than 12.6% – which calls out for a mega-revolution. The fall of 0.6% in female endogamous marriages noted means, in practice, that *five* females out of nearly 1,000 changed their previous pattern of endogamous marriage. This is an alarmingly small number to produce so important a social shift. Third, the quality of the historical exposition seems scarcely adequate. We are warned that 'the nobility of George I was as different from that of Anne as the nobility of Edward VII was from that of the first half of Victoria's reign',[30] but the explanation of this change is that 'it comes on the eve of the industrial revolution, almost as if the structure of society were becoming a little more liberal just in time for that event'. This seems a rather mystical example of historical explanation to derive from so rigorous a statistical analysis.

What Dr Hollingsworth's figures show is not so much a sudden break in the marriage pattern as a steady decline in endogamous marriage during the seventeenth century, followed by a slight rise in the eighteenth century as the peerage became, if anything, more exclusive, followed by another decline in the nineteenth century. A straightforward consolidation of the male and female marriages in Hollingsworth's Table 1 produces the result shown in Table 16.

Refinements to Hollingsworth's methodology and modifications of his conclusions have been offered by D. N. Thomas.[31] He objected to the simple division into noble or common: in the first category, the marriage behaviour of dukes might differ from that of barons, and in the second category one needed to distinguish foreign wives, daughters of baronets and so on in order to yield a more discriminating picture. The marriage

---

[30] *Ibid.*, 10.
[31] 'Marriage patterns in the British peerage in the 18th and 19th centuries', M.Phil. thesis, London University (1969); and 'The social origins of marriage partners of the British peerage in the eighteenth and nineteenth centuries', *Population Studies*, XXVI (1972), 99–111.

Table 16. *Percentage of noble to total marriages, 1600–1899 (based on Hollingsworth)*

	Total no. of marriages	No. of noble marriages	Percentage of noble to total marriages
600–24	1,255	448	35.70
625–49	1,188	420	35.35
650–74	1,142	382	33.45
675–99	1,024	334	32.62
700–24	974	245	25.15
725–49	823	212	25.76
750–74	1,286	338	26.28
775–99	1,447	405	27.99
800–24	1,715	432	25.19
825–49	1,819	469	25.78
850–74	2,038	434	21.30
875–99	1,704	345	20.25

behaviour of eldest sons and heirs might be different from that of younger sons, and the pattern of second and third marriages might differ from that of first marriages.

In one respect Thomas' findings appeared to support Hollingsworth. He accepted the suggestion of a social revolution and produced a cohort whose marriage pattern was significantly different. Unfortunately it was not the same cohort. Thomas' table indicated that the endogamous marriage rate of the cohort born 1720–9 was as low as 17.2%, compared with 34.7% for the previous and 27.5% for the subsequent decades. This cohort would be marrying from 1740 onwards. Since Hollingsworth had identified 'the significant change' as taking place in the middle of the 675–99 cohort, we appear to have rival social revolutions.[32]

[32] Table 3 of Thomas' M.Phil. thesis, 104. The existence side by side of one decade (1710–19) with the highest endogamy of the two centuries surveyed and another (1720–9) with the lowest suggests that decades are too short to avoid distortions of sample. If the same evidence is presented in fifty-year periods, the element of continuity becomes apparent:

Cohort	No. of marriages	No. of in-marriages	Percentage of in-marriages to total
1700–49	543	144	26.5
1750–99	761	214	28.1
1800–49	925	249	26.9
1850–99	704	148	21.0

Thomas was much more sceptical of the liberal view of aristocrati
marriage than Hollingsworth had been. He demonstrated that dukes an
marquises were more likely to marry within the aristocracy than earls o
viscounts, and that the same was true of heirs against younger sons. Bu
his main conclusion was that there existed 'a greater concern with a
ethic of endogamy . . . than is revealed in a simple analysis of in- and out
marriages', and that 'the possibility of one's daughter marrying into th
peerage could not have been an important means of social advancemen
for those families who were on the fringes of, or who lay outside th
"gentlemanly" class'. It could hardly be said, Thomas concluded, tha
'the social exclusivity of the peerage was placed in jeopardy by the natur
of its recruitment of spouses'.[33]

Since a good deal of analytical work has been done on the children c
peers my own survey is confined to the peers themselves. Of the 954, 12
did not marry at all. Four of these were Catholic priests,[34] seven did nc
reach the age of fifteen,[35] and another ten died before the age of twenty
three.[36] The proportion of peers not marrying was therefore 13.4% c
the whole. If the 954 peers are divided into three roughly equal group
we can see the chronological distribution (Table 17).

The marriage rate as a whole is very high, as one would expect, since w
are considering persons who were under great family pressure t
produce legitimate heirs. Thomas found throughout the eighteent
century as a whole a marriage rate of 84% among heirs, and 63% amon
younger sons.[37]

Hollingsworth noted a rather low rate of marriage in the early decade
of the eighteenth century.[38] The nature of my evidence does not allow
exact comparisons to be made, but out of the seventeen peers noted a
dying before the age of twenty-three, eleven were born in the perioc
1690–1729 which saw some virulent smallpox epidemics.

[33] *Population Studies*, XXVI, 109, 99.
[34] The 6th Baron Dormer, d. 1761; the 7th Baron Gerard, d. 1733; the 6th Earl Rivers, d. 1737; th
13th Earl of Shrewsbury, d. 1743.
[35] 4th Duke of Brandon, d. 1769; 3rd Earl of Coventry, d. 1712; 8th Earl of Lincoln, d. 1730; 5t
Baron Lovelace, d. 1709; 8th Baron St John of Bletso, d. 1714; 13th Earl of Suffolk, d. 1779; 5t
Earl Waldegrave, d. 1794.
[36] 3rd Earl of Bath, d. 1711; 6th Baron Brooke, d. 1711; 2nd Duke of Buckingham, d. 1735; 2n
Baron Calthorpe, d. 1807; 9th Baron Clifton, d. 1713; 4th Duke of Dorset, d. 1815; 7th Earl o
Exeter, d. 1722; 5th Earl of Gainsborough, d. 1759; 2nd Viscount Lonsdale, d. 1713; 9th Baro
Teynham, d. 1727.
[37] 'The social origins of marriage partners', Table 2, 101. The basis of Thomas' calculation mean
that his figures are not systematically comparable with my own.
[38] 'The demography of the British peerage', 21.

Table 17. *Percentage of unmarried peers, 1600–1799*

orn	Total of peers in group	Number unmarried	Percentage unmarried
600–89	317	34	10.7
590–1729	341	57	16.7
730–99	296	37	12.5

Of the remaining 826 peers, 224 married twice, and thirty-six three mes. The 3rd Lord Harborough was the only eighteenth-century peer ▸ marry four times: towards the end of his life the search for a male heir ▸came frantic and his third and fourth marriages were at three months' ▸d seven months' intervals from the death of his previous wife. ▸evertheless he died without a male heir, estate and title going to his ▸unger brother. The proportion of second marriages to all marriages ▸as 27.1%, and third marriages 4.35%. Thomas' figures for second ▸arriages of male heirs for the whole century was 22.6%, which is a little ▸wer than mine, as one would anticipate.[39]

The rate of remarriage declined steadily from the seventeenth to the ▸neteenth centuries as the expectation of life for brides increased.[40] This ▸cline does not show up very markedly in my figures for peers, ▸esumably because of the importance of begetting heirs. In the later ▸ars of the eighteenth century, the figures are beginning to be ▸arginally affected by divorce. Before 1740 only three peers obtained ▸vorces, Lord Roos in 1670, Lord Macclesfield in 1698 and the Duke of

'Marriage patterns', Table 16, 188; 'The social origins of marriage partners', Table 2, 101. Figures taken from Hollingsworth's Table 13 give the proportion of second to first marriages (for sons *and* daughters of peers) as 20.3% for the seventeenth, 13.3% for the eighteenth and 12.6% for the nineteenth centuries.

In Table 43 ('The demography of the British peerage', 57), Hollingsworth printed an extremely useful analysis showing the remarkable increase in expectation of life for aristocratic women during the eighteenth century:

1650–74	32.7 years
1675–99	34.2 years
1700–24	36.3 years
1725–49	36.7 years
1750–74	45.7 years
1775–99	49.0 years
1800–24	51.7 years
1825–49	58.4 years
1850–74	62.8 years

See also P. E. Razzell, *The conquest of smallpox*.

Norfolk in 1700. Proceedings were, of course, by private Act of Parliament. After a long gap, the Duke of Beaufort was granted a divorce in 1744. He was followed by Lord Bolingbroke in 1768, to whom we have referred earlier, Grafton (1769), Ligonier (1771), Perc (1779), Carmarthen (1779), Brandon (1794), Cadogan (1796) ar Abercorn, Viscount Hamilton in the British peerage (1799).[41] Five of th last eight remarried. In addition, Lord Tyrconnel, an Irish peer, gained divorce in 1777, and the 10th Earl of Exeter was divorced in 1791 befor succeeding to the title.[42]

Table 18 gives the proportion of remarriages to marriages by dates birth of peers.

Table 18. *Percentage of second to first marriages, 1600–1799*

Born	No. of 1st marriages	No. of 2nd marriages	Percentage of 2nd to 1st marriages
1600–89	283	88	31.10
1690–1729	284	70	24.60
1730–99	259	66	25.50

But Table 19 giving third marriages as a proportion of first marriag shows the declining trend much more clearly.

Table 19. *Percentage of third to first marriages, 1600–1799*

Born	No. of 1st marriages	No. of 3rd marriages	Percentage of 3rd to 1st marriages
1600–89	283	20	7.06
1690–1729	284	12	4.20
1730–99	259	4	1.50

[41] Brandon was Duke of Hamilton in the Scottish peerage.
[42] Exeter was the hero of a real life Gothick romance, turned into unremarkable verse by Tennys in 'The Lord of Burleigh'. In 1789 he appeared in Great Bolas, Shropshire, as a yeoman, under name of John Jones, wooed and married a village girl named Sarah Hoggins. A legal marria later made her Countess of Salisbury. She was then, according to the romantic version, convey unknowing to Burleigh and told she was mistress of all she surveyed.

Birth cohort of peer	1 English peers	2 Scottish peers	3 Irish peers	4 Peerage conn.	5 Foreign nobility	6 Royal	7 Bts	8 Knts	9 Clergy	10 Milit.	11 MPs	12 Others	Total	Columns 1–6 as % of total
1600–09	—	1	—	—	—	—	—	—	—	—	—	—	1	100.0
1610–19	1	—	—	—	—	—	—	1	—	—	—	—	2	50.0
1620–29	3	—	2	2	—	—	1	1	—	—	—	—	9	77.7
1630–39	9	—	—	6	1	—	2	1	—	—	—	2	20	75.0
1640–49	13	—	—	9	—	3	1	1	—	—	—	5	30	76.6
1650–59	8	—	—	10	2	1	3	6	—	—	—	9	39	54.0
1660–69	12	—	—	21	2	1	3	2	1	1	—	10	53	68.0
1670–79	24	—	3	20	—	—	4	2	1	—	1	12	70	71.0
1680–89	21	—	1	17	1	1	4	3	—	2	1	11	60	65.0
1690–99	24	1	1	14	1	—	1	4	1	2	—	21	71	59.2
1700–09	18	2	3	17	1	1	1	1	1	2	2	14	62	66.0
1710–19	21	1	5	22	1	—	2	1	—	—	1	21	75	66.6
1720–29	11	4	—	30	2	—	4	—	1	3	2	17	74	63.5
1730–39	18	3	—	20	—	—	5	1	2	1	3	15	68	60.3
1740–49	19	4	2	21	—	—	3	—	1	2	2	13	67	68.6
1750–59	23	4	2	16	—	—	2	—	3	—	6	14	70	64.3
1760–69	6	—	1	9	—	—	—	—	1	1	1	7	26	61.5
1770–79	10	—	1	1	—	—	—	—	2	—	—	4	18	66.0
1780–89	2	—	1	5	—	—	—	—	—	—	—	2	10	80.0
1790–99	1	—	—	—	—	—	—	—	—	—	—	—	1	100.0
Total	244	20	22	240	10	6	36	24	14	14	19	177	826	

Table 20 gives a detailed breakdown of the first marriages of English peers in the eighteenth century by social origins of their wives' fathers. Priorities are from left to right – i.e. a father who was both baronet and peer will be listed as peer, and a father who was both baronet and MP will be listed as baronet. Column 6 refers to the natural female children of monarchs.

The only column which requires explanation is column 4, labelled 'Peerage connection'. This represents an attempt to get over the difficulty mentioned on p. 79, and to meet comments made by F. M. L. Thompson in his review of Hollingsworth's work.[43] In a comprehensive survey of noble marriage it does not seem sensible to treat as commoner those wives who, though not the daughters of peers, came from families with close peerage connections. A total of 240 wives are therefore included in that category. Of these, the great majority fall into five basic groups: eighty-eight were granddaughters of peers, twenty-seven were nieces of peers, twenty-six were great-nieces of peers, twenty-three were great-granddaughters of peers and twenty-one were cousins of peers. The remaining fifty-five fall into smaller groups such as widows of peers (7), sisters of peers (5), great-great-granddaughters of peers (8), and so on. I am sure that in my zeal I have included some wives whose connection with the peerage will seem too remote to be of consequence. This may well be counter-balanced by the fact that, given infinite time, further research would undoubtedly promote others to closer categories.

The small cluster of marriages in column 6 represents the extra-mural activities of Charles II (4), James II (1) and George I (1). The Stuart marriages, which must have looked sound investments when made, proved liabilities after 1688: the 15th Lord Dacre and the 3rd Lord Anglesey separated from their wives; Jacobite loyalty brought the last Lord Derwentwater to the block, the last Earl of Yarmouth expired with his title in poverty. The 1st Earl of Lichfield's marriage to a daughter of Barbara Castlemaine by Charles II was at least fruitful, since they produced five daughters and thirteen sons. The 4th Earl of Chesterfield married in 1733 the Countess of Walsingham, illegitimate daughter of George I by the Duchess of Kendal. She was extremely wealthy but the marriage produced no children, nor, perhaps, much delight, since

---

[43] *History*, LI (1966), 400. Thompson made the point, later developed by Thomas, that a stark division into noble or common was not helpful: 'if the children of peers were finding their marriage partners either from their own legal group or from the ranks of the landed gentry or from second or subsequent generation descendants of peers, the social historian may legitimately say that the marriages were socially endogamous'.

Chesterfield's views on women were cynical even by eighteenth-century standards.[44]

The group of wives of foreign ancestry in column 5 reflects in the main the unusual degree of involvement by Britain in European affairs between 1688 and 1715. Four of the wives were Dutch. Lord Stafford married in 1694 the daughter of a French count while he was in exile with James II at St Germain. The two husbands in the cohort 1720–9 were both diplomats.[45] At not much more than 1% of total first marriages, the foreign element is small and suggests an insular society.[46]

Though the English peerage showed no great desire to form matrimonial alliances with continental nobles, they were much more willing to marry the daughters of Irish and Scottish peers. In a total of 154 marriages contracted by peers born in the period of 1600–69, only three were to the daughters of Irish or Scottish peers, a mere 1.9%. The Act of Union of 1707 strengthened the ties between England and Scotland socially as well as politically and economically, and in the total of 617 marriages contracted by peers born between 1670 and 1759, there were

[44] 'Women', he told his natural son, 'are only children of a larger growth; they have an entertaining tattle and sometimes wit; but for solid, reasoning good sense, I never in my life knew one that had it . . . a man of sense only trifles with them, plays with them, humours and flatters them, as he does with a sprightly, forward child.' *Letters*, IV, No. 1585.

[45] The 1st Lord Albemarle was a Dutch nobleman who came over with William III. Lord Cholmondeley and Lord North married Dutch wives while campaigning in the Low Countries in the 1700s. The 1st Viscount Hampden was a diplomat at The Hague and married there in 1743. The two husbands of the 1720s cohort were also diplomats: the 2nd Lord Mansfield (then Viscount Stormont) married the daughter of a Saxon count in 1759, and Sir Joseph Yorke, later Lord Dover, married a Danish wife in 1783.

[46] I think this applies also to the group of Catholic peers. Though many of them sent their sons abroad to be educated, only two seem to have married foreign wives, Lord Stafford and the 6th Baron Arundell of Wardour who married in 1716 the daughter of a baron of the Holy Roman Empire, born in Belgium.

Thomas, 'The social origins of marriage partners', Table 6, 105 found rather higher marriages to foreigners among peers' sons, and a substantial increase for the cohort born 1840–59, and marrying from 1870 onwards. I have modified his figures to take note of the ratio of foreign to all marriages:

	Total marriages	No. of marriages to foreigners	Percentage of marriages to foreigners
1700–19	200	8	4.0
1720–39	243	13	5.3
1740–59	221	6	2.7
1760–79	221	6	2.7
1780–99	306	8	2.6
1840–59	379	42	11.1

thirty-six Scottish or Irish matches, a proportion of 5.83%.[47] While a
Irish peer might or might not have much connection with Ireland, th
Scottish peerage was closed and national in character. The figure
therefore show the beginning of an integration of the aristocracy of th
three countries which developed more markedly in the nineteent
century. The absence of Scottish marriages in the last four cohorts
misleading for two reasons. First, the numbers involved are too small t
provide a valid sample. Second, the growing practice of granting Britis
peerages to Scottish peers has distorted the evidence since, to avoi
double counting, such peers have been placed in column 1. There were
in fact, four marriages in the last three cohorts which would otherwis
have appeared in columns 2 and 3. The 5th Duke of Manchester marrie
in 1793 the daughter of the 4th Duke of Gordon, a British peer as Lor
Norwich since 1784; the 11th Duke of Somerset married in 1800 th
daughter of the 9th Duke of Hamilton, who was also Duke of Brandor
the 2nd Baron Montagu of Boughton married in 1804 the daughter c
the 1st Baron Douglas, created a British peer in 1790; and the 3rd Baro
Foley married in 1806 the daughter of the 2nd Duke of Leinster in th
Irish peerage, whose father had been granted a British viscountcy in 174
at the time of his marriage to the daughter of the 2nd Duke c
Richmond.

Table 20 does not do justice statistically to that improvement in th
status of the clergy in the eighteenth century to which Holmes and other
have drawn attention.[48] Since some of the clerical fathers-in-law had als
peerage connections, a number have been promoted to column 4: th
archbishop of Tuam, for example, whose daughter married Lor
Clifford in 1789 was also the 3rd Earl of Mayo in the Irish peerage. If thes
are reinstated to give a more realistic survey of clerical prospects, we se
that of 284 marriages to peers born between 1600 and 1689, only two, c

---

[47] This suggestion is powerfully confirmed by the evidence provided by Dr P. C. Otto in her Ph.D
thesis, Stanford University, 'Daughters of the British aristocracy: their marriages in th
eighteenth and nineteenth centuries with particular reference to the Scottish peerage'. Table 9.
shows a very marked increase in the number of daughters of Scottish peers who marrie
Englishmen:

1690–1749	15.7%
1750–1799	35.6%
1800–49	41.9%
1850–99	50.7%

It was however one-way traffic. Daughters of English peers showed less enthusiasm for marryin
Scots.

[48] G. Holmes, *Augustan England: professions, state and society, 1680–1730*, 87 refers to 'a more marke
upwards shift in the social status of men attracted to the profession' after 1660. It is related to th
infiltration of the church by the aristocracy discussed in Chapter 2.

.7% were to the daughters of clerics: of 531 marriages to peers born etween 1690 and 1779, twenty were to the daughters of clerics, a roportion of 3.76%.[49]

It is less easy to evaluate the standing of the clerics. Some were tutors or rivate chaplains, whose daughters caught the eye of peers' sons at an npressionable age. The 1st Baron Harcourt made a secret marriage at ighteen to the daughter of his father's chaplain,[50] and G. R. St John's narriage in 1783 to the daughter of his tutor has already been referred to. But the twenty-two clerical fathers-in-law included four archbishops, our bishops, and two deans.[51] Not all clandestine marriages were ecessarily imprudent. Lord Southampton's son made a Gretna Green lopement in 1784, but his bride was the daughter of the bishop of Exeter nd a Keppel into the bargain.[52] At the other extreme of life was the 3rd Earl of Egremont who, at the age of fifty married a clergyman's daughter vho had lived with him at Petworth for at least sixteen years and who ore him six children.

The category 'Others' in column 12 is not very explicit. It should not e assumed that the fathers placed there were of no distinction or tanding. The majority of them were of the gentry class. The 2nd Baron Craven, for example, married the sister of Sir Fulwer Skipwith, 2nd Baronet of Newbold Hall, Warwickshire: her mother was the daughter of a knight. The 8th Viscount Hereford married in 1690, when she was welve, the daughter of Walter Norborne of Wiltshire: she was the granddaughter of a baronet, a great-great-niece of 1st Baron Wotton, on er grandmother's side descended from the 1st Earl of Exeter, and after Hereford's death remarried and became the mother of Lord Botetort. Lord Clifton (Earl of Darnley in the Irish peerage) married in 1766 the

It will be seen that seven clerical fathers-in-law, entered in column 4, have been reinstated in column 9 for the purpose of this discussion. One other, whose father was cleric and baronet has been added for column 7. She married Lord Teynham in 1753.

This was in 1680, many years before he was raised to the peerage. Harcourt's father was a knight and lived at Stanton Harcourt, Oxon., which had been in the family hands since the thirteenth century.

The 3rd Baron Edgecumbe married the daughter of John Gilbert, archbishop of York in 1761 and the 8th Viscount Stormont (also Earl of Mansfield) married the daughter of William Markham, archbishop of York in 1797; John Parker, later 1st Lord Boringdon married in 1764 the daughter of the archbishop of Tuam, and the 2nd Lord Clifford married in 1789 the daughter of another archbishop of Tuam. Lords Arundell of Trerice (?1700), Harrowby (1762), Jersey (1770) and Southampton (1784) married the daughters of the bishops of Llandaff, London, Raphoe and Exeter respectively. Lord Paget (1767) married the daughter of the dean of Clonmacnoise and Lord Seaforth (1782) the daughter of the dean of Lichfield.

Walpole to Mann, 8 July 1784: 'Mrs Keppel has been persuaded to pardon her; but Lady Southampton is inexorable; nor can I quite blame her, for she has thirteen other children, and a fortune was very requisite.' Corr., xxv, 508.

granddaughter of the bishop of Elphin. The wife of the 4th Earl c
Berkeley, Elizabeth, daughter of Henry Drax, had connections with th
peerage families of Granville, Seymour, Leveson-Gower, Wyndhan
and Fiennes, without getting into a higher category than column 12

Two general conclusions may now be drawn. First, that the marriage
of the peers under review were overwhelmingly within their own socia
group. We should disregard the first four and last four cohorts a
containing too few marriages to be statistically safe. For the remainin,
twelve cohorts, covering peers born between 1640 and 1759, at no poin
do the first six columns account for less than 54% of total marriages an
for most of them the proportion is well above 60%. If columns 7 and
are included, as other analysts suggest should be done to represent
'wider aristocracy', no cohort falls below 66% and the average for all o
them is 72%. It is difficult to see how a much higher proportion o
endogamous marriage could be achieved in a free society. It is, I am sure
true, as Stone, Trumbach and others have maintained, that parents gav
their children considerably more freedom of choice in marriage in th
eighteenth century than earlier.[53] But there is no reason to believe tha
most aristocratic sons and daughters did not subscribe to the prevailin{
ethic in favour of marriages of equal rank, nor that they did not attacl
similar importance to considerations of status and fortune. The increase
freedom expressed itself as a personal rather than social factor, a freedon
within acceptable limits. When Viscount Perceval obtained the hand o
Lady Catherine Cecil in 1737 she, at the age of seventeen, confessed tha
she would not have been coerced into marriage: 'She told him, among
other things, that she would have refused the Earl of Berkeley and th
Duke of Leeds if they offered.'[54]

The second inference is that, on the basis of this evidence, there is littl
reason to believe in fluctuations in the marriage pattern. In the twelv
cohorts, the degree of endogamous marriage (taking the first si:
columns) never falls below 54% nor rises much above 76%. I hav
already expressed the view that ten-year cohorts are scarcely adequate fo
analysis. If we present the same information in twenty-year cohorts, th
regularity of the overall pattern becomes quite clear (see Table 21).

Support for my contention that the pattern of aristocratic marriage ii
the eighteenth century was relatively stable comes from the work of D

[53] L. Stone, *The family, sex and marriage in England, 1500–1800*; Trumbach, *The rise of the egalitaria
family*.   [54] *HMC. Egmont*, II, 329.

Table 21. *Percentage of endogamous to total marriages, 1640–1759*

orn	Total marriages	Total from columns 1–6	Columns 1–6 as percentage of total
640–59	69	44	63.7
660–79	123	86	69.9
680–99	131	81	61.8
700–19	137	91	66.4
720–39	142	88	61.9
740–59	137	91	66.4

Table 22. *Percentage of daughters of Scottish peers marrying sons of peers, 1700–1899*[55]

Born	Percentage marrying sons of peers
1700–19	28.1
1720–39	37.0
1740–59	38.5
1760–79	29.0
1780–99	25.9
1800–19	16.7
1820–39	26.2
1840–59	40.5
1860–79	23.9
1880–99	31.6

. C. Otto.[56] She agrees that *mésalliances*, though giving vast pleasure to etter-writers and commentators, were rare.[57] The proportion of the aughters of Scottish peers marrying sons of peers increased slightly in he course of the eighteenth century and was running at a high level well to the nineteenth century as shown in Table 22. Dr Otto argues that the ohesion of the peerage was in no way undermined or placed in jeopardy y its choice of marriage partners and suggests that continuity rather than hange is the factor to which attention should be directed.[58] If the efinition is extended to include baronets, knights and gentry as part of a wider aristocracy', then 83.7% of the marriages of daughters of Scottish eers were endogamous throughout both centuries, and 87.9% of the narriages of the daughters of English peers.[59]

[55] *Ibid.*, Table 6.9. [56] See p. 88, Note 47. [57] *Ibid.*, 369.
[58] *Ibid.*, 178. [59] *Ibid.*, 385.

Finally, we must examine a piece of evidence which, at first sight
threatens to undermine the case for the exclusiveness of the marriage
pattern of the English peerage. Table 20 is open to the by now routine
objection that by including all peers we are taking into account men who
were neither peers nor the heirs of peers at the time of their marriage, but
ennobled subsequently. Their marriages, it may be objected, tell us
nothing about the habits of the peerage. There are 219 peers in this
category out of the 826 examined on p. 85. It is a comparatively simple
matter to subtract their marriages from the totals given. The rest will
then be the core peerage.

One would necessarily expect that the subtraction of those persons
whose marriages had been made prior to their becoming peers would
increase considerably the endogamous character of the remainder. There
is in fact some increase but it is very small. Taking the twelve central
cohorts as the most reliable, the proportion of endogamous marriages
before subtraction was 67.9%. After subtraction, it has risen to 68.6%.

This seems puzzling. If one of the defining characteristics of the
peerage as an elite is its tendency to marry relatives of peers, it is a
tendency which can hardly be shared with the non-elite as well. But it
will be remembered that in Chapter 1 we saw that the new recruits to the
peerage came from very much the same class and social background as
the others and that what was taking place was a topping-up process. This
is true of the 219 peers we have subtracted. No fewer than 165 of them
already had connections with the peerage. 59% of their marriages were
within columns 1 to 6. They were therefore rather strange commoners
since it can hardly be argued that 59% of all marriages in eighteenth
century England were to members of the close aristocracy. The stage
army of chapter 1 is on the march again. The 219 'newcomers' to the
peerage turn out to include more than thirty grandsons of existing peers,
sixteen younger sons of peers, twenty-three Irish peers or heirs to Irish
peers, fourteen Scottish peers or heirs to a Scottish peerage, fourteen
nephews of peers, four members of foreign nobility, twelve great
grandsons of peers, and so on. Their elevation to the peerage was to a
great extent an acknowledgement that they shared its characteristics and
their subtraction therefore makes little difference to the overall pattern.
The impression of an exclusive peerage with relatively few genuine
newcomers is therefore reinforced.

4

THE SINEWS OF POWER: POLITICAL

In his excellent book on the Secretaries of State, Mark Thomson offered 'the paradox of continuing domination of the aristocracy and the simultaneous insignificance of the House of Lords, *per se*'.[1]

It is true that, by the beginning of the eighteenth century, the supremacy of the House of Commons in financial matters was a well-established convention. The claims of the Commons to an undisputed control over money matters, which had been urged before the Civil War, were resumed immediately after the Restoration and a protracted dispute with the House of Lords began. In 1661 the Lords resolved that there were no precedents in history for this new claim by the House of Commons. In 1671, the Commons retorted that taxation ought not to be questioned by the Lords and in 1678 they reiterated that supply was 'the undoubted and sole right of the Commons' and 'ought not to be changed or altered by the House of Lords'.[2] The Lords' attempt in 1692 to assess their own taxes was also abandoned, though they retired under cover of a rather insubstantial smoke-screen that they maintained their power of amendment to be a 'fundamental, inherent and undoubted right from which their lordships can never depart'.[3] That established, they departed. Geoffrey Holmes quotes a nice example from 1702 when the bishop of Carlisle found himself the only peer answering to a money bill, 'no other lord in the House regarded what was doing, this being only (pro forma) to preserve a seeming right to dissent from, or amend, any part of a money bill'.[4] Their lordships' successful resistance to tacking in Anne's reign was a defensive victory only, preventing the Commons from making an excessive use of their superior position. Seventy years later, Lord Shelburne was still gallantly defending an

[1] *The Secretaries of State, 1681–1782*, 56.
[2] *Lords Journals*, XI, 328; *Commons Journals*, IX, 235, 509.
[3] *Lords Journals*, XV, 191.   [4] *British politics in the age of Anne*, 397.

abandoned fortification, assuring the House in 1782 that it retained 'a clear, indisputable right to alter any bill of supply whatever'.[5] His lordship had never been celebrated for his grasp of political reality.

Concession on so important a matter as the power to tax was bound to weaken the House of Lords' constitutional position. All the privileges of the Lords, declared Addison, writing in 1719 as *An Old Whig*, did not equal that of the Commons in 'commanding the purse of the community'. The Lords had already given way on a matter of even greater importance – the nature of the government itself. Though in 1688 the bishops and peers had played a crucial role in inviting over William III and for a brief moment in December 1688 the twenty-nine peers at the Guildhall were virtually the government of the country, in the Convention of 1689 the House of Lords held back from pronouncing on the settlement and allowed the Commons to make the running. Halifax and Devonshire argued that the House should not 'proceed upon any public business till they saw what the Commons did', and carried a motion to that effect.[6] Although this was part of a Whig manoeuvre to thwart the probable Tory majority in the Upper House, the constitutional effect was to yield priority in this vital area to the House of Commons. Perhaps the last chance for the Lords to remain on equal terms with the Commons vanished with the defeat of the Peerage Bill in 1719 which, though a party proposal, would certainly have increased noble influence by removing the power of the crown to override opposition through the wholesale creation of peerages, such as had been effected in 1712 and was threatened in 1832.

This does not, of course, imply that the House of Lords did not stand in need of care and attention from ministers. The fact that so many ministers were themselves peers gave weight and authority to the House's debates, and new recruits were brought in from time to time to make sure that the government's case was adequately put. The House provided a platform for those peers who wished to make a contribution to public life. From the continent, the Comte de Ségur watched in envy: 'la vie brillante, mais frivole, de nôtre noblesse, à la cour et à la ville, ni pouvait plus satisfaire nôtre amour-propre lorsque nous pensions à la dignité, à l'indépendance, à l'existence utile et importante d'un pair

---

[5] *Parliamentary history*, XXIII, 143.

[6] *The Correspondence of Henry Hyde, Earl of Clarendon*, ed. S. W. Singer, II, 252–4. Clarendon's account of Devonshire's argument on 25 Jan. 1689 was 'the House of Commons had appointed to go upon that business on Monday; and therefore he moved, the Lords would not enter upon it till Tuesday; by which time we should be able to gather some lights from below, which might be of use to us'.

Angleterre'.[7] The right of the minority in the House to publish protests was an opportunity to influence opinion that no opposition could ignore, and a further privilege, the use of proxies, meant that ministers must always be on guard against ambushes. Nevertheless, the weight of opinion has been that the House of Lords became, in the course of the century, more picturesque than important, and defeat in the Lords was rarely a major hazard for ministers. The number of peers holding government office, court place or pension, augmented by most of the bishops and a majority of the Scottish representative peers, gave administrations an almost automatic majority in a House which, until the mid-1780s, numbered little more than two hundred, with far fewer normally attending.[8]

Building on his own research into electoral history, Geoffrey Holmes devoted a chapter of his book on Queen Anne's reign to the House of Lords. He pointed out that contemporaries might well have thought that the Lords were gaining in importance and he did not deny that its role in the party struggle was of real significance. Nevertheless, the ingredients were already there for bringing the House under government command. The sixteen Scottish representative peers, who arrived in the House in 1707 after the Act of Union, were particularly anxious to receive favours and, 'after 1710, the docility of the Scots peers became proverbial'. In 1714, according to Holmes' estimate, the party of the crown was some seventy strong. Fifty Lords held places of profit under the crown and another nineteen held positions of trust. A further seventeen held pensions.[9] The government had other cards to play if necessary. On occasions the queen was willing to attend debates and there was little doubt what her wishes were. Lastly, there was the reserve power of creating peers, done on a small scale in 1703 and on a grand scale in 1712.

Mémoires, I, 89.

D. Large, 'The decline of the "party of the crown" and the rise of parties in the House of Lords, 1783–1837', *English Historical Review*, LXXVIII (1963), 669–95. From the grand total of peers, one must subtract peeresses, Catholics who would not take the oath, minors and, until 1782, Scottish peers holding British peerages. In addition, there were always peers who were too old or ill to attend, and others who were abroad on pleasure or on military or diplomatic service. The largest vote cast was 176 (including forty-two proxies) on Repeal of the Stamp Act in 1766. Other large divisions were 171 on the India Bill in 1783 (thirty-nine proxies), 168 on the Malt Tax in 1713 (forty-one proxies), and 167 on the motion in 1741 to remove Sir Robert Walpole (thirty-one proxies).

Holmes, *British politics in the age of Anne*, App. B. For purposes of comparison, we should subtract from Holmes' figures three peers who were Privy Councillors only. This honour, given to major politicians, did not really command any political loyalty. I have excluded them from my own subsequent calculations. Holmes' total may, for our purposes, be taken as about sixty-seven.

The main reason for the Tory government's difficulties in the Lords w: that the bench of bishops was not sufficiently malleable: the ministe were confronted by a number of Whig bishops, who put party loyalt above their prospects of translation. This was one of the reasons why th Tories were forced to resort to a wholesale creation of peers in 1712 twelve in all – which so shocked some of their countrymen.

There were special circumstances in Anne's reign that explain th problems facing ministers in controlling the Lords. The swift transitio of administrations was bound to cause trouble in building up suppor The precariousness of political life meant that more peers and bishop than usual might choose to gamble on the future. Most of all, th prominence in the reign of religious issues made it less likely that th bishops could tack and turn. As religious questions ceased to dominat politics, the bishops became the most reliable of the government troops.

The evidence indicates that this 'party of the crown' increase considerably in strength as the century progressed. An analysis for 1752 designed to coincide as closely as possible with that of Holmes, suggest that the number of peers holding offices or positions of trust had risen t about ninety. At that time, the total peerage (excluding royal dukes) wa about 178. But, of course, from the total peerage we must subtrac twelve Catholics, eleven minors and two ineligible, leaving 153. Thos who had a specific interest in supporting the administration wer therefore nearly 60% of the effective membership of the House. / further analysis for 1769 suggests that the number had swollen to mor than ninety, and a third for 1777 puts it at about eighty-six. One reaso for the increase from Anne's reign is that George II and George III as ma monarchs had Lords of the Bedchamber. There were eleven in 1752 wh were members of the House of Lords, thirteen in 1769 and twelve i 1777. In personal attendance on the king, the Lords of the Bedchambe were peculiarly open to persuasion and were watched as barometers o royal opinion.[10]

---

[10] 1752 Ashburnham, Clinton, Dunmore, Fauconberg, Fitzwilliam, Hertford, Mancheste Poulet, Rochford, Rockingham, Waldegrave.
   1769 Bolingbroke, Botetort, Bruce, Buckinghamshire, Denbigh, Eglinton, Ker, Mancheste March, Masham, Orford, Pomfret, Willoughby de Broke (Eglinton and March bein Scottish representative peers).
   1777 Bolingbroke, Buckinghamshire, Denbigh, Jersey, Ker, March, Orford, Osborne, Oxfor Pembroke, Pomfret, Willoughby de Broke.

Some confirmation of these analyses comes from a list made by John Robinson in 1774.[11] Robinson had taken over as Secretary to the Treasury in 1770 and was facing his first general election. His total of peers holding office included seventy-seven English peers and ten representative Scottish peers, making an aggregate of eighty-seven.

In addition to places, there were pensions. Holmes identified some seventeen peers in 1714 as in receipt of pensions. Namier, in a famous analysis for 1754, drew attention to a dozen peers in receipt of financial assistance. Namier was, of course, at pains to emphasise the benevolent and charitable character of these payments and called his section 'the aristocratic dole'.[12] Several of these pensions were to peers who, through the vicissitudes of inheritance, had become parted from the bulk of their estates. Namier has always had something of a reputation as a cynic and I would be uneasy to appear even more cynical than he was. Yet I cannot help feeling that, on this occasion, Namier's comparative indifference towards the House of Lords, and his desire to prove the innocence of the secret service payments, led him to be less perceptive than usual. I do not deny, of course, that there was a benevolent aspect nor that monarchs and ministers felt the need to maintain the dignity of the peerage. But you will not think me a monster of machiavellian guile if I observe that, were I to wish to suborn the House of Peers (which God forfend), I would start with the needy rather than the affluent. One of Namier's dozen, Lord Saye and Sele, explained to Newcastle that he would attend the House of Lords if he could afford to. He was given a pension of £600 p.a. It would be strange if, under those circumstances, he had developed into a troublesome critic of government. Of another of his dozen, the Earl of Warwick, Namier remarked that he took no part in politics. This was quite wrong. Warwick held the very important office of chairman of committees in the House of Lords for more than twenty-five years until

---

[1] *Parliamentary papers of John Robinson, 1774–84*, ed. W. T. Laprade, Camden Society, 3rd series, XXXIII, 12–14, 'List of peers who hold offices'. We need to make some slight adjustments to Robinson's lists. He omitted the Duke of Richmond, who was a Lieutenant-General, Lord Lieutenant of Sussex and a Privy Councillor; Cleveland, who held the sinecure of Controller of the Seal of Greenwax Office and Receiver of Profits of Seals of King's Bench; the Duke of Leeds, who was Chief Justice in Eyre, north of Trent, and a Privy Councillor; the Duke of Rutland, who was Lord Lieutenant of Leicestershire and a Privy Councillor; Lord Wycombe, a Lieutenant-General and Privy Councillor; and Lord Lovel, who was Lord Lieutenant of Somerset. Queensberry was included since he was also Duke of Dover, but because of the ruling in the Brandon case, did not sit, save as a Scottish representative peer. There are also errors of transcription. 'Earl of Ferres' should read Earl Ferrers, and three lines from the bottom of page 12 should read Lord Orford, *not* Oxford.

[2] *The structure of politics at the accession of George III*, 2nd edition, 221–5.

his death in 1759. Hardwicke and Newcastle then negotiated
replacement for him in the shape of Lord Willoughby de Parham
another of Namier's dozen. When Lord Willoughby de Parham died, h
was replaced by yet another needy peer, Lord Delamer. Delamer
cousin, the Earl of Warrington, had been until his death in 1758 anoth(
of Namier's dozen, and Delamer himself was given a pension of £60
p.a. from 1761.[13]

I am afraid that I became nearly as obsessed with Namier's dozen 'non
political' peers in receipt of pension as he did. It is not difficult to trac
them down since the *Lords Journals* list the attendance for every day.
took the liberty of checking on Namier's year of 1754. Warwick an
Willoughby de Parham were, as you will have gathered, among th
most regular attenders in the whole House. But eleven of the twelv
attended, most of them frequently. In a small House, on 12 February
Lord Hardwicke could look out on thirty-five other peers, six of whor
were bishops, five Scottish representative peers and four of our friends
Warwick, Willoughby de Parham, Saye and Sele and Raymon
(another whom Namier described as taking no part in politics). A wee
later, Newcastle and Hardwicke confronted sixty-three peers, of whor
ten were bishops, eight Scots and six (no less than half) of our dozen. A
the opening of the next session, on 14 November 1754, there was a grea
get-together of the pensioners, with seven of the twelve in attendanc(
Lords Warwick, Willoughby de Parham, Warrington, Halifax, Dudley
Raymond and Radnor. One wonders whether they ever found out wha
they had in common.

From the last of Namier's dozen, Lord Peterborough, Newcastle di
not seem to be getting his money's worth. I wondered whether he was
serving officer, like his grandfather, but he was not. Perhaps he was age
and infirm. He was forty-eight and vigorous. Then I stumbled across
clue in *The complete peerage* for 1775 which described him as 'uxorious t
excess'. I do not wish to blacken a man's character, particularly after 23
years, but I suspect that, in eighteenth-century parlance, uxorious ofte
meant a fondness for other people's wives, as well as one's own. Perhap
that was what he was doing. He did, however, pop in on 25 March 175
and took the oath – belatedly – but did not stay. The House then went o
to discuss a bill to allow a bridge 'over the water or haven between th

---

[13] For the role of chairman of committees, see J. C. Sainty, *The origin of the office of chairman*
committees in the House of Lords, HoL RO Memo, 52. For Willoughby de Parham, see P. J. W
Higson, 'Lord Willoughby de Parham: a neglected Society president', *Antiquaries Journal*, L
(1972), 169–84.

own of Sandwich and', they added solemnly, 'the opposite shore'. I wonder he could tear himself away. However, it is a story with a happy ending. Lord Peterborough turned up again seven months later (but did not stay) and by March 1756 was attending quite regularly. Perhaps Newcastle had had a word with him. In case you feel – with some justice – that the illustration has got out of hand, I suggest that these examples add a little to our understanding of 'non-political' peerage pensions.

I have now to strike a cautious note. These lists are highly seductive to historians looking for certainty amid the confusions and complexities of the real past. Holmes' list for February 1714, quite rightly, includes a dozen peers who, while holding offices or positions of trust, remained in Whig opposition. In the same way, my list for 1777 must include Lord Rockingham, a Privy Councillor and Lord Lieutenant of the North Riding, and Lord Shelburne, a Lieutenant-General in the army and a Privy Councillor: both were leading a sustained opposition to His Majesty's government. Lord Pembroke in 1777 was a Lord of the Bedchamber, Lord Lieutenant of Wiltshire, and a Lieutenant-General. That, according to the cruder theories of political motivation, should have been enough to secure his loyalty to any royal government. In fact he was a furious critic of Lord North, alluding to the 'infamy, disgrace, folly and obstinacy' of the government. In February 1780 he voted against it, resigned his Bedchamber post, and was dismissed his Lord Lieutenancy.[14]

Recent studies have reinforced the need for caution. Professor W. C. Lowe prefaced an investigation of the behaviour of bishops and Scottish representative peers with an implied rebuke to me for once referring to the 'automatic majority' which the party of the crown could attain.[15] It is a well-merited reproof and I hang my head. Professor Lowe pointed out that neither bishops nor Scottish representative peers were particularly good attenders and that, during the short ministry of 1766 and 1767, some bishops were frequently in opposition. Although I concede the point that there is no such thing as a normal situation, the circumstances of the 1760s were rather unusual. The Duke of Newcastle, who had taken greater interest in ecclesiastical matters than any other eighteenth-

---

[4] *The Pembroke papers*, ed. Lord Herbert, 225, 405–6. The Rockinghams insisted in 1782 on his reappointment to the Lord Lieutenancy but the king would not have him back in the Bedchamber, *The Correspondence of King George III*, v, No. 2940. For Queensberry in 1789 and Amherst in 1804, see *Later correspondence of George III*, ed. A. Aspinall, I, 422–4; IV, 208, Note 1.
[5] 'Bishops and Scottish representative peers in the House of Lords, 1760–1775', *Journal of British Studies*, XVIII, 1 (Fall 1978), 86–106.

century politician, had gone into opposition after forty years in government: it is hardly surprising that some of 'his' bishops stayed with him.

Lowe asserted that 'the best measure of political participation' is to be found in attendance. No one is very likely to quarrel with that, since there is not much point in having supporters who are not present. There was, however, a good deal of absenteeism among all the other groups making up the House of Lords, and, in fact, Lowe concluded that the bishops were 'the most regular' in their attendance. The falling away in the attendance of the bishops which he noted between 1772 and 1774 was probably due, less to lack of loyalty, than to the remarkable success of Lord North's early years in office, which produced as a consequence a low level of political activity.

The performance of the Scottish representative peers has also been subjected to scrutiny. Professor M. W. McCahill argued in 1972 that, in the later years of the century at least, they were by no means docile troops.[16] The parliamentary position of the Scots changed, however, after the Lords' resolution of 1782 allowing Scottish peers holding British peerages to take their seats. Once there was the possibility of permanent British seats in the House, the representative peerages became less attractive and the government's hold was correspondingly weakened.[17]

Professor McCahill developed his ideas at greater length in a book published in 1978.[18] He broadened the thesis into a substantial revision suggesting that the degree to which the House of Lords was under the control of government has been much overstated, and maintaining that it was still an 'active, independent branch of the constitution', able to sustain its traditional role of balancing the other two branches. That the peers who composed the party of the crown were capable of acts of rebellion and disobedience may readily be conceded: they were not guardsmen to be marched into the lobby at will. But, although many of McCahill's observations are of value, in general he seems to push his case too hard. It was surely excessive, for example, to claim that the Lords in

[16] 'The Scottish peerage and the House of Lords', 172–96.
[17] G. M. Ditchfield, 'The Scottish representative peers and parliamentary politics, 1787–93', *Scottish Historical Review*, LI (April 1981), 14–31, analysed the voting on Stormont's motion of 13 Feb. 1787, and concurred with McCahill that it helped to rescue the Scots from 'the more extreme charges of servility made against them'. But as a piece of evidence, it is weakened by the fact that the division was on a Scottish matter and affected the privileges of the Scottish peers themselves – i.e. it was of all issues the one when some independence might reveal itself.
[18] *Order and equipoise: the peerage and the House of Lords, 1783–1806*.

the eighteenth century had prevented the Commons 'from becoming the dominant house'.[19]

McCahill claimed that the House of Lords did discharge its traditional function of balancing the constitution. But the working of a balance presumes that it acts both ways. That their lordships, on the two occasions McCahill cited, protected the crown scarcely proves the point, unless one can show that they were prepared, if necessary, also to resist the crown, as they had done in 1688. If it is counter-objected that circumstances gave them little opportunity to resist the crown, this suggests less that they were performing their theoretical functions than that the descriptions of those functions had become anachronistic and irrelevant. Certainly McCahill persuades us that the House of Lords was a highly conservative body, but, in a period with a highly conservative monarchy and a highly conservative Lower House, what distinctive role did that give for their lordships? Instead of a balance, they were a drag-chain on a coach already proceeding at a very leisurely pace.

In fact, Professor McCahill followed the passage in which he asserted the independence and importance of the House of Lords by another drawing attention to 'the extraordinarily low attendance' of the nobility on most occasions.[20] It is not easy to understand how their lordships could perform so vital a task as preserving the constitution by planting trees and hunting foxes. Admittedly, he suggested that they could be induced to attend their parliamentary duties on occasions of political importance but he added a remarkable gloss which went far to destroying his own case: 'It was not usually their object to evaluate the merits of those policies whose fate they would decide. Instead, the majority used these occasions to demonstrate their continuing loyalty to the King's government and their willingness to support whatever projects his ministers recommended.'[21]

It will, I hope, be helpful at this stage to look at some of the more important occasions after 1714 when ministers found themselves in a minority in the House of Lords. In May 1733, immediately after the Excise crisis, Walpole's opponents in the Lords pressed him hard over the confiscated estates of the South Sea Company directors. The Duke of Newcastle handled the main debate on the 24th rather badly, though Walpole was in attendance at the bar of the House to offer advice: the voting on the previous question was seventy-five against seventy-five, and the government was technically defeated. Sir Thomas Robinson, in

[19] *Ibid.*, 212.   [20] *Ibid.*, 15.   [21] *Ibid.*, 18.

a long account to Lord Carlisle, described it as 'the first question that has been lost by the Court in the House of Lords during the two last reigns, and in a very full House, and upon a known debate, and great pains taken'. The bishops stayed solid at twenty-four votes to one, but the Scottish representative peers split evenly, seven and seven.[22] The opposition failed to follow up their advantage, and Walpole counter-attacked with vigour. Four new peers were created for the next session, more to boost debating talent than to swell the numbers; there were several dismissals; and at the general election of 1734 Lord Islay's stern methods brought the Scots brigade into line once more.[23] The election at Edinburgh took eight hours, there were sixty peers present with another sixteen proxies, and Walpole's men took all sixteen places. When the opposition tried its strength in the new Parliament by dividing on the Address, it was beaten by eighty-nine votes to thirty-seven. Although the episode certainly points to the need for constant attention to the House of Lords, it also suggests what could be achieved by resolute management.

The next great opposition onslaught on Sir Robert came early in 1739 with an attack upon the Convention of Prado. This was of crucial political importance because it represented Walpole's last chance to negotiate an understanding with Spain and avoid the war which, in the end, brought him down. In the House of Lords the ministers survived by ninety-five votes to seventy-four (proxies twenty-four and sixteen). The bishops divided seventeen to five in favour of government and fifteen of the Scottish representative peers turned out in support.[24] Opposition claimed that, of the ninety-five majority, only twenty-one were without places, pensions or favours, and that of the seventy-four minority, only eight held places, pensions or favours.[25]

The Pelhams had a very secure hold upon the Lords and divisions fell

---

22 *HMC. Carlisle*, 116–21. On page 118 Robinson gives six of the seven Scottish peers in opposition.

23 Lord Hervey was one of the peers created on this occasion though his father, Lord Bristol, expressed surprise that he should wish to 'exchange the important House you was a member of' for such an 'insignificant' one as the House of Lords. *Hervey Letter Books*, III, No. 963.

24 There is no division list in the *Parliamentary history*, and J. C. Sainty does not give one, but *An Authentick List of the House of Peers as they voted For and Against the Convention* is in the British Library.

25 Bishops were not regarded as holding places as such, but only if, in addition, they held prebendaries, deaneries and the like. The leading opposition peers still holding places were the Duke of Argyll, Field Marshall, not dismissed from his colonelcy of the Horse Guards until 1740, and Lord Scarborough, who retained his regiment. The list includes a calculation that the places and pensions on the government side cost the taxpayers £209,400 p.a. The Prince of Wales voted in opposition.

to an all-time low, but the rekindling of political excitement in the 1760s produced another government defeat. Rockingham's administration was beaten in February 1766 on two votes concerning American policy, prior to the repeal of the Stamp Act. The motions were, in themselves, of little significance, though the defeats were mortifying.[26] The revolt was, in the main, due to suspicion that the king was hostile to the American policy of his ministers: 'Most of Your Majesty's servants', wrote Grafton reproachfully, 'were in the Majority.'[27] Rockingham obtained authority to contradict these rumours and the repeal itself was carried on 11 March by one hundred and five votes to seventy-one.[28]

A better-known defeat was that sustained by the Coalition in December 1783 when its India Bill was rejected in the Lords. Reports of the king's dislike of the Coalition and its bill were well founded and the expected government majority melted away like summer snow. 'The bishops waver and the thanes fly from us', wrote Richard Fitzpatrick, 'in my opinion, the bill will not pass.'[29] He was quite right. The ministers lost the first vote on 15 December by eighty-seven votes to seventy-nine (proxies eighteen and twenty-two). The bishops divided twelve to eight against the government, the Lords of the Bedchamber five to six against, and the Scottish representative peers seven to six in favour. On this occasion, the king refused to countermand the rumours and in the second division on 17 December a further shift took place, the government losing by ninety-five to seventy-six (proxies nineteen and twenty).

The first thing to remark is the comparative rarity of major defeats. The second is that the last two involved the use of the king's name to influence votes. Throughout the century there remained considerable ambiguity about the extent to which the government was royal or ministerial. Most of the time this ambiguity was dormant, though it was a commonplace of politicians in both houses to insist that their allegiance was personal to the king. Not only did any rumour about the king's doubts towards his ministers pluck at the political conscience of members, it also advertised to time-servers that the days of the

---

[26] The first, on 4 Feb., amended by sixty-three votes to sixty a government motion recommending governors in America to compensate riot victims, substituting the word 'required'. Two days later, voting was fifty-nine to fifty-four on a motion thanking the governors for enforcing the laws: opposition carried a specific reference to the Stamp Act. See P. D. G. Thomas, *British politics and the Stamp Act crisis*, 199–205.

[27] *The correspondence of King George III*, I, No. 230.

[28] There were thirty-two proxies on the court side, ten for opposition. This was the largest division in an eighteenth-century House of Lords and corrects my note in *The Fox–North Coalition*, 139, Note 2. *The correspondence of King George III*, I, Nos. 242, 248, 249.

[29] *Memorials and correspondence of Charles James Fox*, II, 220.

administration were almost certainly numbered. Rockingham's ministry outlasted the crisis of February 1766 by only four months, the
Coalition that of December 1783 by one day. Neither episode, in my
view, does much to establish the genuine independence of the House of
Lords. Fox denounced the last incident as a gross and 'impudent avowal
of political profligacy', whereby the opinion which peers held in the
morning, they renounced by noon. It would, said Fox, vilify the House
of Lords 'to the latest posterity'.[30]

Few resolutions can have been less regarded than that passed in 1701 by
the House of Commons that for a Lord of Parliament to concern himself
with the election of any member of the Lower House constituted 'a high
infringement of the liberties and privileges of the Commons of
England'.[31] The resolution seems not even to have had a momentary
effect, for, in the general election of 1705, it was complained that the
intervention of the peerage was greater than ever. All the evidence
suggests that the resolution was not merely ignored, but increasingly
ignored. At most, it was dragged in to embarrass or torment a few
aristocratic patrons, like Newcastle at Seaford in 1747 or Lord Falmouth
at Truro in 1780.[32] The quality of non-intervention the resolution
produced may be judged by the Duke of Chandos, Lord Lieutenant of
Herefordshire, to his agent in 1722: 'be cautious not to use my name in
speaking to any of the gentlemen or freeholders. You know the votes of
the House of Commons don't allow Lord Lieutenants to interfere in
elections, but your appearing for Sir Hungerford will be a sufficient
indication.'[33]

There are, of course, a number of analyses, contemporary and
subsequent, designed to demonstrate the electoral influence of the
peerage. Unfortunately they are rather difficult to use. The contemporary estimates are, for the most part, tendentious and partisan. Two well-
known examples for the later period – the lists drawn up by T. B. H.
Oldfield in 1792 and by George Tierney on behalf of the Society of the
Friends of the People in 1793 – originated in the campaign for reform of
Parliament.[34] They are, of course, of great interest, but they must be used

---

[30] Parliamentary History, XXIV, 211. [31] Commons Journals, XIII, 648.
[32] The House of Commons, 1715–54, I, 370; The House of Commons, 1754–90, I, 241–2.
[33] The House of Commons, 1715–54, I, 257–8.
[34] Oldfield was a member of the Society for Constitutional Information and published his findings
    originally under the title History of the boroughs. For information about him, see E. C. Black, The
    Association, App. A, and my own Parliamentary reform, 1640–1832, 122, Note 3. Tierney's work
    was largely a digest of Oldfield. But see pp. 111–12 below.

as sources, not as uncontaminated evidence. Namier offered the warning that no two historians would reach agreement on the distinction between nomination and influence, and, indeed, the distinction is hard to uphold save in extreme cases.[35] The electoral situation fluctuated all the time. Open boroughs fell under influence and even apparently secure boroughs sometimes bolted and made their escape – if not into independence, at least to another patron. Contemporaries did not even know for certain what influence they themselves possessed, and could be both delighted and mortified.

To avoid at least some of these difficulties, it seemed wisest to base our analyses on the evidence now provided by the History of Parliament Trust. Interested parties can then, at least, make their own estimates and draw their own conclusions. The information available now covers the period 1715 to 1790. Our immediate task, therefore, is to establish the position in Anne's reign so that we can be reasonably sure of the base-line. Fortunately, we have an expert guide.

Geoffrey Holmes, in his thesis on the electoral influence of the peerage in Anne's reign, warned us that the situation was extremely volatile.[36] Electoral interests were established and overthrown very quickly, in comparison with the Hanoverian period. The frequency of general elections before the Septennial Act exposed patrons to constant challenge. Though some substantial electoral empires were founded, and peers like Beaufort, Lansdowne, Somerset and Wharton spent much money, results were uncertain and success fleeting. On the basis of Holmes' work it looks as if, in 1702, there were some twenty boroughs under lay peerage control, returning some thirty-one MPs.[37] By 1713, the number of boroughs under patronage had risen to twenty-eight,

---

[35] *Structure of politics*, 144.

[36] G. S. Holmes, 'The influence of the peerage on English parliamentary elections, 1702–13', B. Litt. thesis, Oxford University (1952).

[37] Sir Jonathan Trelawney, bishop of Exeter until 1707 and thereafter of Winchester until his death in 1721, had considerable electoral influence but I have not taken this into account. The rest are as follows:

Aldborough	2	(Newcastle)	Huntingdon	2	(Sandwich)
Andover	2	(Bolton)	Ilchester	2	(Poulet)
Appleby	1	(Thanet)	Lymington	1	(Bolton)
Arundel	1	(Scarborough)	Morpeth	2	(Carlisle)
Banbury	1	(Guilford)	Richmond	1	(Wharton)
Beeralston	2	(Stamford)	Stamford	1	(Exeter)
Bishop's Castle	1	(Bradford)	Warwick	2	(Brooke)
Christchurch	1	(Clarendon)	Westbury	2	(Abingdon)
Eye	2	(Cornwallis)	Wootton Basset	1	(Rochester)
Helston	2	(Godolphin)	Wycombe	2	(Wharton)

returning some forty-five MPs.[38] In addition, there were perhaps five counties in which the peerage might be said to command one seat.[39] The explanation of this rise in the number of boroughs under the patronage of peers is less an extension of their activities than the fact that several of the peers created in Anne's reign had boroughs at their disposal.[40] Though it would not be prudent to attempt to quantify too exactly, Holmes concluded that the overall position reflected 'a steady rise in the proportion of the House elected by aristocratic influence'.

From 1715 to 1790, I have based my estimates on the History of Parliament. To minimise uncertainty, I have adhered very strictly to the dates of peerage creation, even where this produces apparent absurdity. I have disregarded the electoral influence of Irish peers since, when they sat in the Commons, it is hard to establish whether they were patrons or candidates. I have excluded the two universities, though peers, particularly as Chancellor or High Steward, exerted great influence, and the sons of peers were much favoured as candidates. In 1715, according to my computation, forty-eight of the English boroughs were under partial or total peerage control, returning sixty-eight members. This, it will be noted, represents a sharp increase on Holmes' assessment for 1713, which itself was a sharp increase on the estimates for 1702. In addition, I would add twelve seats in English counties, one Welsh borough and one Welsh county, seven Scottish boroughs and sixteen Scottish counties, making a grand total of 105 seats under peerage control. This constituted one-fifth of the whole House of Commons. By 1747, the total had risen to 167, the

[38]

Aldborough	2	(Newcastle)	Helston	2	(Lansdowne)
Andover	2	(Bolton/Beaufort)	Ilchester	2	(Poulet)
Appleby	1	(Thanet)	Lewes	2	(Pelham)
Arundel	1	(Scarborough)	Launceston	1	(Rochester)
Banbury	1	(Guilford)	Lymington	1	(Bolton)
Bishop's Castle	1	(Bradford)	Malmesbury	2	(Wharton)
Bossiney	2	(Radnor/Lansdowne)	Morpeth	2	(Carlisle)
Brackley	2	(Wharton/Bridgwater)	Monmouth	1	(Beaufort)
Beeralston	2	(Stamford)	Richmond	1	(Wharton)
Bury St Edmunds	2	(Hervey)	Stamford	1	(Exeter)
Camelford	2	(Lansdowne)	Radnor	1	(Oxford)
Cirencester	2	(Bathurst)	Warwick	2	(Brooke)
Eye	2	(Cornwallis)	Westbury	2	(Abingdon)
			Wootton Basset	1	(Rochester)
			Wycombe	2	(Wharton)

[39] Hunts., Lancs., Lincs., Northd and Staffs., commanded by Manchester, Stanley (Derby), Ancaster, Somerset and Paget respectively.

[40] E.g. Lansdowne, created 1712, controlled two at Helston and one at Bossiney; Hervey, created 1703, commanded two at Bury St Edmunds; Bathurst, created 1712, commanded both seats at Cirencester; Pelham, created 1706, had two seats at Lewes; Oxford, created 1711, had a seat at Radnor; Granville, created 1703, had two seats at Camelford.

reater part of the increase taking place in the English counties and oroughs. By 1784, the total had risen again to 197, almost all the increase eing in the English boroughs. If we extend the survey to the end of 1784 he total would rise to about 207 seats, since Sir James Lowther, who ommanded nine seats and Charles Cocks, who was patron of one eat at Reigate, were raised to the peerage just after the 1784 election. If ve go up to 31 August 1786, the total rises to 210, since Lord Surrey, who ad been building up a powerful interest since 1780, inherited the ukedom of Norfolk, and passes into our statistical ken, bringing with im three more seats and the prospect of others to come. The degree of eerage patronage would appear, therefore, to have doubled between 715 and 1785, and had probably quadrupled since the beginning of the ighteenth century.

I have no doubt that in some respects these figures exaggerate the lectoral influence of the peerage. In some places, where there appears to ave been a commanding interest, further evidence would reveal doubts nd complexities. But to some extent this must be counter-balanced by he under-estimate of peerage influence in those constituencies where it ell short of command. The important Abingdon interest at Oxford, the 'avendish interest at Lancaster after 1756, the Coventry interest at 3ridport and the powerful Hobart interest at Norwich go unrecorded in ur statistics, as well as a vast amount of influence in county elections.

The evidence may also be presented in a different way. In 1715, the ighty-two English and Welsh seats under peerage control were shared y forty-eight noblemen. The Duke of Newcastle already had by far the argest total, with twelve seats, followed by Wharton with six and omerset with four. The twenty-three Scottish seats were shared by eventeen Scottish peers, Argyll having command of six. By 1747, sixty-ix English peers shared 156 seats. Newcastle had added to his electoral mpire, which then totalled thirteen, but new patrons were moving up o rival him. Lord Edgecumbe commanded seven seats. The Bedford nterest, which in 1715 had been worth only two seats, had been built up y John Russell, the 4th Duke, and was worth five seats; Falmouth had ive, Beaufort five, and Grafton, Buckinghamshire, Orford, Gower,)orset and Lonsdale four each. The Scottish peers still controlled wenty-three seats, but Argyll's share had moved up to eight. By 1784, eventy English peers shared 169 seats. The Newcastle empire shrank fter 1768, though the 2nd Duke still commanded seven seats. An mportant new empire was that of Eliot, ennobled in 1784, with six seats t his disposal. Two emerging interests were Northumberland and

Rutland with seven seats. Bedford retained his five, Falmouth ha‹ increased to six, having gained control of one at Mitchell and another a Tregony to compensate for the loss of one at Penryn; Edgecumbe wa‹ down to five, having lost one seat at Grampound, Penryn and Plympto‹ Erle against one gain at Bossiney; Marlborough could claim five Abingdon five, Fitzwilliam four, Devonshire four and Gower fou‹ Twenty Scottish peers shared twenty-six Scottish seats, Argyll and But‹ having three each.

Some check upon the validity of these figures can be provided b‹ comparing the estimate for 1747 with the assessment made for 1761 b‹ Namier in *The structure of politics at the accession of George III*. Adjustment are of course necessary. Certain peerages had become extinct in th‹ meantime – the Lonsdale peerage, for example, in 1751 and th‹ Burlington peerage in 1753; others had come into existence subsequen‹ to the general election of 1747 – Archer in July 1747, Wycombe in 176c Boston and Melcombe in 1761. The main difference in our calculations ‹ that Namier did not include the English counties or the Wels‹ constituencies. It is certainly true that no peer could establish comman‹ of a county in the way he could buy up a burgage borough or pack corporation. The sensible ones behaved with great discretion, affecte‹ diffidence even if they did not feel it, consulted and negotiated a goo‹ deal, and rarely jeopardised their influence over one county seat b‹ attempting both.[41] Nevertheless, any overall survey of aristocrati influence which did not acknowledge the dominant position obtained b‹ certain peers in some counties would be incomplete. Since there wer‹ only three noble estates in Rutland and no more than eight hundred or s‹ freeholders, the influence of the Finches, Noels and Cecils counted fo‹ much. Thomas Noel succeeded his brother as knight of the shire in 172‹ held the seat for forty-eight years, and passed it on at his death to a cousir‹ Gerard Noel Edwards, who held it for another forty-four year‹ Huntingdonshire was dominated by the two branches of the Montag‹ family, one at Kimbolton, the other at Hinchingbrooke. In Derbyshir‹ one seat was, by common consent, left to the Cavendish family. In Cam‹ bridgeshire, in 1754 and 1761, the two knights of the shire were the Mar‹ quis of Granby and Viscount Royston, eldest sons of the Duke of Rutlan‹ and the Earl of Hardwicke respectively. Even in a large county lik‹ Gloucestershire, with an electorate of six thousand or more, the influenc‹

---

[41] Among examples of peers who were not so wise, see Lord Darlington, who attempted to bring ir two for Co. Durham in 1761 and the Duke of Northumberland, who tried to carry two in hi‹ own county in 1774.

of the Beauforts on the hill and the Berkeleys in the valley was paramount.

Namier conceded that his list for 1761 would require correction and that the degree of aristocratic control would be greater if one counted constituencies in which two noble patrons struggled for superiority. His assessment for 1761 was that fifty-five English peers influenced the return of 111 members.[42] To make comparison with my own assessment possible, we should then add thirty-two seats in English counties and in the Welsh constituencies, and a further five peers who were not previously patrons, bringing it to some sixty peers returning 143 members. The shortfall of a dozen or so on my own assessment disappears if I am permitted to suggest further small adjustments to Namier's list for 1761. We should remember that the History of Parliament, on which my own assessment is based, incorporated another thirty years of Namier's diligent research, compared with *The structure of politics*, which came out in 1929.[43]

A check upon my assessment for 1784 is provided by the work of Professor McCahill, which I mentioned earlier.[44] My assessment for English and Welsh borough seats under patronage was 138: Professor McCahill's was 124. To bring our lists into line, I subtract from McCahill three peers, Lonsdale, Bulkeley and Somers, who were created just subsequent to the general election and who shared some seven borough seats at that time. I would then wish to add some twenty seats to his list.[45]

---

[42] This is the figure given in the second edition, published 1957. The original edition of 1929 had suggested fifty-one peers commanding 101 seats. The figures for commoners' patronage also increased as more evidence became available, from fifty-five commanding ninety-one seats to fifty-six commanding ninety-four seats.

[43] I would *delete* from Namier's list Lord Boston, who seems not to have been a patron in his own right at Bodmin; I would *add* to Newcastle's empire both seats at Lewes and at East Retford, and both seats at Seaford; Bolingbroke had both at Wootton Bassett; Townshend one at Great Yarmouth; Halifax one at Northampton; Northampton one at Northampton; Orford one at Great Yarmouth and one at King's Lynn; Monson and Scarborough one each at Lincoln; Grosvenor, who commanded both seats at Chester, was made a peer on the day of election, 8 April 1761, and I would include him.   [44] See pp. 100–1.

[45] From McCahill, *subtract* Lonsdale 5, Bulkeley, Somers. To McCahill, add:

Rutland	Leicester 1, Scarborough 1, Cambridge 1
Abingdon	Wallingford 1
Fitzwilliam	2 seats at Malton
Orford	Callington 1
Falmouth	Mitchell 1, St Mawes 1
Sydney	2 seats at Whitchurch
Beaulieu	Windsor 1
Milton	Dorchester 1
Godolphin	Helston 2
Suffolk	Castle Rising 1
Northampton	Northampton 1
Irwin	Horsham 2
Bute	Bossiney 1

Some of these, I am sure, Professor McCahill would readily agree to. There is little doubt that Lord Fitzwilliam commanded both seats at Malton; there had been no contest in the borough since 1715 and no list of which I am aware had ever questioned it. The Suffolk family should be credited with one at Castle Rising, where the member returned, Walter Sneyd, was nephew to the patron, Lady Andover. Less certain is a seat for Northampton which, with an electorate of well over one thousand, might be regarded as too large for patronage. Nevertheless, the Compton family had held a powerful interest since 1727 and their successful candidate in 1784 was Lord Compton himself, who held the seat until 1796, when he succeeded as 9th Earl of Northampton.

We have now established, with, I hope, some approximation to historical truth, the position towards the end of the eighteenth century. Although it is not strictly part of my brief, it may be of value to know the trend up to 1832. Fortunately, we have recently been provided with a scholarly survey by J. Sack – and, even more fortunately for my sake, there is a good deal of correspondence between our assessments.[46] Sack's main purpose was to discuss the relationship between patron and member – an important and interesting theme, which I do not propose to pursue here. My own analysis, up to 1786, suggested 210 seats under patronage. Sack's figure for 1802 is 221.[47] Of course, since we are comparing different periods there will be a number of gains and losses as interests crumbled and new ones were created. But the degree of difference between our figures is fairly easily explained. The Norfolk interest which, when we left it in 1786, had only three secure seats, had, as the result of assiduous electioneering, climbed by 1802 to eight, and by the Duke's death in 1815 had risen to eleven. Another developing interest was that of Robert Smith, whom we have met before as a rare example of a banker elevated to the English peerage in 1797 as Lord Carrington. In 1802, he had five seats at his command. These two interests alone bring us roughly into line. Though it would be imprudent to attach too much significance to exact numbers, the degree of peerage patronage seems to have peaked in 1807, when Sack suggests 236 seats were under command. There was a slight subsequent falling-off, but the figure up to 1830 remains at over two hundred. In the last general election, that of 1831, the number dips to 191. The nature of the 1831 general election,

---

[46] 'The House of Lords and parliamentary patronage in Great Britain, 1802–32', *Historical Journal*, XXIII (1980), 913–37.

[47] There seems to be a slight discrepancy between the figures Sack offers in his Table 1 and those which can be derived from his Appendix. I have taken the Appendix as a guide.

which I have discussed elsewhere, led to a number of previously secure interests being overthrown.[48]

I mentioned a number of contemporary assessments in the 1790s and up to 1832, particularly the remarkable series offered by Thomas Oldfield. I cannot, however, call them in here as independent corroborative evidence, since they have been used by the History of Parliament, McCahill and Sack.[49] One, however, is somewhat discrepant and calls for a certain amount of explanation. This is the list published in February 1793 on behalf of the Society of the Friends of the People and intended to prepare the ground for Charles Grey's motion for a reform of parliament. The author was George Tierney, though the work was clearly based upon Oldfield, whose *History of the boroughs* came out the year before. It has been remarked that Tierney's assessment was rather smaller than most others. This is in itself curious because one might have suspected that an avowedly propagandist work would seek to exaggerate the extent of peerage control. But before we salute George Tierney as a man of firm principle, we should pause to consider the situation. The Rockinghams and their successors the Foxite Whigs were always in some embarrassment over parliamentary reform since their own leaders owned so many of the boroughs complained of. Tierney was therefore in a delicate position and he rose to the challenge like a good party man. He cheated. The Duke of Portland was head of his party. His family had had influence in Cumberland since the 1690s. Nobody was likely to forget it, since in the 1760s and 1770s there had been a much publicised struggle for supremacy, involving legal actions, between him and Sir James Lowther. Oldfield recorded it. Tierney had never heard of it. The Duke of Bedford was another leader: Tierney did not believe that he had influence in Bedford borough. The Duke of Norfolk was a third leader and, as we have seen, on the way to becoming something of an electoral heavyweight. Oldfield gave him five seats in 1792, rising to nine in 1797 and eleven by 1816. Tierney could only remember one seat – conceding, grudgingly, that the Duke of Norfolk did have a certain influence at Arundel. The completeness of Tierney's political amnesia is awesome. He even managed to forget that Lord Derby had influence in Lancashire and that the Duke of Northumberland had influence in Northumberland – as, indeed, he still has, being, among other things, chancellor of my

---

Parliamentary reform, Chapter 10.
In general they run parallel to our findings. The *Black Book* for 1820 suggested eighty-seven English peers returning 213 members. Sack's estimate for 1820 is eighty peers returning 175 members.

own university of Newcastle upon Tyne. Under these circumstances, the shortfall on Tierney's list of some thirty seats is less inexplicable Tierney's biographer, H. K. Olphin, was most impressed: 'he rendered to the cause of reform a lasting service . . . Proprietors of all the rotten boroughs, if they wished to deny the title, could find their name in the published list.'[50] Not all proprietors, and not all names.

You will, I am sure, have detected in these remarks about patronage a certain defensiveness and I must again remind you that there is a subjective element in all these assessments. But, again, we are fortunate There is a method of checking, not indeed on the exact figures, but on the overall trend, which is our primary interest, and that method is, luckily more precise in its exploitation. If we are correct in postulating a vast increase in the control exercised over the electoral system by the peers we would expect this to be reflected in the membership of the House of Commons. It is a laborious but straightforward matter to ascertain whether there was a corresponding increase in the number of peers' son finding their way into the Lower House.

There are certain methodological problems which make it difficult to use other people's assessments, save for checking. My analyses are confined to members returned at general elections: unlike some other analyses, they do not include members returned at by-elections. Where there has been a 'hedge' or a disputed return, the member finally returned for the seat is the one scrutinised. Illegitimate sons have not been included: fortunately the number is not so great as to ruin statistical comparisons. Sons of peeresses in their own right have been included But the main reservation to be borne in mind is that the composition of the House changed at the Act of Union with Scotland in 1707 and again at the Act of Union of 1801, which added one hundred Irish members Only the general elections from 1708 to 1796 are therefore strictly comparable.

According to my calculation, the grand total of peers' sons and Irish peers returned in 1708 was seventy. The House numbered 558. In 1710 it fell to fifty-four and in 1713 to forty-eight. There followed a steady increase until the middle of the century: fifty-three in 1715, eighty-two in 1722, ninety-three in 1727, down to seventy-seven in 1734, up to one hundred in 1741, to one hundred and twelve in 1747 and one hundred and thirteen in 1754. It stayed around that level until the end of th century, rising to one hundred and nineteen in 1790 and to one hundred and twenty in 1796. If we isolate the sons of English peers, thirty-two

[50] *George Tierney*, 20.

were returned in 1713, fifty in 1734, seventy-two in 1768 and eighty-two in 1796. For those who prefer their history even more quantified, it means that what we may call the peerage element of the House of Commons rose from just over 8% in 1713 to 21% in 1796.

With rather less certainty, we can trace the previous and subsequent positions. Keeler's analysis of the Long Parliament of 1640 suggests that there were forty-four peers' sons and Irish peers in a substantially smaller House of Commons of 507 members – i.e. roughly 8.7%.[51] In 1701, the last Parliament of William III's reign, there had been fifty-five in all – nearly 11%. After 1801, the House of Commons numbered 658 MPs. Geritt P. Judd IV's figures for 1802 were 143.[52] This gives a percentage in the larger House of 22%, compared with my estimate of 21% for 1796. The subsequent figures from Judd are as follows:

1806	162	1820	147
1807	159	1826	165
1812	143	1830	155
1818	157	1831	137

The falling-off in 1831 corresponds with the decrease in patronage which we noted earlier.

There are a number of articles covering the period from 1832,[53] and they make use of contemporary estimates. But to make sure that the same terms of reference are still being employed, I propose to stick to my own assessments. For 1841, I make the total 127, which suggests a considerable falling-off from the peak of 1826.[54] By 1874 a great shift was taking place and the total is down to ninety-two.[55]

Of course, these figures do not in any sense reflect the true noble element in the Lower House and their purpose is to point a trend. They exclude many peers' sons who came in at by-elections. In order to proffer strict statistics, they also exclude many members who were obviously part of the peerage element but who were not sons of peers when elected. The member for Sutherland in 1727 was William Sutherland, Lord Strathnaver, but his father died young before inheriting the title, so that

[1] M. F. Keeler, *The Long Parliament, 1640–41: a biographical study of its members.*

[2] *Members of Parliament, 1734–1832*, App. 6, 84.

[3] E.g. S. Woolley, 'The personnel of the Parliament of 1833', *English Historical Review*, LIII (1938), 240–62; W. O. Aydelotte, 'The House of Commons in the 1840s', *History*, XXXIX (1954), 249–62; W. L. Guttsman, *The British political elite.*

[4] Sons of English peers 100; Irish peers 4; sons of Irish peers 13; sons of Scottish peers 9; sons of peeress 1.

[5] Sons of English peers 62; Irish peers 5; sons of Irish peers 14; sons of Scottish peers 10; sons of peeress 1.

technically he was not the son of a peer and is excluded.[56] Similarly, Lord Charles Manners, returned from Cambridge University in 1774, was in the direct line of the Dukedom of Rutland which he inherited in 1779, but his father (the famous Marquis of Granby of public-house fame) died aged forty-nine before he succeeded.

To trace all the relationships which made the opening of an eighteenth-century Parliament a family reunion for many members would be impossibly time-consuming. Yet some indication must be provided if we are to focus the genuine aristocratic influence in the Lower House. Let us take, for example, the House returned at the general election of 1784. Our basic category of sons of peers and Irish peers was 107. This was rather lower than usual, a statistical hiccough explained by the fact that the Coalition, which was shattered by the election, was an uncommonly aristocratic body. A good many peers' sons were among Fox's Martyrs. Lord John Cavendish, for example, who had sat since 1754 when he was twenty-one, was defeated at York: he retired from the world, wrote Burke (note the phrase) 'exceedingly irritated at the triumph of his enemies'.[57] In addition to 107, counting each member in one category only, there were twenty-six grandsons of peers, one great-grandson of a peer, twelve nephews of peers, one great-nephew, five brothers of peers, three brothers-in-law of peers, one cousin of a peer and nineteen who were married to the daughter of a peer. This increases our noble element by sixty-eight.

This impression of a Lower House more and more dominated by a particular group is both reinforced and modified if we extend our survey into other classes of member. It is modified because it reminds us that it was really the landed interest as a whole which monopolised power, with the peerage, as no doubt they thought of themselves, as the *crème de la crème*. The 1784 House, which I have just described, included a further eighty-four baronets, sixteen sons of baronets, eighteen whose mothers were daughters of baronets, eleven who were married to the daughters of baronets and so on – a further 129.[58]

The cohesiveness of the eighteenth-century House of Commons, from which sprang a sense of common values and a sense of confidence, made it one of the most exclusive ruling elites in human history. In 1715 out of 558 members, no fewer than 234 had fathers who had also served in

---

[56] His father was returned for Tain burghs in 1707 but disqualified as the eldest son of a Scottish peer.
[57] *The House of Commons, 1754–90*, II, 205.
[58] The comparable figures for 1715 are as follows: basic peerage 53; related to peers 75, baronets or related to baronets 158.

e House: by 1754, the number had grown to 294, well over 50%. Even
1784, by which time the figure had started to decline, it was 214. This,
;ain, was by no means the whole story. In 1754, in addition to the 294
ferred to, another twenty-nine members of the House had grand-
thers who had served. A further forty-two had brothers serving with
em or who had already served.[59] There were three Beckford brothers
d three Colebrooke brothers in the House; Henry Beauclerk, fourth
n of the 1st Duke of St Albans who served for Thetford, had five
others who had already been members.[60] The marriage connections
e too many and too complex to be quantified, but another twenty-two
embers had uncles or great-uncles who had served, and ten more had
usins who were or had been members. The grand total of additions is
erefore 103 which, added to the previous 294, gives 397 members who
d or had had close relatives in the House – well over 70%. Nor should
be presumed that the remaining 25–30% of the House were men of
umble antecedents or lacking in good connections. Thomas Potter, not
cluded in any of the above categories, was the son of the archbishop of
anterbury, and compensated, as is sometimes the case, by being quite
markably lewd; John Fitzpatrick was son of an Irish baron, married to
e daughter of an earl and brother-in-law to a duchess; Robert Lee was
n of an earl and another illegitimate grandson of Charles II; William
nsonby was son of a British baron and Irish earl and married to a
ughter of the 3rd Duke of Devonshire. In contrast, H. R. G. Greaves
ggested that by 1909 the number of members whose fathers had been
the House had fallen to 11% and by 1928 it was down to 2%.[61]

he influence of the peerage, as exercised through the House of Lords
d augmented through the House of Commons, palls, in my
dgement, in comparison with the power they wielded directly as

Another fifteen MPs, whom I do not include, had brothers who sat subsequently.
Beauclerk and his patron the Duke of Grafton had an unusual relationship: each could claim
Charles II as grandfather, Beauclerk's grandmother being Nell Gwynn and Grafton's being Lady
Castlemaine. Considering their female ancestry, the Beauclerks were an uninteresting fraternity,
distinguished mainly by their ability to wheedle pensions and honours from the state. The Dukes
themselves were Hereditary Grand Falconers at £2,500 p.a., which they augmented with further
pensions.
'Personal origins and interrelations of the Houses of Parliament since 1832', Economica, IX (1929),
174–84.
    I do not doubt that these relationships will seem to some readers tenuous and the product of
statistical zeal rather than historical importance. But in the eighteenth century, as I have already
suggested, family relationships, to a degree surprising to a modern mind, were of significance. Let
me rest my case on one example, relating to Audley End in Essex. John Whitwell was born the
son of a Northamptonshire attorney, but his mother was the daughter of an impoverished baron,
the 2nd Lord Griffin, who had married the daughter of the 3rd Earl of Suffolk. In 1742, when his

office-holders, in day-to-day charge of the country, with a firm grip o
the executive. It is surprising how frequently historians point to tl
monopoly of office-holding in continental countries as a fact
promoting revolutionary discontent yet fail to acknowledge the positio
in England. It is true that, unlike many continental countries, there w
no formal and legal monopoly of high office. It was possible for men
humble birth to rise to positions of great importance in public life. Tl
position is further obscured by the fact that the four great first ministe
of the century – Walpole, Pelham, North and Pitt – who between the
held the office for nearly sixty of the one hundred years, sat in the Hou
of Commons. But three of the four were only technically commoner
being sons of peers, while the fourth, Walpole, finished up in the Hou
of Lords.

When we start with the cabinet itself, we are confronted by a boc
which was evolving through most of the century. It is only from 178
onwards that we can trace the membership with reasonable certainty.
seems therefore best to offer selected examples up to 1782 and to de
with the great offices of state separately.

Pelham's cabinet in the summer of 1744 is put by Wilkes at fiftee
members.[62] Six of them were Dukes – Argyll, Devonshire, Dorse
Grafton, Newcastle and Richmond. When a reshuffle took place
November 1744, Pelham took the opportunity to increase the duc
element, bringing in Bedford. Since the archbishop of Canterbury w
very much an honorary member of the cabinet, this means that one-ha
of that body were dukes.

When Newcastle took over on the death of his younger brother, the
was an inner cabinet of six and an outer cabinet of fourteen. The onl
non-peer in the inner cabinet was Sir Thomas Robinson, Secretary o
State for the South, and brought in to lead the Commons. In the outo
cabinet in 1755, there were two commoners, Robinson and Henry Fo:
George Grenville, in the mid-1760s, had an efficient cabinet of nine, i
which he was the only commoner.[63]

uncle died, Whitwell inherited Audley End, changed his name to Griffin – or, rather overdoin
it, to Griffin-Griffin – entered Parliament, inherited a barony, and was given a further baron
For good measure he became a Field Marshall. When he died in 1797 Audley End went tc
second cousin from Berkshire, Richard Aldworth Neville, who also became 2nd Lo
Braybrooke, and who also changed his name to Griffin. The relationship between the 2nd Lo
Braybrooke and the former owners of Audley End, the Earls of Suffolk, was fairly remote. B
the property was agreeable.
[62] J. W. Wilkes, A Whig in power, 58.
[63] I. R. Christie, 'The Cabinet during the Grenville administration, 1763–1765', English Historie
Review, LXXIII (1958), 86–92.

Between 1782 and 1820, sixty-five individuals held cabinet office. Of these forty-three were peers, and of the remaining twenty-two, fourteen were the sons of peers. Of the remaining eight, C. P. Yorke was the son of Charles Yorke, whose patent of nobility was made out in 1770 when he died; Tommy Grenville was the grandson of a peeress, one of his brothers was a marquis and another was a baron. Genuinely non-aristocratic were Henry Dundas, William Windham, Henry Addington ('The Doctor'), George Canning (whose mother had been an actress, as the fashionable world never forgot), Nicholas Vansittart and Charles Bragge-Bathurst. Three of these finished up in the House of Lords.

The erosion of peerage influence in the cabinet was gradual and undramatic. The growing complexity of government reduced the value of the well-meaning amateur peer and enhanced the need for full-time politicians and men of business. The first cabinet in which peers seem to have been in a minority was that of Palmerston in June 1859, with seven peers against eight commoners; the balance was soon restored in 1860 and 1862 when Sidney Herbert and Lord John Russell were moved to the Lords. By 1892, in Gladstone's fourth cabinet, the balance had tipped 5 : 12 against the peers. In the Asquith cabinet, which declared war on Germany in August 1914, there were only four peers out of a total of twenty members. Thus, slowly, in F. M. L. Thompson's happy phrase, the gentlemen gave way to the players.

Of the great offices of state, some can be dismissed summarily. The Lord Lieutenant of Ireland, the Lord Chamberlain and the Lord President of the Council were always peers. The Lord Chancellor, head of the legal profession and dispenser of much ecclesiastical patronage, was almost invariably a peer: only two of the fourteen holders of the office were not, Sir Nathan Wright, Keeper of the Great Seal from 1700 to 1706, and Charles Yorke, whom I mentioned before, and who would have been a peer had he lived a day longer. It should however be noted that Robert Henley had to wait three years before receiving his barony in 1760. Of the thirty-six Lords Privy Seal, thirty-five were peers, the exception being John Robinson, bishop of London, who was given that office in 1711 to conduct the peace negotiations at Utrecht. Of twenty-two First Lords of the Treasury, sixteen were peers and four were sons of peers: the exceptions were James Stanhope, grandson of a peer and Walpole, created a peer. Next to the First Lord, the most important executive officers were the Secretaries of State for the North and the South. There were forty-nine altogether, of whom twenty-eight were peers, five were sons of peers and five were grandsons of peers. Six of the remaining eleven were created peers. The Secretaryship for the South was held for sixty-three of the one hundred years by a peer: that for the North for sixty-five years. Between Craggs, who died in 1721, and Henry Fox in 1755, no commoner held either office. There was, of course, no great civil service machine to provide a rival source of power to ministers; in 1800, the Foreign Office had only eleven clerks and the War Office only six.

Next we have control of the armed forces. First Lordship of the Admiralty was held by twenty-three men, of whom sixteen were peers, one a prince of the royal blood (Prince George of Denmark, in Anne's reign), one son of a peer (Keppel) and another (George Grenville), son of a peeress. The remaining four were Leake, Wager, Saunders and Hawke. Sir Charles Saunders held the position for only four months in Chatham's ministry of 1766, and Sir John Leake was never quite First Lord, but acted in Anne's reign as chairman of the Navy Board. Before Sir Charles Wager accepted the post in 1733, he pointed out to Walpole that the First Lord was normally a peer of the realm.

Life on an eighteenth-century man-of-war was not all that appealing to most aristocrats. Nevertheless, a number of peers or peerage connections did make careers in the navy. Promotion from post-captain to admiral was automatic and it was therefore of importance to attain post-captain as soon as possible. This depended upon a certain amount of sea time – i.e. ocean experience. But officers with sufficient interest could get off to a flying start. It is amusing in Russian history to read of Cyril Rassumovsky who was commissioned at the age of nought, thus enabling him to retire as a Field Marshall at the age of twenty-three. But Thomas Cochrane, Lord Dundonald, was entered on the books of his uncle's vessel when he was four, and, when he took up his career in earnest, he was posted to the flagship of Admiral Keith, also the son of a Scottish peer. To his father, Cochrane wrote in 1798: 'I cannot tell how I stand as to promotion . . . There are no less than eleven lieutenants on board . . . Most of them, however, I believe have little or no interest.'[64] A. D. Harvey suggested that the navy contained a higher proportion of noble officers than the regular army,[65] while D. A. Baugh, in his study of naval administration, wrote that 'there were enough external connections to keep the navy securely within the aristocratic network'.[66]

---

[64] J. Sugden, 'Lord Cochrane, naval commander, radical, inventor: a study of his earlier career, 1775–1818', Ph.D. thesis, Sheffield University (1981).

[65] *Britain in the early nineteenth century*, 23–4.

[66] *Naval administration, 1715–50*, Navy Records Society (1977), 5.

The system of purchase in the army, which survived until Cardwell's reform of 1871, was the nearest thing in England to the sale of office which was so prominent a feature of the *ancien régime* in France. We should note, however, that the abolition of purchase in the French army was begun in the 1770s and completed during the Revolution, almost one hundred years before it was implemented in England. As a legally recognised institution, purchase of commissions dated from the decision in *Ive* v. *Ashe* in 1702. It played into the hands of young men of wealth and connections and was an essential part of aristocratic control of the army. A commission as Lieutenant-Colonel in the cavalry at the end of the eighteenth century cost more than £5,000 so that there was little chance of outsiders infiltrating. There was a bitter struggle in Victoria's reign over Cardwell's reform which, having been thrown out by the House of Lords, had to be effected by the use of the royal prerogative.[67]

It should be remembered that the army had an important police role within the state. The forces of law and order at the disposal of most magistrates were derisory and the only way of dealing with persistent rioting was to ask for troops. This is not to suggest that army officers were keen to become embroiled with the civil population. Hayter has shown that, for the most part, officers and men found such duties disagreeable and riots were usually handled lightly.[68] But at times, during the Wilkite riots for example, the role of the army became an important political issue, and the attitude of the army, had there been widespread disaffection, would have been as crucial as it turned out to be in France in 1789.

Political interference in the army needs little elaboration. William Pitt was dismissed from his cornetcy in 1736 for opposing Walpole; in 1764 Henry Seymour Conway, colonel of the First Dragoons, lost his regiment for opposing George Grenville on the Wilkes issue. When Edward Harvey obtained the coveted post of Aide de Camp to the new king in 1760, a friend wrote, bluntly: 'let me tell you to whom alone you are obliged for this – Lord Bute, Lord Fitzmaurice and your brother Will'. Major-General A'Court, MP for his family borough of Heytesbury, impatient at not getting a regiment in 1762, threatened to go into opposition, did so, and lost his lieutenant-colonelcy in the 2nd Foot Guards.[69]

[7] An excellent account of the subject is A. Bruce, *The purchase system in the British army, 1660–1871*.
[8] T. Hayter, *The army and the crowd in mid-Georgian England*.
[9] *The House of Commons, 1754–90*, II, 594, 5.

The *Court and City Register* for 1769 lists 102 colonels of regiment Forty-three of them were peers or sons of peers, seven were grandsons c peers and four more were married to the daughter of a peer – i.e. ove half the colonels had direct peerage connections.[70] It continues with a li of the governors of thirty-three garrisons in Britain – some of ther lucrative places bringing in more than £1,000 p.a. Fifteen were in th hands of peers or peers' sons, one was held by the grandson of a peer, an two more were commanded by the brothers of peers – eighteen out c thirty-three, or 55%. In the upper ranks of the army, the peers clustere thickly. Ten per cent of the Major-Generals were peers; 16% of th Lieutenant-Generals; 27% of the full Generals. The rank of Fiel Marshall was given very sparingly in the century. Of twenty Fiel Marshalls, fourteen were peers – i.e. 70%.[71] There was little likelihoo that the higher ranks of the army would be badly out of step wit Parliament. Of the 102 colonels previously referred to, twenty wer peers, and another thirty-four sat at some time in the House of Common – more than half the total. According to the History of Parliament, ther were fifty or sixty army officers in each of the Parliaments from 1715 t 1790.[72]

The large number of peers' sons in the Commons and the growin; influence of the aristocracy in the church was defended on the ground that, by reconciling power and property, it provided ballast to the ship c state. Similar arguments were adduced to defend the system of purchas in the army. Palmerston, as Secretary at War in 1827, warned the cabine that it was 'of great constitutional importance that the military force o this country should be identified in feelings and interest with our civi and political institutions, and this can best be effected by introducin; among its officers, and especially among those who fill its *higher* ranks, large infusion of men belonging to the aristocracy, that term bein; understood to refer to the possession of wealth as well as of rank'.[73]

Lastly, in our survey of high office, we may glance briefly at th diplomatic service. D. B. Horn, in his *British diplomatic service* list seventy-seven individuals who served as ambassadors between 1689 an 1789. Of these, forty-seven were peers, just over 60%. But this under estimates aristocratic influence in the service. Many of the commoner

---

[70] Excluding royal dukes, but including Scottish and Irish peers.
[71] It should be noted that these figures refer to peers only. If the sons of peers are brought in, th proportion of Generals rises to well over 40%.
[72] See Table in *The House of Commons, 1715–54*, I, 155 and in *The House of Commons, 1754–90*, I, 14 [73] Cabinet memorandum, Broadlands MSS WO 51, 1 quoted by Bruce, *The purchase system*, 176

rved as ambassadors to Turkey, where the salary until 1803 was paid by
te Levant Company and became steadily less attractive.[74] The really
nportant embassies were those of Versailles, Madrid and Vienna: of the
tirty-four ambassadors serving there, twenty-six were peers – more
an 75%. Of course, several of the ambassadors categorised as non-peers
ad, nevertheless, close peerage connections. Sir Joseph Yorke, British
presentative at The Hague for thirty years, was the son of Lord
ardwicke, and finished up in the Lords himself as Baron Dover;
/illiam Stanhope was cousin to James, 1st Earl Stanhope, who
pointed him envoy to Madrid in 1717; he also ended up in the Lords as
arl of Harrington. Edward Wortley Montagu, ambassador to the Porte
om 1716 to 1718 was a grandson of the Earl of Sandwich, and his wife,
te redoubtable Lady Mary, was daughter of the Duke of Kingston.

It may, of course, be objected that I have fallen a victim to twentieth-
ntury assumptions which automatically give priority to central
overnment and regard its work of supreme significance, whereas in the
ghteenth century, in most parts of Europe, local government was of
reater importance. I do not propose to embark upon the same kind of
chaustive survey for the shires, counties and boroughs of England.
idicial and administrative power was in the hands of the justices of the
eace. The justices were appointed by the Lord Chancellor on the advice
f the Lord Lieutenant of the county. We have already seen that the Lord
hancellor was almost invariably a peer. We may now look briefly at the
ords Lieutenant.

J. C. Sainty lists 294 men who were Lords Lieutenant in England and
/ales in the eighteenth century. Of these, 255 were peers or sons of
eers. Of the remaining thirty-nine, two were special cases, being
ishops of Durham in the county palatine, and, in any case, they were
embers of the House of Lords. Of the other thirty-seven, twenty-five
ere from Wales and Monmouth, where there was an acute shortage of
eers.[75] That leaves twelve Lords Lieutenant. Of these, five – Bromley,
oddington, Herbert, Lowther and Pulteney – were subsequently created
eers. Norborne Berkeley, Lord Lieutenant of Gloucestershire 1762–6,
as brother-in-law of the Duke of Beaufort and subsequently estab-

A. C. Wood, 'The English Embassy at Constantinople, 1660–1762', *English Historical Review*, XL
(1925), 533–61.

J. C. Sainty, *Lists of the Lieutenants of the Counties of England and Wales, 1660–1974*. In due course,
even Wales succumbed to the aristocratic embrace. In 1769, of the thirteen counties including
Monmouth, peers held four and commoners nine. By 1808 the position was reversed, with peers
holding ten and commoners only three.

lished his claim to the barony of Botetort, which had been in abeyan
for 250 years. Sir William Courtenay of Powderham Castle, who w
Lord Lieutenant of Devon 1714–16, was the brother-in-law of a pee
George Dodington, Lord Lieutenant of Somerset 1715–20, was
cousin of Lord Cobham, and his great Somerset and Dorset esta
eventually descended to the Temple family. Sir William Lowther, Lo
Lieutenant of Westmorland 1753–6, was a grandson of William, 2r
Duke of Devonshire, and his successor, Sir John Pennington was create
an Irish peer in 1783. This leaves two. Sir Charles Hanbury-William
Lord Lieutenant of Herefordshire from 1742 to 1747, was married to tl
daughter of Earl Coninsby, and held the property of Hampton Cou
eight miles north of Hereford. The remaining Lord Lieutenant, Hen
Compton, was of Tower Hamlets and a special case. Even our non-pee
were very well connected.

There are two points which are worth noting. The first is that the Lo
Lieutenant's exclusive power of recommending justices was yet anoth
example of the eighteenth-century tendency towards monopoly
power. Whereas in the seventeenth and early eighteenth centuries it w
not uncommon for the Lord Lieutenancy and the Custos Rotulorum
be held by different individuals, increasingly the Lord Lieutenant too
over both functions. Earlier, recommendations for appointment to tl
bench came to the Lord Chancellor from a variety of local sources, but b
the second half of the eighteenth century the Lord Lieutenant, acting
Custos Rotulorum, had managed to exclude all others.[76]

In addition to the nomination of justices, there were other areas
patronage which made the Lord Lieutenant a key figure in the shires ar
helps to explain the intense rivalry for the position. The Lord Lieutenan
as we have seen, wielded considerable electoral power. 'We have f
some time expected a dissolution of this Parliament', wrote Sir Robe
Davers from Suffolk in 1710, 'but if the Lord Lieutenants of son
counties be not turned out, and particularly ours, matters will not go
well as we wish.'[77] In the same year, the Duke of Beaufort complaine
that the mere report that his Gloucestershire rival, Lord Berkeley, was
have the Lord Lieutenancy made 'the greatest hardship' in electionee
ing.[78] The electoral importance of the Lords Lieutenant seems to ha
declined later in the century, probably because the number of coun

[76] L. K. J. Glassey, *Politics and the appointment of the justices of the peace, 1675–1720*, 13–15. The Cus
Rotulorum for Co. Durham remained separate and was usually held by the bishop, while t
Vane family of Raby Castle held the Lord Lieutenancy.
[77] *HMC. Portland*, IV, 590.   [78] *Ibid.*, 611.

ontests fell so dramatically. Nevertheless, John Robinson, in preparing or the general election of 1774, made notes to consult several Lords Lieutenant.[79] The Lord Lieutenant also had decisive patronage over the militia. In 1661, when the militia was established, the House of Lords ucceeded in carrying, against the Commons, that senior appointments n the militia should be in the hands of the Lords Lieutenant.[80] Lastly, the ord Lieutenant had important responsibilities for the preservation of w and order and could call upon troops to assist him.[81] The key overnmental positions in the localities were therefore firmly in the rasp of the aristocracy.

n the introductory essay of *The historian at work*, I suggested that an mportant task of the historian was to stand back from the evidence he ad painstakingly compiled and ask irreverent questions. The time has ow come to practise what I preached, though you must not expect rreverent answers. Do not these lists exaggerate the command which the eighteenth-century peerage exercised? Am I not in danger of seeing peers under the beds? My first answer is that many of these lists do not really ttempt to quantify influence: the intention has been to demonstrate *rends* and to suggest that the parrot cry in the eighteenth century that the nfluence of the crown had increased, was increasing, and ought to be liminished, served to mask the fact that it was the influence of the obility that was increasing. I doubt whether the historian ever has the vidence to assess influence as such, since much of it must be ephemeral, ersonal and unrecorded. My second answer is that, in some respects, the ists do exaggerate. It is in the nature of statistical or structural analysis of his kind that it tends to simplify and to choke out the subtleties and omplexities of real life. The exceptions to the rule are often the most nteresting and important. The nobility did not, always, act as a group or ake one view of public events. Even when they came nearest to doing so, n their drawing together in outrage at the atrocities of the French Revolution, there were still individual peers like Lauderdale and Stanhope who found merit in the French example. Their unanimity was frequently threatened by party rivalry. It would not have been easy for an observer to perceive in March 1784 that Fox, North and Pitt, all sons of peers, were really 'on the same side' – though this was a line of attack

[9] *Parliamentary papers of John Robinson*, 20–3.
[0] J. R. Western, *The English militia in the eighteenth century: the story of a political issue, 1660–1802*, 14.
[1] See, e.g., E. A. Smith, *Whig principles and party politics: Earl Fitzwilliam and the Whig Party, 1748–1833*, 244–6 for Fitzwilliam's work as Lord Lieutenant of the West Riding in the late eighteenth and early nineteenth centuries.

increasingly made by radicals such as Horne Tooke, Cobbett and Hazlitt. The unity of the nobility was masked by fierce dynastic rivalries: the Dukes of Chandos and Bolton in Hampshire, the different branches of the Montagus in Huntingdonshire – Montagu versus Montagu rather than Montagu versus Capulet. There were celebrated instances when families split: the eccentric Tom Hervey stood against his brother at Bury St Edmunds in 1747 and lost the family one of its two seats in the borough; Charles Francis Greville quarrelled in 1784 with his brother Lord Warwick and defeated him in his own borough. There were important electoral areas where the influence of the peerage did not penetrate. Though the famous independency of Wiltshire was something of an illusion, the freeholders of Somerset, Devon and Cornwall were genuinely independent. Many of the large parliamentary boroughs, like Bristol, Liverpool and Newcastle, were outside the aristocratic embrace and were run by their own financial and commercial oligarchs. Nor could so small a peerage have functioned without clients, subordinates and supporters, and it is in the nature of things that such people often acquire power for themselves, sometimes biting the hand that feeds them in the process. But, when these and other reservations are made – some of which must apply to any regime – one wonders if any ruling group could have been more cohesive or better integrated.

There is a further objection which, at first sight, threatens to tumble our structure of statistics like a pack of cards. Is is not, to a great extent, a statistical illusion based upon the fact that the nobility was increasing markedly in numbers, particularly towards the end of the eighteenth century? In fact the objection has already been anticipated. Geritt P. Judd IV compiled a list of analyses in the 1950s and observed: 'A more obvious explanation of the increase of peers' sons in the Commons is simply that the peerage itself almost doubled in size between 1780 and 1832.'[82] Fortunately, for your peace of mind, I do not think that this objection is insuperable. In the first place, many of the developments we have noted may be traced much earlier than the increase in the total number of peers – control over boroughs, for example, or the increase in peers' sons in the Commons. Second, the rise in the total of the peerage in the later decades scarcely kept pace with the rise in population generally. In other words, all groups were increasing in numbers. But there was only a limited number of boroughs and seats and, to a considerable extent, of places and honours, and if the peerage was adding to its share, other groups were losing.

[82] *Members of Parliament*, 32.

Let us now look back on our opening paradox – that the power of the House of Lords declined while the influence of the peerage increased. We can now see that it was less a paradox than a truism – or even a consequence. There was hardly any major role for the House of Lords to play. They were firemen in a town without fires and, consequently, they could allow their hoses to rot. Just occasionally, when danger threatened, their reserve powers could be brought into use. But other historians have pointed out how weak was the radical challenge in the eighteenth century and what there was was fairly easily contained.[83] Just as the crown had found more subtle weapons than its power of veto, the eighteenth-century peerage had better methods of control than rejecting bills and budgets in the House of Lords. Our analysis, however laborious, also helps to explain why the army, which had cut loose in the seventeenth century with devastating results, was reliable one hundred years later. Christopher Clay has drawn attention to the importance of the methods adopted after 1660 to ensure regular pay for the troops.[84] To this we may add a political explanation. What, in the eighteenth century, could army officers have rebelled against and, if they had taken over, how could they have constructed a society more congenial to their own aristocratic views and interests?

[83] See, for example, the remarks by F. O'Gorman in the final discussion in my *The Whig ascendancy*, Chapter 8.
[84] C. Clay, *Public finance and private wealth: the career of Sir Stephen Fox, 1627–1716*, 72–4.

5

THE SINEWS OF POWER: ECONOMIC

Few will wish to deny the proposition that wealth contributes to political power. We must therefore try to establish how much wealth, in relation to other groups, the peerage commanded, how that wealth was acquired and how it could be deployed for political purposes. We also need to know, if possible, how political power itself contributed to wealth.

These are by no means easy questions. Though it is not hard to obtain guesses of some rentals, and newspapers and magazines were always speculating on the wealth of the departed or the portion of the bride-to-be, estimates of rentals, even if accurate, mean little unless carefully related to debts, obligations and outgoings. The number of such studies is slowly increasing,[1] but so far we have insufficient to quantify. There were large disparities between poor peerage families like the Lincolns, the Warwicks, Montforts and Yarmouths and the great magnates like Bedford, Portland, Devonshire, Bridgwater and Northumberland. Even among the dukes, there were marked differences: neither the Beauclerks, Dukes of St Albans, nor the Fitzroys, Dukes of Grafton, were well endowed with land. When the 2nd Duke of Manchester died in 1739, Mrs Osborn, who had an eye for such things, put the estate at no more than £4,000 p.a., out of which £2,000 a year jointure was to be paid 'to a young woman [who] may live this fifty year', and reckoned that the new duke would have, net, no more than £3,000 p.a.[2] Her forecast was almost uncannily accurate: the dowager duchess lived to be eighty and died forty-seven years later. When the 4th Duke died in 1788, Wraxall noted that his fortune bore no proportion to his dignity.[3]

[1] Smith, *Whig principles and party politics*: R. Kelch, *Newcastle – a duke without money: Thomas Pelham-Holles, 1693–1768*; R. A. C. Parker, *Coke of Norfolk: a financial and agricultural study, 1707–1842*; Wordie, *Estate management in eighteenth-century England*.
[2] *Political and social letters*, 65.
[3] Wraxall, *The historical and posthumous memoirs*, v, 172.

We have to bear in mind, not only the disparities between aristocratic families, but the vicissitudes within families. Much depended upon medical and genetic luck, the length of dowagerships, as well as unexpected inheritances. Stone has traced the difficulties of the Cecils, Earls of Salisbury, who, during the 1740s, were paying half their income to meet the interest on debts and mortgages.[4] The experiences of the Brydges family were peculiarly frenetic. The 1st Duke of Chandos made a famous killing as Paymaster-General during Marlborough's wars and became a titan of wealth. Nevertheless he managed to dent his vast fortune, losing heavily in the South Seas Bubble and proving the softest of touches for confidence men of every kind. He invested in building projects in Bath and Bridgwater, in oyster fishing, in bottle manufacture, copper-bottoming, lead, gold, American lands, coal anywhere, even in Steele's dreaded fish-pool – and everywhere he lost. 'He was a bauble to every project', wrote his biographers, and his schemes form a kind of compendium of early eighteenth-century bucket shops. Three years after his death, the demolition of his famous house at Cannons commenced.[5] There are many examples of unexpected bequests. William Pitt gained a very acceptable addition to his fortune in 1765 at the expense of his rival, Lord North, when Sir William Pynsent, an eccentric Somerset baronet, left him a large estate in honour of his stand against general warrants. The following year, the indefatigable Mrs Osborn noted a reversion of £9,000 p.a. to come to Pitt should George Villiers, the fifteen-year-old son of Lady Grandison, die under age: 'He is inclined to be wild, and has not had the small pox, and Pitt is lucky. Therefore everyone concludes the boy is to die.'[6] He did not and Pitt was disappointed. Six years later, Mrs Boscawen reported of the young Villiers that 'his lordship is very ingenious in the art of wasting the most possible money in the least possible time'.[7]

The marked disparities within the peerage suggest that it may be unwise to attempt to treat it as an economic bloc, and it is certainly true that many untitled landlords were far wealthier than the lesser peers. But Mingay and Thompson are agreed in warning us against regarding the peerage and the gentry as one landed group.[8] The lifestyle of the average peer and the average squire, if such creatures existed, were very different.

[4] L. Stone, *Family and fortune: studies in aristocratic finance in the sixteenth and seventeenth centuries.*
[5] Baker and Baker, *The life and circumstances of James Brydges, first Duke of Chandos.*
[6] *Political and social letters*, 145.
[7] *Autobiography and correspondence of Mrs Delany*, 2nd series, I, 464.
[8] Mingay, *English landed society in the eighteenth century*, 9–10; F. M. L. Thompson, *English landed society in the nineteenth century*, 20.

So was their social role. The function of blunting the cutting edge o envy by absorbing rising aspirants, though often regarded as th characteristic peculiar to the peerage, was accomplished, so far as it wa accomplished at all, by the gentry. Responsibility rather than absorp tion, wrote Thompson, was the role of the peerage. Of course, traditio insisted that there was a recognised path to the peerage through th gentry, by means of a country estate, a county seat, a baronetcy, an Iris peerage and, at length, an English peerage. It could be done. The Cus family provides a notable example. In the early seventeenth century the were prosperous Lincolnshire yeomen. Richard Cust, a lawyer, becam MP for Lincolnshire in difficult times in 1653 and gained a baronetcy i 1677. The second baronet married the sister and heiress of an Irish pee the third became Speaker of the House of Commons; the reward fo being by common consent the least distinguished Speaker of the centur was a barony for his son in 1776, and his son, in turn, was raised to a earldom in 1815. But even here the process took more than a centur before completion. At every stage there were formidable obstacles, i addition to the scorn one might encounter. Since land was prized, no only as an investment, but for the political and social position it gave, i was an expensive commodity and purchasers were often willing to pa above the strict economic rate for it. To buy straight in at the to required a vast fortune, even if the opportunity was there. The bes estates did not change hands often. The development of entail was, as w shall see, designed to keep great estates intact. When it failed of it purpose, the landowner naturally enough sold off his outlying propertie and poorer estates before parting with the family's heartland. Nor was i easy for new men to establish themselves in county society. The office o sheriff was tedious and irksome and was sometimes given to newcomer: hence Richard Smith, an Indian nabob of humble origins was able to become sheriff of Berkshire in 1779. But the next step wa difficult. There is clear evidence that the county representation was mor and more confined to a small group of well-established families. Th number of county contests declined very markedly in the course of th eighteenth century and any attempt to thrust oneself in by challengin established interests was increasingly resented. Twenty-six of the fort English counties were contested in 1705, but in 1747 there were no mor than three contests in all, and in 1780, at the height of the economica reform campaign, only two. The length of service as county members o the knights of the shire elected in 1705 was 11.5 years: by the 1790 genera election, it had more than doubled to 23.91 years.

et us see what we can establish about the general position of the peerage
the eighteenth century. At first sight, the problem does not look too
nmanageable. There are three contemporary calculations extant,
aced at remarkably convenient intervals in 1696, 1760 and 1803. Each
ffers some estimate of the total national income and of the shares falling
particular groups. They are by Gregory King, Joseph Massie and
atrick Colquhoun.[9]

King's calculations, probably the best known of the three, were
ublished in 1696 but, in fact, refer back to the situation in 1688. He
iggested a total of 160 temporal peers with an average income of
2,800, making a grand aristocratic income of £448,000, or about 1%
f the national income. The latter he put at £44 million. This appears to
ive us a firm foundation at the beginning of the period in which we are
iterested.

There is little difficulty in accepting King's number of peers. It is rarely
ossible to agree on a precise figure, since a certain amount depends upon
efinitions of abeyances, attainders, doubtful claims and the like. My
wn estimate is 153, which is a discrepancy of little consequence. On the
ther hand, King's other figures look rather suspect. One wonders about
1e roundness of some of the estimates: 16,000 families of persons
minent in arts and science, 50,000 tradesmen's families and the like.
)ther categories seem hard to establish: King distinguishes between
minent and lesser clergy and one wonders how he counted 30,000
ypsies, thieves, beggars, etc.

King's analysis has, in fact, been subjected to careful scrutiny by
rofessor Geoffrey Holmes, who pointed out that it was far from King's
rimary purpose to produce his famous Table. King himself seems to
ave entertained doubts about the average income allotted to peers, and
ibsequently raised it to £3,200. Even the revised proposition was, in
Iolmes' judgement, a ludicrous under-estimate and is certainly at
ariance with many individual incomes that can be established.[10]
dward Chamberlayne in his *Angliae Notitia*, published in 1669, had
uggested £10,000 p.a. as a plausible guess, a distressingly large

[9] G. King, *Scheme of the income and expense of the several families of England for the year 1688*; J. Massie, *A computation of the money that hath been exorbitantly raised upon the people of Great Britain*; P. Colquhoun, *Treatise on indigence* and *Treatise on the population and resources of the British Empire*.

[10] 'Gregory King and the social structure of pre-industrial England', *Transactions of the Royal Historical Society*, 5th series, 27 (1977), 41–68. G. Aylmer, *The king's servants*, 329 calls King's estimates 'fantastically low'. For further discussion, see Mingay, *English landed society in the eighteenth century*, 21 and D. V. Glass, 'Two papers on Gregory King', in D. V. Glass and D. E. C. Eversley, eds., *Population in history: essays in historical demography*.

difference of opinion, even though he subsequently reduced it to £8,00
in later editions. A proposal in the House of Lords in 1701 was tha
viscounts should be worth at least £4,000 p.a. and barons at leas
£3,000.[11] Admittedly this was to some extent motivated by fears tha
the peerage should be brought into disrepute by meagre lords, but it als
suggests that the average income must have been substantially highe
than King allowed. The base of our computations turns out to be suspect

Massie's analysis in 1760 did not suggest very marked changes.[12] H
did not follow King's allocations in detail, but lumped together the to
six in King's group – i.e. the aristocracy and gentry. Massie calculated th
national income to have risen some 36% – from £44 million to abou
£60 million. The share of the top groups had risen very slightly from
14.1% in King's survey to 14.3% in Massie's. The total numbers o
temporal peers in 1760 was 181 – again, a modest increase on the 168
total. If inference can legitimately be drawn, it would be that the lande
class had shared in the steady increase of wealth throughout the period
but had hardly changed its position in relation to other groups.

Colquhoun's calculation for 1803 however suggested very consider
able changes. The peerage itself had expanded markedly since 1760 and
according to Colquhoun, stood at 287. The estimated family income wa
£8,000, giving a group aggregate of £2,296,000. This was nearly fiv
times the aggregate which King had suggested. The national wealth wa
presumed to have increased by roughly the same extent, standing a
£209 million instead of £44 million. The share of the peerage in th
national income seems therefore to have remained steady at about 1%
But significant changes were suggested for other groups. The big gainer
were merchants and shop-keepers, whose collective wealth appeared to
have risen by seven and six times respectively, and manufacturers, who
appeared for the first time in Colquhoun's Tables and were allotte
nearly 10% of the total national income. The aggregate income fo
artisans had increased by ten times but this is accounted for mainly by th
vast increase in the numbers placed in that category – 446,000 familie
against 60,000 families in King's lists. Their income per family was u
merely from £40 to £55.

The general position which may cautiously be inferred is that th
temporal peers and the landed classes maintained their share of th
expanding national income, but that some other groups had don

[11] Quoted A. S. Turberville, *The House of Lords in the reign of William III*, 168.
[12] P. Mathias, 'The social structure in the eighteenth century: a calculation by Joseph Massie', in his *The transformation of England*, 171–89.

significantly better and were beginning to close the gap. The new class of manufacturers was accredited with an income of £20 million, as against £28 million for the landed classes excluding fundholders. King's survey had suggested an income of £2,400,000 for merchants (as against £6,285,000 for the landed classes); Colquhoun's merchants, manufacturers, shipbuilders and shipowners combined totalled £39 million to the landed classes' £28 million.

The same evidence can be presented in a rather different fashion by offering peers' incomes as a ratio to others. Within the ranks of the landed classes, they roughly maintained their position – bishops, baronets and esquires gained ground slightly against peers, while knights and gentlemen lost ground. The ratio of peers' incomes against greater merchants worsened significantly from 7 : 1 to 3 : 1. But their position relative to the lower orders improved. Their ratio against artisans more than doubled, while that against labourers increased some 40%.

If the rise from, say, £3,200 to £8,000 per peerage family is anything like true, it suggests a very substantial increase in personal standards of living. There is, of course, the question of prices to consider, but there was no dramatic increase between the late seventeenth and late eighteenth centuries, although there were undoubtedly some fierce temporary fluctuations. If, of course, we are dealing with relative proportions of the national income, prices may be disregarded, and in view of the dubious nature of the statistics, it might be wise not to attempt to correlate with prices too closely.[13]

A brave attempt to summarise the broad movements in landed property over some four centuries was made in 1966 by F. M. L. Thompson.[14] He was at pains to point out the extremely tentative character of his findings and the amount of guesswork involved. His conclusions are not totally adapted for our purposes since he maintained, quite rightly, that many large gentry landowners had more acreage than some peers, and that the topmost category is better described as 'landed aristocracy', of which the peerage formed a substantial part, between one-half and two-thirds. Though he did not deny that there was a

[13] For price changes, see C. B. Behrens, 'Nobles, privileges and taxes in France at the end of the ancien regime', *Economic History Review*, 2nd series, xv (1962/3), 451–75, and Mingay, *English landed society in the eighteenth century*, 44–51.

[14] 'The social distribution of landed property in England since the sixteenth century', *Economic History Review*, 2nd series, xix (1966), 505–17. The article should be read in conjunction with J. P. Cooper's commentary in 'The social distribution of land and men in England, 1436–1700', *ibid.*, xx (1967), 419–40.

gradual move towards great estates in the course of the eighteenth century, the figures he put forward would make it somewhat undramatic in character. The percentage of cultivated land in England and Wales in the hands of the landed aristocracy was, in Thompson's view, between 15% and 20% in 1688, rose to between 20% and 25% by 1790, steadied out in the nineteenth century, and went into a fairly sharp decline towards the end of the nineteenth century. Hence, when we are attempting to account for the rise of great estates in the earlier eighteenth century, it may be worth remembering that the shift in the landed balance of power may have been a comparatively modest one.

If we are correct in inferring a distinct improvement in the financial position of the peerage in the eighteenth century, we must now attempt some kind of explanation. A good deal of work has been done on this problem, particularly for the earlier eighteenth century, but, as not infrequently happens, it does not make it easier to construct an overall picture.

Perhaps the most convenient starting-point is a distinguished and influential article in 1940 by H. J. Habakkuk, which argued that the 'general drift of property in the sixty years after 1690 was in favour of the large estates and the great lords'.[15] A factor which Habakkuk regarded as of 'fundamental importance' was the increasing use made of the strict settlement, which afforded the core of the family estate some protection against extravagant heirs. The redefinition of the entail, after a long period during which both crown and courts had been hostile to the device,[16] Habakkuk attributed to the lawyer and conveyancer Sir Orlando Bridgeman, who had suggested trustees to preserve contingent remainders. Habakkuk did not maintain that the strict settlement could create great estates – merely that it helped to preserve them. The more positive factors assisting the larger landowners were the pressure placed upon their smaller competitors by fierce wartime taxation during the struggle against Louis XIV's France, exacerbated by rising living standards which tempted many of them into debt. The larger landowners, with better access to government office, could survive more easily.

Habakkuk's thesis held the field for many years and hardened into accepted opinion. It was always, however, rather precariously based

[15] 'English landownership, 1680–1740', *Economic History Review*, 1st series, x (1940), 2–17.
[16] Discussed in J. P. Cooper, 'Patterns of inheritance and settlement by great landowners from the fifteenth to the eighteenth centuries', in *Family and inheritance: rural society in Western Europe, 1200–1800*, ed. J. Goody, J. Thirsk and E. P. Thompson, 192–327.

upon his investigations into only two counties, Bedfordshire and Northamptonshire. Moreover, in detail the argument was not totally convincing. It did not adequately distinguish between the creation, consolidation and preservation of great estates, nor, perhaps, could a study of just two counties make such a distinction. Habakkuk did not offer any explanation why the courts, which had disavowed previous limiting devices, should have accepted Bridgeman's. Moreover, he admitted that a high proportion of the land changing hands between 1680 and 1740 'came into the hands of families who already in 1680 owned large estates'. This merely moved the whole problem back a few decades and made the process seem much less dramatic. The explanation which Habakkuk offered, that dowries were turned into landed properties,[17] masked a truism that if, in any period, husbands choose to invest dowries in land, more land will be acquired: it did not explain what made them do so.

Habakkuk supported his thesis in a further article in 1950, in which he drew attention to an increase in the size of dowries in relation to jointures, suggesting that this might have helped prestigious families, which could attract generous dowries and use the proceeds to buy still more land.[18] It is not easy to see why this should necessarily have helped large landowners. It would scarcely have worked in favour of Daniel Finch, 2nd Earl of Nottingham, who had seven daughters to dispose of, presumably with inflated dowries.[19] The hazards of life were so great in the eighteenth century that an anticipated gain might well be wiped out by an unexpectedly long widowhood, with a consequent drain upon the estate.[20]

In recent years, Habakkuk's original thesis has been increasingly challenged. Christopher Clay, in an important revisionist article in 1968,[21] while not disputing that the trend favoured large estates, doubted whether any one factor could sustain the role which Habakkuk

[17] 'English landownership', 7.

[18] 'Marriage settlements in the eighteenth century', *Transactions of the Royal Historical Society*, 4th series, 32 (1950), 15–30.

[19] See Habakkuk's own article. 'Daniel Finch, 2nd Earl of Nottingham: his house and estate', in *Studies in social history: a tribute to G. M. Trevelyan*, ed. J. H. Plumb, 141–78. There is some confusion how many children Nottingham did have, but it seems to have been eight by his first wife and at least seventeen by his second. The daughters collected three dukes, two marquises, one earl and one baronet. Their portions seem to have cost Nottingham £52,000, a good deal more than the building of his splendid house at Burley-on-the-Hill.

[20] C. Clay, 'Marriage, inheritance, and the rise of large estates in England, 1660–1815', *Economic History Review*, 2nd series, XXI (1968), 505, Note 4 quotes an example where the Grimstones lost an inheritance to the Barringtons and in addition had to pay a jointure of £1,600 p.a. for no fewer than twenty-seven years.   [21] *Ibid.*

had suggested for the strict settlement. He did not like Habakkuk's suggestion that the landed classes, by amassing dowries by means of loans in order to invest the proceeds in land, were 'raising themselves by their own bootstraps'. On the contrary, Clay argued, at a time when interest charges were normally higher than the yield from land, such a policy would be economic folly. By no means all portions were raised by mortgage; they were often raised by the sale of land; nor did husbands necessarily spend dowries on land purchase. Clay's lone voice subsequently became something of a chorus. In 1974 Holderness objected that his own investigations into Lincolnshire did not reveal the importance of entail.[22] J. V. Beckett joined in the discussion in 1977 with an excellent article based upon his study of Cumbria.[23] In particular, he offered important methodological reservations. The distinction between large and small landowners was by no means easy to make, while the practice of concentrating upon individual counties for purposes of analysis ran the risk of distorting the overall picture. A landowner might well be building up an estate in one county by selling off elsewhere. Like Holderness, Beckett found the strict settlement was used considerably less than Habakkuk had implied. Lloyd Bonfield, in 1979, pointed out that the strict settlement came into operation only provided that the father survived until his heir's marriage, a condition frequently not met.[24] R. A. C. Parker, in a study of the estates of Coke of Norfolk, agreed that entail had played a relatively minor role in building up that property, pointing out that Lord Lovel's strict settlement of 1718 had never come into operation,[25] and he confirmed that for many years the owners of the Holkham estate had pursued a policy of selling off their outlying properties in order to concentrate their strength in Norfolk.

In three successive presidential addresses to the Royal Historical Society, Habakkuk took the opportunity to restate and revise his thesis.[26] His first lecture emphasised the importance of credit in enabling large landowners to survive crises that would bring down smaller men. The example of the 1st Duke of Newcastle might serve to convince

---

[22] 'The English land market in the eighteenth century: the case of Lincolnshire', *ibid.*, XXVII (1974), 557–76.
[23] 'English landownership in the later seventeenth and eighteenth centuries: the debate and the problems', *ibid.*, XXX (1977), 567–81.
[24] 'Marriage settlements and the "rise of great estates": the demographic aspect', *ibid.*, XXXII (1979), 483–93.
[25] *Coke of Norfolk*. Further criticism of the Habakkuk thesis may be found in P. Roebuck, *Yorkshire baronets 1640–1760: families, estates and fortunes*.
[26] 'The rise and fall of English landed families, 1600–1800'; *Transactions of the Royal Historical Society*, 5th series, 29 (1979), 187–207; *ibid.*, 30 (1980), 199–221; *ibid.*, 31 (1981), 195–217.

anyone who doubted the point. His shaky finances have been patiently examined by Ray Kelch.[27] For forty years the Duke tottered under vast mountains of debt yet, somehow, survived. But easier access to credit must surely apply to all great men in most periods? It is hard to regard it as a factor that could operate only in these few crucial decades. Moreover, it is a circular argument, in that one has to have the great estates before one can obtain the credit to preserve them. Easy credit might have enabled a great estate to survive but it could hardly, in itself, have allowed one to be built up. Habakkuk's second article, technical in nature, analysed acts to sell estates to pay debts and pointed out that few large landowners were forced to resort to that remedy, even during the pressures of the wars against Louis XIV. In his third article, Habakkuk seemed to have retreated a good deal from his original position, placing little emphasis on entail as a factor encouraging the growth of great estates.

But while Habakkuk's three reviews were helping to draw the threads together, a fresh bout of academic warfare had broken out. English and Savile combined to criticise the critics and suggested that Bonfield's objections to Habakkuk's thesis were less damaging than might at first appear.[28] Their argument was that the strict settlement was not as vulnerable as Bonfield had maintained. It might take place at the coming-of-age of the heir, several years before marriage: this would increase the chance of the father remaining alive to negotiate a settlement. Moreover, settlements could be drawn up to include a son and grandson and another party unborn for twenty-one years – so that the estate might be protected for forty years or more. Bonfield retorted that English and Savile had produced little evidence that, in the period 1680–1740, settlements usually took place at coming-of-age, and argued from demographic evidence that only in a comparatively small number of cases did the landowner survive to see his grandson born and therefore have the opportunity to negotiate a long-term settlement.

It is distinctly imprudent to enter other people's affrays, whether as second or umpire. There seems little doubt, however, that Bonfield's critics did not produce sufficient evidence to support their rival interpretation. Moreover, as we have seen, Bonfield was by no means alone in feeling that Habakkuk had overplayed the importance of the strict settlement, and Habakkuk himself seemed inclined to accept the

---

[27] *Newcastle: a duke without money.* Newcastle was very lucky. He had no children to provide for, access to the very best legal and financial advice, and high social and political rank to draw upon.

[28] B. English and J. Savile, 'Comment on Bonfield's "Marriage settlements and the 'rise of great estates'"'; and Bonfield's rejoinder, *Economic History Review*, 2nd series, XXXIII (1980), 556–63.

point. Nevertheless, the fresh controversy made it even harder for the onlooker to perceive where truth lay.[29]

Another factor to which attention has been drawn is the effect of the abolition of the Court of Wards in 1660. Sir William Blackstone was perhaps over-exuberant when he described the abolition as 'a greater acquisition to the civil property of this kingdom than even *Magna Carta* itself'.[30] Nevertheless, it is true that the activities of the Court of Wards before the Civil War were greatly resented and contributed to the souring of relations between the monarchy and the peerage. Even if the family succeeded in retaining control of its own minor, it could prove an expensive business outbidding others, to whom the acquisition of guardianships was a mere investment. At worst, control of the estate, for a critical period, could finish up in the hands of a court favourite, one of his supporters, or a complete stranger to whom he had sold the wardship. In the hands of a sober and responsible group of trustees, appointed by the family, a minority could be a period of retrenchment and recovery, with a skeleton staff looking after the deserted hall and little more than school fees to pay. Peter Roebuck pointed out that the basis of the sound condition of the Holkham estate was the work of the trustees during the minority in the 1700s.[31] He argued further that minorities were more likely to occur in the late seventeenth and early eighteenth centuries. I am not myself certain that the demographic and genealogical evidence is sufficiently reliable to allow comments in terms of particular decades. But there seems little doubt that minorities were rather more frequent in the earlier part of the eighteenth century than in the later.[32]

Bearing in mind that we do not necessarily have to explain a vast shift in favour of great landlords and that a number of factors were probably at work, it seems possible that the abolition of the Court of Wards may

[29] It is possible to contribute a mite of information on the chances of a landowner surviving to see a grandson born to him in direct male line and therefore having the opportunity to negotiate a strict settlement of the kind English and Savile describe. Of course there is no guarantee that people would be in a condition to take advantage of the situation: the grandfather might himself be on his deathbed and in no state to negotiate anything, and the grandson might survive a few days only. I have analysed the 954 English peers, dividing them into those born before 1720 and subsequently, 575 and 379 respectively. In the first group, 19.8% survived to see a grandson born in direct male line: in the second group, it rose to 27.4%. The evidence is, alas, not decisive. Few peers could have been in a position to make the kind of settlement discussed, yet it could have made some difference in the protection afforded some estates.

[30] *Commentaries on the Laws of England*, II, Chapter 5: 'Of the Antient English Tenures'.

[31] 'Post-Restoration landownership: the impact of the abolition of wardship', *Journal of British Studies*, XVIII, 1 (Fall 1978), 67–85.

[32] Of ninety-nine minority successions in the eighty-four families mentioned below, fifty-eight were before 1750 and forty-one afterwards.

have given a push in that direction. There is no doubt that the chance of a minority was of real concern to a large number of families. The total number of families who held a peerage throughout the eighteenth century was eighty-four. Of these, only twenty-five did not have to face a minority at some stage. Two families, the Earls of Plymouth and the Lords Clifton, had to face four minorities in the course of the century. Seven others had to face three minorities.[33] Of the three hundred successions in these eighty-four families, exactly one-third were of minors. Four families had to face the possibility of minorities of twenty-one years,[34] and the Petre family had to face two such possibilities, in 1713 and again in 1742. The estates of the Petre family were in minority for no less than forty-six of the one hundred years, the Russells of Woburn for thirty-four years, the Shaftesbury family for thirty years, the Beauforts for twenty-eight years and the Keppels, Earls of Albemarle for twenty-six years.

I hope I shall not be thought wanting in respect to brothers in the profession, if I say that economic historians have not so far agreed upon an explanation of the growth of the great estates or the prosperity of the eighteenth-century peerage. If what was once 'received opinion' is now, in Habakkuk's phrase, to be regarded as 'an open question', non-experts may venture to join in and to emphasise non-economic factors. Habakkuk suggested, for example, that one factor might be decreased provision in the eighteenth century for younger sons, who were left to make their way in the world. If this can be substantiated, it might be because of the considerable increase in professional opportunities as a result of the commercial revolution and the expansion of the armed forces and civil service.[35]

In discussing the financial difficulties facing large estate owners in the earlier seventeenth century, Habakkuk placed emphasis on the high interest rate of 8% or 10%: once entrapped in borrowing, to which their extravagant lifestyle tempted them, they found their financial burden accumulating at frightening speed, forcing them to sell land.[36] However, he did not pursue the argument into the eighteenth century when interest rates were usually low and when the position of landlords may

---

[33] Beaufort, Bedford, Bridgwater, Brooke, Grey of Ruthin, Lincoln, Petre.

[34] Albemarle, Dudley, St John of Bletsoe and Suffolk. Dudley and Suffolk were born posthumously. I say 'possibility' because the infant lord might die before coming-of-age.

[35] See Geoffrey Holmes, 'The achievement of stability: the social context of politics from the 1680s to the age of Walpole', in my *The Whig ascendancy*, 1–27.

[36] 'The rise and fall of English landed families' (1981), 201–6.

have been correspondingly easier. It is certainly hard to imagine Newcastle surviving in heavy debt for forty years had the interest rate been 10% instead of the 4% he was usually called upon to pay. It is true of course that low interest rates would be of benefit to all landowners, but the great landlords were better placed to take advantage of them since they had so much more security to offer.

There is, I think, widespread agreement that there was at least a move towards the consolidation of large estates (not the same thing as the growth). Consolidation, as has been suggested, can hardly be studied on a county basis, but will be revealed only by examination of the many estates of great landed families. There were sound economic reasons, much canvassed in the century, for the consolidation of estates. It made for more effective administration and supervision. There may also have been non-economic factors at work and what we are trying to explain may have been less the result of changing conditions than changing objectives. In particular, the substitution of Parliament for the court as the centre of political power can scarcely have failed to produce economic consequences. The young men who thronged Elizabeth's or James' court were not seriously handicapped in trying to catch or retain royal favour by the fact that their estates were scattered. But with Parliament's position greatly enhanced after 1688 and annual meetings taking place, electoral power became of increasing importance. To some extent we can gauge this from the remarkable increase in the cost of a seat throughout the century.[37] If land was to be translated into effective electoral and political power, there was much to be said for concentrating it. Sometimes, of course, property in distant parts gave command over parliamentary boroughs and here the property was usually retained: the Russells held on to their Devonshire estates, which gave them complete command of two seats at Tavistock, and the Duke of Newcastle kept his Yorkshire' property at Boroughbridge and Aldborough, though his main estates were in Sussex and Nottinghamshire. But in relation to county elections, scattered holdings were a positive nuisance, dragging landowners into disputes they would rather avoid, without any assurance that they would have a decisive voice. Coke of Norfolk represented his own county for forty years and it seems likely that the consolidation which he and previous owners had pursued was primarily for political purposes. Undoubtedly most of the substantial debts he ran up were for electoral reasons. In other words, instead of politics following economics, it was, in this instance, the other way

[37] Cannon, *Parliamentary reform*, 34–5.

round. After all, Arthur Young upbraided landowners for reluctance to maximise their profits by raising rents when they had the opportunity and deplored the fact that they so often put local popularity and political influence before good husbandry. In consolidating, good husbandry and good politics went hand in hand.

I am not sure that what discussion has taken place of the political factors encouraging aristocratic prosperity has been particularly illuminating. It has usually taken the form of debating to what extent individual family fortunes could be based upon the fruits of office. No one would wish to deny that this was important for some families. The perquisites of high office were the foundation of the Orford and Holland fortunes. In addition to direct salaries, there was the benefit of reducing family commitments by placing members in snug sinecures. Free parking has always been a great privilege. The Gothicking of Strawberry Hill and the private printing press was the result of Sir Robert Walpole appointing his youngest son Horace to three lucrative sinecures at the age of twenty-one: Usher of the Exchequer, Comptroller of the Pipe and Clerk of the Estreat. The Comptroller of the Pipe, we are told, 'keeps an exact copy of the great roll of the pipe'. It sounds very onerous. 'The Clerk of the Estreats receives the Estreats every term and writes them out . . . he is, as it were, an Assistant to the Comptroller of the Pipe.'[38] These and another nice little place in the Customs, which fell in when Lord Orford died, brought in some £3,300. This was a little less than the emoluments of the Captain-General and Commander-in-Chief when there was one. It inspired Horace Walpole to a piece of redoubtable self-righteousness at his forbearance: 'From that time', he wrote proudly, 'I lived on my own income and travelled at my own expence . . . I was content with what [my father] had given to me, and from the age of twenty, I was no charge to my family.'[39] Since he had the places for life and lived to be eighty, he cost the public well over £150,000. He tried repeatedly to obtain better financial provision, while expressing a noble disdain for money and a determination never to ask favours: 'contempt of money' he assures us, was his passion.[40] His brother, Sir Edward, was Clerk of the Pells for life,

[38] *True state of England* (1729).
[39] 'Account of my conduct relative to the places I held under government and towards ministers', *Works* (1798), II, 363–70.
[40] *Memoirs of the reign of George II*, ed. Lord Holland, III, 158–63; *The House of Commons, 1715–54*, II, 510–13.

which brought in £3,000 p.a. at first, rising to £7,000 p.a.: in addition two little places, Master of Pleas and Escheats and Joint Collector in th Customs House, brought in another £400 each. He did not do mucl with his life, but he found time to beget three illegitimate daughters, wh married one son of a peer, one English earl, one Scottish earl and on royal duke (one of the daughters marrying twice). Horace Walpole' uncle, Old Horace, a superannuated diplomat, had another life sinecur as Teller of the Exchequer, bringing in a comfortable £3,000 p.a. It i unfair, however, to single out the Walpoles. The Grenvilles, withou shining talent, did very well for themselves later in the century, while th two sons of the Earl of Egremont, appointed to colonial sinecures at th age of six and three respectively, were said to have drawn more than on million pounds, over more than fifty years.[41] No wonder Cobbett, i the early nineteenth century, was provoked to describe the aristocracy brutally, as 'a prodigious band of spungers, living upon the labour of th industrious part of the community'.[42]

Nevertheless, it is possible to exaggerate the importance of office holding generally. Sir Robert, after all, had been first minister for ; record twenty-one years, and it is scarcely surprising that his famil should do uncommonly well. On the other hand, Coke of Norfolk whose increase in wealth was spectacular, never held office at all. Th more remarkable instances of fortunes amassed through office derive from the Paymastership, especially in time of war, since the balances i hand could be lent on short-term loans for the Paymaster's persona profit. Walpole, Chandos and Holland had all been Paymaster. Th other offices did not pay to anything like the same extent. North's twelv years as first minister did not leave him a wealthy man, and Pitt, wh spent almost all his adult life as first minister, died hopelessly in debt Nobody in the century held high office for a longer period than the Duk of Newcastle, yet his finances remained in stubborn disarray. This was i part because salaries could by no means be regarded as gross profit. Cour attendance and high political office involved considerable expense i maintaining a London house, entertaining lavishly, and often cultivating rapacious voters.

But, in any case, this is not necessarily the best way of approaching th problem. It is bound to yield only individual, fitful and somewha inconsequential evidence. It is more instructive to see whether th peerage used its political ascendancy as a class to create favourabl

---

[41] Cobbett's Political register, XLV, 110–11.
[42] Quoted G. Spater, William Cobbett: the Poor Man's Friend, I, 293, Note 88.

conditions for itself. This leads us to a discussion of taxation policy. It is he more important since there has been a good deal of mythologising on he subject. Too often a crude contrast has been drawn between an English nobility manfully shouldering its burden of taxes while continental nobles shamefully passed them on to the poorest groups in society. Even the best of scholars have inclined to take a kindly view of he English nobility in this respect. 'Unlike their continental counter-parts', wrote G. E. Mingay in 1963, 'they were prepared to tax hemselves heavily when the need arose.'[43]

It is far from my wish to try to reverse that picture. The Prussian *Junkers* and the Polish *szlachta* certainly did their best to shuffle taxation off on to the towns. Nevertheless, it has been drawn too sharply and a good deal of research on both sides of the Channel has substantially modified the position. There is certainly much greater recognition of the virtues of the *ancien régime* in France than has hitherto been the case. Derek Jarrett, in an impressive pioneering work, which has perhaps not received the attention it deserves, pointed out that the anomalies of tax assessment in Hanoverian England were, in some respects, as indefensible as the immunities and exemptions which riddled the French taxation system.[44] French noblemen, he warned us, had they paid all they were supposed to would have paid *more* in direct taxation than their English counterparts, and, though he added that evasion was rife in France, one could hardly maintain that it was unheard of in Hanoverian England. C. B. Behrens, while admitting that continental taxation hung like a millstone round the necks of the peasantry, added, 'and contrary to what is generally believed, round the necks of most noble landowners'.[45]

It would be hard, if not impossible, to offer precise comparisons with tax burdens in different European countries, since the regional and local variations within each country, including Britain, were so great. However, there is little reason to believe that Britain was the most heavily taxed nation. That ability to wage war, which astonished eighteenth-century Europe, was based upon the ability to raise loans rather than taxes – in contrast to the seventeenth-century position at the end of the second Dutch war, when the Dutch fleet raided and burned in the Thames Estuary while our own seamen mutinied for lack of pay, and the government was reduced to borrowing from its own employees like Pepys. By contrast, the Seven Years War, unprecedented in scale and cost, was supported almost entirely by borrowing from the public.

[43] *English landed society in the eighteenth century*, 115.
[44] *The begetters of revolution*, 228.   [45] *The ancien régime*, 32.

The landed classes complained, of course, most bitterly that they wer subject to crushing levels of taxation, particularly during the wars c Anne's reign. Their chorus was sufficiently shrill and well-orchestrate to impress not only contemporary ministers, but also posterity. Part c their irritation, however, was the suspicion that financial and commer cial wealth was not bearing its fair share of the burden. In fact, fev eighteenth-century administrations had the expertise to tax commercia wealth, save by an excise which, for political reasons, was extremel unpopular in Britain.

A comparison by Gregory King in 1688 suggested that Britain pai rather less per head than the French and substantially less than the Dutch Under pressure of warfare, the gap closed in the 1690s, but the Dutcl continued to be the most heavily taxed country in Europe.[46] Through out eighteenth-century Europe there was a steady increase in taxation a armies and fleets grew bigger and as governments increased thei commitment to education. Though British governments of the perio did not spend on education, Britain shared in the general trend. Pete Mathias has suggested that, whereas national income doubled betweer 1700 and 1790, revenue per capita increased more than two and a hal times. In 1700, the government was taking some 9.1% of the nationa income, but by 1790 it had risen to 15.0%.[47]

Comparison of tax levels between Britain and France causec confusion in the eighteenth century and is still giving trouble today Necker and Arthur Young, on either side of the channel, were ir agreement that the French nobility was more lightly burdened, but, a often happens, they seem to be agreed in being wrong.[48] The exemptior of the French nobility from the *taille* – the most important direct tax – seems a rock of certainty in a confusing world, and is certainly a rock tc which generations of hard-pressed undergraduates have clung. But, alas it is not so simple. The nobility was by no means the only group to be exempt from the *taille*. Moreover, since, for the most part, they rentec out their lands rather than cultivated them directly, the obligation of the tenant to pay the *taille* was usually taken into account when fixing a realistic rent – so that some of the burden, at least, was carried by the landowner. A succession of French finance ministers had been increasing the amount of the *capitation* and the *vingtième* – introduced in 1695 and

---

[46] *Natural and political observations*, quoted P. Deane in 'The implications of early national incomé estimates', *Economic Development and Cultural Change*, 4, 1, Part 1 (Nov. 1955).
[47] 'Taxation and industrialization in Britain, 1700–1870', in *The transformation of England*, 121.
[48] Behrens, 'Nobles, privileges and taxes in France at the end of the ancien regime', 451–75.

1750 respectively – since those taxes were paid by the privileged orders. There were, in fact, three doses of the *vingtième* running side by side in the 1780s and producing, it was suggested, the equivalent of the English Land Tax at its peacetime level of three shillings in the pound. The essential difference between the two countries was that a far greater proportion of total revenue in France was levied in the form of direct taxation. C. B. Behrens' conclusion, at the end of her investigation, was that the French nobility was certainly required to pay more in taxes than its British counterpart, often did so, and in some cases paid a great deal more.

Miss Behrens' findings were confirmed in a further careful examination of the problem by Peter Mathias and P. O'Brien.[49] They showed that 75% of the extra finance needed to fight the four major wars between 1702 and 1783 was raised in Britain by loans. A much larger proportion of the French revenue was raised in the form of direct taxation, and their conclusion was that 'the failure to tax wealth and rising income effectively in Britain was at bottom a political decision'.

With these warnings ringing in our ears, we can turn more closely to taxation of the peerage, noting that it by no means follows that the position in Anne's reign held true for the rest of the century. There was a marked falling-off in the proportion of revenue raised by direct taxation, and, in particular, through the Land Tax. Direct taxation declined from producing, in Anne's reign, about one-third of the total yield to 17% or 18% immediately before the Revolutionary wars. As a percentage of the national income, it fell from 3.0% or 3.5% in Anne's reign to 2.3% in the 1770s. The greater part of the revenue, and an increasing part, came from indirect taxation and fell upon the mass of the people.

This analysis confirms what we might have suspected from other sources. W. R. Ward's account of the operation of the Land Tax does not bear out the more sentimental views of the landed interest.[50] When the Land Tax was first mooted in 1692 to raise money for the war against Louis XIV, the House of Lords insisted upon amending the bill, demanding that the assessments for the peerage should be made by five out of twenty-six of their number and that the collection should be in the hands of an official nominated by themselves. The House of Commons

[49] 'Taxation in Britain and France, 1715–1810', *Journal of European Economic History*, v, 3 (1976), 601–40. There is a comment on the article by Donald McCloskey, *ibid.* (1978), 209–10, but it does not challenge the basic conclusion.
[50] *English Land Tax in the eighteenth century.*

protested that its monopoly of financial control was being challenged and, in the public interest, the Lords were forced to give way. But the key person in the collection of taxes was the Receiver-General of each county and Ward tells us that, by the middle of the eighteenth century, that official was firmly under aristocratic nomination.[51] The Receiver-General-ship was lucrative and sought after: it is unlikely that the office holder would have hounded noble defaulters too savagely. Nor would the assessors who were local men, 'unpaid, probably with a somewhat limited education, and subject to local pressures'.[52] The extent of the under-valuation throughout the whole country can be gauged from the fact that the yield from the new Income Tax, at two shillings in the pound, *efficiently collected*, amounted to £6 million – equivalent to the Land Tax at twelve shillings in the pound, which was, of course, an unthinkable rate. Colin Brooks, in a discussion of the Land Tax in the early part of the eighteenth century remarked that 'under-assessment was tolerated by the central government'.[53] This slightly misrepresents the real position. The concept of a central government in Hanoverian England is something of a misnomer – certainly in comparison with France: there was no separate bureaucracy which might claim to represent the interests of the state. Since central and local government in England were run by very much the same people, what existed was an amiable willingness to tolerate their own under-assessment.

The reluctance of the landed classes to pay direct taxation is too well authenticated to demand elaborate proof. Linda Colley noted a remarkable outburst of candour from Lord Hardwicke, not normally a harsh critic of aristocratic supremacy. He referred to 'the bargain, which the nobility and gentry made with the crown soon after the Restoration when they purchased out their own burdens by the tenures and wardships by laying an excise upon beer and ale to be consumed by the common people; for those liquors, when brewed in private houses, are not subjected to it'.[54] Sir Robert Walpole's political acumen persuaded him to keep Land Tax as low as possible. In one of the rare government defeats of the century, Chatham's administration was beaten in February 1767 and the Land Tax reduced to three shillings. Among the consequences which flowed from this decision was Charles Townshend's

[51] *Ibid.*, 110–11.
[52] J. E. D. Binney, *British public finance and administration, 1774–1792*, 58.
[53] 'Public finance and political stability: the administration of the Land Tax, 1688–1720', *Historical Journal*, XVII (1974), 281–300.
[54] P. C. Yorke, *The life and correspondence of Philip Yorke, Earl of Hardwicke*, III, 34, quoted Colley, *In defiance of oligarchy: the Tory party 1714–60*, 11.

pledge to find alternative revenue in the American colonies: the results of that pledge were not unimportant. Charles Fox's strident objections to the introduction of a form of Income Tax in 1797 are well known – 'profligate contempt of property'[55] – and one of the first acts of the post-war House of Commons in 1816 was to defy the Chancellor of the Exchequer, Nicholas Vansittart, and to insist upon the abolition of the Property Tax as one of the horrors of war.

The leader for many years of the most avowedly aristocratic party of the century was the 1st Marquis of Rockingham. The Rockinghams' concern for the mercantile interest of the country has often been the subject of approving comment and the Rockinghams prided themselves upon their sensitivity to public opinion. It was not, however, allowed to get out of hand and prompt them to deeds of heroic self-sacrifice. Lord North's proposal to raise a tax on absentee Irish landlords was enough to rouse the Marquis from his normal lethargy: he joined with his fellow peers in a vigorous campaign of resistance, wondering whether North's involvement might not constitute grounds for impeachment.[56] As for English taxation, one of the best-known features of the Land Tax is that its assessments were erratic: London was substantially over-taxed, while other areas, particularly Yorkshire, were seriously under-assessed. Rockingham was not enthusiastic about any changes in the operation of the Land Tax. Indeed, one of his chief objections to any reform of Parliament was that it might weaken Yorkshire's privileged position. In March 1780, he warned against the more advanced proposals of the Association movement: 'Yorkshire sends thirty-two members, sixteen of which may be deemed to come from what are called *rotten boroughs* . . . I dare say you know very well that the *counties*, etc. . . . which are *low rated to land tax* have found some security from their being very *numerously* protected by having a pretty large proportion of members of Parliament.'[57] He concluded with an ironic flourish: 'I think a *little attention* to the *security of property* is not beneath the consideration of the gentlemen and freeholders in Yorkshire.' What Rockingham called grandly 'the *security of property*' was the ability to wriggle out of his share of the national tax burden. Lord Rockingham was certainly not unique in his willingness to see other people paying his taxes. The Cardiff collectors' book for 1788 showed that the Earl of Plymouth and Lord

---

[5] *Parliamentary history*, XXXIII, 1111–12.

[6] R. J. S. Hoffman, *The marquis: a study of Lord Rockingham, 1730–1782*, 285–9.

[7] *Memoirs of the Marquis of Rockingham and his contemporaries*, ed. Lord Albemarle, I, 405–6. I was reminded, however, in the discussion at Belfast, that a number of the Yorkshire freeholders, in the West Riding especially, could be the owners of urban property.

Cardiff had paid no tax on their local properties for ten and twenty years respectively.[58] The French nobility was entitled to feel a little irritation when English noblemen read them lectures on the need for patriotism.

Let us see if these very general observations can be supported in individual cases. One of the fullest studies of an estate throughout the whole century is one I have already mentioned, by R. A. C. Parker, on Holkham Hall in Norfolk. He noted that, though the incidence of the Land Tax in Anne's period was sharp, it fell throughout the rest of the century despite persistent warfare, and that comparable rates of taxation were not reached until the last decade, during the Revolutionary war. Even then, it did not follow that taxation was crippling, certainly by modern standards. Dr E. A. Smith, in his study of Lord Rockingham's heir and nephew, Earl Fitzwilliam, showed that in 1796, in the middle of the war, the Wentworth Woodehouse property had a rental of £20,000 p.a. On this, Fitzwilliam was paying £721 in taxes, i.e. about 3.5%.[59]

With levels of taxation like this, it was possible for a well-run estate to show the most remarkable returns. In Chapter 3 we saw how Sir Hugh Smithson succeeded to the Percy estates in Northumberland after a fortunate marriage to the Duke of Somerset's daughter. The 6th Duke, whose interests lay in the south, had neglected the Percy estates and his irascibility made it impossible for him to find stewards or bailiffs who could work with him. The estates were said to have a rental of £8,607. By systematic exploitation of their potential, particularly in coal-mining, the new Duke was said to have raised the revenues to £50,000. It would be unwise to rely much upon the figures, but the tendency is not in dispute.[60] Evidence which is much more reliable comes from modern studies. The rental income from the Russell estates rose from about £15,000 in 1692 to more than £37,000 by 1739. By 1771 it had reached more than £51,000.[61] At Holkham, there was a steady rise in total rental from £5,800 in 1707, to £9,000 by 1720, and to £14,400 by 1749. After that, a rise in prices demands some adjustment, but Parker's estimate is that between 1776 and 1816 there was a genuine increase in rental of 105%. Of course it is not difficult to find estates which were badly administered and where comparable gains were not achieved, and it may be objected that I have quoted the one estate which is famous for it

[58] Ward, *English Land Tax*, 88.   [59] Smith, *Whig principles and party politics*, 52.
[60] G. Brenan, *History of the House of Percy*, II, 446.
[61] This was only part of the ducal income. E. C. Johnson, 'The Bedford connection: the 4th Duke of Bedford's political influence, 1732–71', Ph. D. thesis, Cambridge University (1980).

xcellent husbandry under Coke of Norfolk. But the point which Parker
as at pains to establish was that Coke was following traditional
methods and has been unduly credited both with striking originality and
ith striking results. Lord Fitzwilliam inherited in 1756 property in
Northamptonshire rented at about £6,900 p.a., but with heavy charges
n it and an outstanding debt of some £45,000, requiring £3,300 p.a. to
rvice it. He sold land to pay off that debt. In 1782 he inherited the great
orkshire estates of the Marquis of Rockingham, which included
aluable coal mines, together with another 66,000 acres in Ireland. The
al mines doubled and redoubled in value, from £1,480 in 1780 to
6,000 in 1801 and £22,500 in 1825. By 1827, Lord Fitzwilliam
timated his income at £115,000.[62]

Two of the examples we have quoted included mineral resources but
arker pointed out that the increase in value of the Coke estates owed
ttle to outside investment or to resources other than agricultural. The
ntext in which vast fortunes could be amassed was an economic policy
vourable to them, and this, in the last analysis derived from political
mmand. Mathias' summary of taxation policy was that 'the over-
helming conclusion is the absence of the levies falling upon wealth and
cumulated capital'. Indeed, he was inclined to find economic
dvantage in the inequalities and anomalies of the tax system: 'the
rophy of land tax valuations . . . thus benefited processes of accumula-
on'.[63] That the system therefore played some part in bringing about an
dustrial revolution may be credited and, to that extent, it can be said to
ave been to the advantage of the nation. That it was to the advantage of
e peerage, Castle Howard, Chatsworth, Petworth, Althorp, Burley,
aston Neston, Heveningham, Bowood, Wilton and Kedleston, testify
loquently enough.

[2] Smith, *Whig principles and party politics*, 11–12, 30–1.
[3] 'Taxation and industrialization in Britain, 1700–1870', in *The transformation of England*, 125–6.

6

THE SINEWS OF POWER: IDEOLOGICAl

The riots of 1981 in Toxteth and Brixton, in Bristol and Manchester – t
say nothing of the abiding difficulties in Northern Ireland – remind u
how fragile is domestic tranquillity, how thin the veneer of civilisatior
how little obedience to the law can be taken for granted. It was a though
never far from the minds of the propertied classes in the eighteent.
century, for two reasons. First, because they looked back to a world
that of their grandfathers and great-grandfathers in the mid-seventeent'
century – when the whole social order had seemed likely to collaps
around their ears. By the time the ghost of Oliver and the Major
Generals had been well and truly laid, there were new, and even mor
fearful, spectres to terrify moderate men – Tom Paine and Jean-Pau
Marat, Danton and Robespierre and Anacharsis Cloots. Second, becaus
the inequalities in society were probably greater than at any time befor
or since. In the earlier seventeenth century, possessions – even for th
well-to-do – were scarce and crude; but by the later eighteenth century
for the lucky few, luxuries and delicacies from all parts of the globe cam
flooding in: exotic trees for the park, strange birds and creatures to diver
visitors, exquisite porcelain from Delft, Meissen and Sèvres, perfume:
fruits, wines, elegant tables and chairs, vases from China, statues fror
Italy (some of them genuine), paintings, tapestries – all the worldly good
that made a Robert Adam mansion so different from the plain, simpl
and empty rooms of the early Jacobean houses. Samuel Johnson, wh
had known dire and pitiful poverty, expressed both points in hi
inimitable way. The Civil War period he described as 'that age whe:
subordination was broken and awe was hissed away', and in anothe
passage he wrote: 'It seems impossible to conceive that the peace c
society can long subsist; it were natural to expect that no man would b

ft long in possession of superfluous enjoyments, while such numbers
re destitute of real necessaries.'[1]

This was the problem to which David Hume addressed himself in 1741
a his essay *Of the first principles of government*. He gave his answer in terms
f ideology. Bearing in mind that in most societies the governed far
utnumber the governors, how is it that the few can control the many?
We shall find that, as force is always on the side of the governed, the
overnors have nothing to support them but opinion. 'Tis therefore on
pinion only that government is founded; and this maxim extends to the
nost despotic and most military governments, as well as to the most free
nd most popular.' Johnson, in a conversation with James Boswell, put
he point even more bluntly: 'What is it but opinion, by which we have a
espect for authority, that prevents us, who are the rabble, from rising up
nd pulling down you who are the gentlemen from your places, and
aying, "We will be gentlemen in our turn".'[2]

The methodological difficulties involved in trying to identify a
upporting ideology reveal the historian at his most vulnerable. It is
loubtful whether any single consensus ever exists. Nor is it likely that,
ven in the most stable regimes, more than a handful of subjects can offer
n articulate and rational defence of their institutions or explain why they
bey the law. Indeed, such a state of affairs, however irritating to
listorians, may be very satisfactory to the authorities if it implies that the
reat majority take the regime for granted. Although we talk of the
cceptance of a regime, it is a vague concept: acceptance can range from
urly acquiescence to cheerful enthusiasm, often in the same individual.
ince few people are sufficiently obliging as to set down why they accept
he regime under which they live, historians are driven back on the
ublished views of scholars and polemicists, without much confidence
hat they represent the opinions of ordinary citizens. Passionate and
ystematic defences of a regime are peculiarly suspect since they are often
roduced when it is under challenge, or even beginning to break down.
The most memorable defence of the old order, Burke's *Reflections on the*

'Life of Samuel Butler', in *Lives of the English poets*; Johnson's contributions to the Vinerian
Lectures of Robert Chambers, identified by E. L. MacAdam, *Dr Johnson and the English Law*, and
quoted J. Wain, *Samuel Johnson*, 280.
Boswell's *Life of Johnson*, ed. G. B. Hill, II, 153. I use the word 'ideology' in this chapter in a very
general sense to mean no more than a set of assumptions or beliefs, as the modern equivalent of
what Hume and Johnson meant by 'opinion'. The beliefs may, of course, be ill-defined and
implausible, they are unlikely to be shared by everyone in society, and they may well seem absurd
to subsequent generations.

Revolution in France, came in the 1790s, towards the end of the period of
stability, and took the form of a counter-attack.[3]

Hume's remarks, which I quoted, may appear provocatively extreme
– under-estimating the strength of the sanctions that governments can
bring to bear. But we must remember that eighteenth-century governments, of which he was primarily thinking, had little of the apparatus of
persuasion, control and coercion which the modern state can wield. Two
pieces of evidence seem to suggest at least tacit acceptance by the
majority of Englishmen in the eighteenth century of their government
and institutions. The first is that, in the very middle of the period, a
sensational opportunity came for the mass of the English people to throw
off their allegiance to the Hanoverians if they felt the regime to be
intolerable – the Jacobite invasion of 1745. Not a mouse stirred.[4] Second,
the forces of law and order in the period were tiny. Tony Hayter, who
investigated the role of the army in the maintenance of order, has written
that the inequalities in society were so glaring that, at other periods, they
would seem to necessitate a system of terror and repression to sustain
them. 'Yet the governments of the age seemed curiously casual about
security.'[5] His work certainly gives no support to the view that a detested
regime was engaged in the ruthless subjection of a surly and discontented
populace.

The upheavals of the seventeenth century meant that the problems of
sovereignty and obedience had received vast attention from political
philosophers. But few ordinary people, if and when they thought about
the problem, did so in terms of scholarly controversy. Despite the sharp
decline of belief in the divine right of kings and its corresponding tenet of
non-resistance, their answer would probably have still been formulated

---

[3] Burke attempted to erect unthinking acceptance into a philosophical system: 'instead of casting
away our old prejudices, we cherish them to a considerable degree, and, to take more shame to
ourselves, we cherish them because they are prejudices . . . It is the misfortune (not, as they
gentlemen think it, the glory) of this age, that everything is to be discussed, as if the constitution of
our country was to be rather a subject of altercation than of enjoyment.'
    For a simple introduction to the concept of ideologies, see John Plamenatz, *Ideology*. The matter
is also discussed in W. L. Guttsman, *The British political elite*, Chapter 3: 'The self-legitimation of a
ruling class'. Mark Goldie, 'The Revolution of 1689 and the structure of political argument: an
essay and an annotated bibliography of pamphlets on the allegiance controversy', *Bulletin of
Research in the Humanities* 84, 4 (Winter 1980), 473–564, has some helpful comments on evaluating
public opinion.

[4] W. A. Speck, *The butcher: the Duke of Cumberland and the suppression of the '45*, 203, commented: '. . .
demonstrated as nothing else could have done just how firmly established the Hanoverian regime
was'.

[5] *The army and the crowd in mid-Georgian England*, 1.

in religious terms: that civil society formed part of God's plan and purpose for mankind, that it was natural and inevitable, that it was sanctioned by time, justified by prescription, and exemplified in microcosm in the family. 'The obedience of children to their parents is the basis of all government', wrote *The Spectator*, 'and set forth as the measure of that obedience which we owe to those whom Providence has placed over us.'[6] It is because they explained civil society within a religious context that Locke and Burke were so unyielding towards atheists, regarding them as men who would destroy the whole social order and who should therefore be put down without mercy.[7]

In this general context, inequalities were largely taken for granted. Isaac Watt, the hymn writer, maintained that 'the great God has wisely ordained in the course of his providence in all Ages, that among mankind there should be some rich and some poor' – sentiments which he turned into verse.[8] Henry Fielding, fifty years later, offered a similarly simple explanation: 'to be born for no other purpose than to consume the fruits of the earth is the privilege (if it may be really called a privilege) of a very few. The greater part of mankind must sweat hard to produce them, or society will no longer answer the purposes for which it was ordained. *Six days shalt thou labour*, was the positive command of God in his own republic.'[9] The greatest prudence was therefore to accept one's station in life with becoming humility rather than try to change it.

Religion provided not merely the sanction for authority and for inequality, but consolation as well. It was held out as the opiate of the masses decades before Marx hit upon the phrase. The argument was put by Addison at the beginning of the century and by Burke at the end. Virtue, Addison noted sadly, was often oppressed and Vice triumphant:

---

[6] 6 Oct. 1711.
[7] 'We know', wrote Burke, 'and what is better, we feel inwardly, that religion is the basis of civil society and the source of all good and of all comfort . . . God is the awful author of our being and the author of our place in the order of existence . . . his eternal law gives to all our conventions and compacts all the force and sanction they can have.' *Reflections*. 'The theoretical centrality' of religion is attributed to Locke by John Dunn, *The political thought of John Locke: an historical account of the argument of the 'Two Treaties of Government'*, pp. xi–xii.
In *A letter concerning toleration*, Locke wrote: 'Those are not at all to be tolerated who deny the being of a god. Promises, covenants and oaths, which are the bonds of human society, can have no hold upon an atheist. The taking away of God, though but even in thought, dissolves all.' Burke's view was 'better this country should be sunk to the bottom of the sea than that (so far as human infirmity admits) it should not be a country of religion and morals.'
[8] Among his less well-known stanzas is the following:
   What though I be low and mean, I'll engage the rich to love me,
   Whilst I'm modest, neat and clean; And submit when they reprove me.
Divine Songs for Children, Moral Songs, vi: 'Good Resolutions'.
[9] *An enquiry into the causes of the late increase of robbers*, 7.

'The last Day will rectify this disorder, and assign to everyone a station suitable to the dignity of his character; Ranks will be then adjusted, and Precedency set right.'[10] You will note that in Addison's vision even Heaven will be hierarchical, though it will be a hierarchy of virtue rather than of rank. In the meantime it was advisable for those in authority to practise humanity in order to 'make their superiority easy and acceptable to those who are beneath them'. Burke's advice to the lower orders was even more forthright: 'They must labour to obtain what by labour may be obtained; and when they find, as they commonly do, the success disproportioned to the endeavour, they must be taught their consolation in the final proportions of eternal justice.'[11]

The role of the church in helping to shape a conformist opinion can scarcely be exaggerated. Until the change in the social structure brought about by the growth of the great manufacturing and industrial towns, the only representative of authority whom the ordinary citizen was likely to see with much regularity was the parish priest. Often the parish priest must have been the only person with any pretensions to learning in the whole village. The only sustained and coherent discourse on public affairs likely to be heard was the weekly sermon. In 1700, when he began his history of Myddle in Shropshire, it seemed natural to Richard Gough to adopt a plan based on the seating and pew-ownership in his local church. When children went to a church or sunday school, they were taught a catechism in which the virtues of obedience were strongly emphasised. Most country grammar schools and public schools were staffed by clerics, and the Fellows of colleges at Oxford and Cambridge were required to be in Holy Orders. If the villager went to the county town to see something of the assizes, which, in many places, remained an important social as well as political and legal occasion, the assize sermon often reinforced the exhortation to submit.[12] John Foxcroft, preaching at Leicester Assizes in 1697, took the opportunity to denounce any ideas of social levelling. 'There is no governing upon even ground', he told the congregation, 'since equality contradicts and destroys the very name and

---

[10] *The Spectator*, 10 Nov. 1711.

[11] *Reflections on the revolution in France* (Everyman edition), 240–1.

[12] See B. White, 'Assize sermons, 1660–1720', Ph.D. thesis, Newcastle Polytechnic (1980). Dr White writes that the preachers 'reiterated, irrespective of party and with a certain monotony, sermons suitable to the occasion, on obedience to the higher powers and against all they recognised as posing a threat to this sense of order' (252).

notion of government. Where all govern, there is no government; and where all are chief, there can be no order.'[13]

It is in part because organised religion was expected to be a prop of the social order that the authorities were so suspicious of the tendencies of the early Methodist movement. Old Dissent had shown what it could do as the driving force behind radical change in the seventeenth century and Methodism seemed at first to be heading in the same direction. Vast open-air meetings of enthusiasts – some like the Kingswood or Newcastle colliers the least tractable and most lawless of men – were worrying in themselves. But even more subversive was the doctrine of the vanity of riches and, above all, the emphasis placed upon the equality of believers in the sight of God. On a famous visit to Bath in June 1739, Wesley preached that 'we were all under sin, high and low, rich and poor, one with another'. Not surprisingly he clashed with Beau Nash. The Duchess of Buckingham rightly perceived hidden dangers when, in a celebrated letter, she offered a stinging rebuke to Selina, Countess of Huntingdon, for encouraging ideas 'so much at variance with high rank and good breeding'.[14] But although Wesley told some well-dressed ladies 'I do not expect the rich of this world to hear me', he was at pains to preach political obedience. 'We of the clergy', he declared in an address to George II in March 1744, 'continually declare, "Ye must needs be subject, not only for wrath, but also for conscience's sake".'[15]

Within the broad framework of tradition and prescription, there were more specific justifications of the governmental arrangements, derived from what Hume called 'opinion of interest': 'The sense of public advantage which is reaped from government; along with the persuasion, that the particular government, which is established, is equally advantageous with any other than could easily be settled. When this opinion prevails among the generality of a state . . . it gives great security to any government.'[16] As the eighteenth century progressed and the wars, plots and coups of the Stuart period were left behind, such an opinion began to form until, for most people, it blossomed into an almost hysterical regard for the constitution. By the accession of George III, admiration for the

[13] 'The Beauty of Magistracy with other observations concerning government', preached at St Mary's, Leicester, 26 March 1697. See also E. Gibson at Surrey Assizes, Croydon on 7 March 1706 in a sermon 'Against speaking evil of princes and those in authority under them'. The congregations were larger and more miscellaneous than one might have expected, and publication often brought the sermons to a wider audience.

[14] *The life and times of Selina, Countess of Huntingdon, by a member of the Houses of Shirley and Hastings*, I, 27.

[15] *The letters of John Wesley*, ed. J. Telford, II, 18.   [16] *Of the first principles of government.*

constitution seems to have reached a peak. The last Jacobite challenge had been beaten off in 1745, and the victories of Clive, Wolfe and Hawke in the following decade laid the foundations for world power. The new mood of national confidence was caught by 'God Save the King', 'Rule Britannia' and 'Hearts of Oak'.[17]

The intellectual crown was put on these achievements by the course of lectures begun at Oxford in 1758 by Professor William Blackstone, and published from 1765 onwards as *Commentaries on the Laws of England*. Blackstone's chapter on the nature of laws in general offered proof of the perfection of the English constitution. Gentlemen did not take much convincing that they had discovered an ideal political formula. To George III it was 'the noblest constitution the human mind is capable of framing'; to Junius, it was 'the wisest of human institutions'; to John Wilkes, 'that perfection of human wisdom, that noblest work of mankind'.[18] In the nineteenth century, even after heavy criticism by Bentham, Godwin, Paine and others, the constitution continued to attract the most fulsome panegyrics. 'We have attained', wrote Francis Jeffrey, editor of the *Edinburgh Review*, 'a greater proportion of happiness and civil liberty, than have ever before been enjoyed by any other nation; and that the frame and administration of our polity is, with all its defects, the most perfect and beneficial of any that men have yet invented and reduced to practice.'[19]

The aspect of the constitution which was so much admired was its self-regulating mechanism, that balance of forces which would enable it to avoid ultimate breakdown, and keep it functioning smoothly. This would allow it to escape the fate which had overtaken all previous political regimes. The concept of a mixed constitution was not, of course, new. Aristotle had distinguished three basic political forms – monarchy, oligarchy and democracy – and Polybius had suggested that by a suitable blend of each a permanent equilibrium might be established. Otherwise, monarchy would inevitably degenerate into despotism, aristocracy into oligarchy, and democracy into anarchy and confusion.[20] Blackstone insisted that the English constitution had 'long remained a

---

[17] 'Rule Britannia', first performed in 1740, composed by Thomas Arne for the masque 'Alfred'; 'God Save the King', origins obscure, but popularity owed to performances during the Jacobite invasion; 'Hearts of Oak', written in the year of victories, 1759, music by Boyce.

[18] J. Brooke, *King George III*, 56–7; *Letters of Junius*, ed. J. A. Cannon, 22; quoted C. C. Weston, *English constitutional theory and the House of Lords, 1556–1832*, 150.

[19] 'Cobbett's *Political Register*', *Edinburgh Review* (July 1807), 406.

[20] F. W. Walbank, *Polybius*, 131–9. Walbank suggests that the idea originated with Thucydides and was something of a commonplace by the time Polybius developed it.

tanding exception to the truth of this observation' and that the machinery of government was 'so admirably tempered and compound-ed, that nothing can endanger or hurt it, but destroying the equilibrium of power between one branch of the legislature and the rest'.[21]

In England, the concept of a mixed constitution had been developed by a number of Tudor writers, usually as part of an argument in favour of limited monarchy and some degree of religious toleration. It was given a great impetus when Charles I included it in his *Answer to the Nineteen Propositions*, in June 1642. For our purposes it is of little consequence whether Charles was sincere in his exposition or whether it was merely a useful debating point at a moment of crisis: it received more public notice than could have been obtained in any other way. Charles identified King, Lords and Commons with monarchy, aristocracy and democracy, traced the characteristics of each, and argued that the constitution would work only 'as long as the balance hangs even between the three estates'. The crucial function in the balance was awarded to the House of Lords, in words which Blackstone later paraphrased, as 'a screen and bank between the prince and people, to assist each against any encroachment of the other'.[22]

After the Restoration, most royalists quickly lost interest in the theory of a mixed constitution, and it was kept alive by the Shaftesbury Whigs, being much deployed in the controversy over the Exclusion Bill. The concept continued to be the subject of vigorous debate in the decades after the Glorious Revolution, the trial of Dr Sacheverell in 1710 being a kind of grand inquest on the principles at stake in the revolution.[23] But with the successful establishment of the Hanoverian dynasty, the bottom dropped out of the argument about resistance and obedience. In the course of time, the theory of a balanced constitution, which had once been a daring and radical assertion, became no more than a constitutional commonplace. Chatham dismissed it in 1770 as 'a common school-boy position' and apologised to their lordships for his tediousness in reminding them of it.[24]

One feature of the constitution which helped to commend it to eighteenth-century Englishmen was the praise and admiration it received from abroad. From the 1690s onwards, a series of eminent foreigners testified, in the most flattering way, to the brilliance of the

---

[21] *Commentaries*, Section II: 'of the nature of laws in general'.

[22] It was drafted by Colepeper and among those who were unenthusiastic at the time was Edward Hyde.

[23] G. S. Holmes, *The trial of Dr Sacheverell*.   [24] *Parliamentary history*, XVI, 818.

English political solution. They did not necessarily analyse it in the sam
way, nor was there any guarantee that their enthusiastic descriptions bor
much relation to actual practice, but the result could hardly be other tha
gratifying. Voltaire and Montesquieu were among the major intellectua
figures whose testimony helped to spread the message. Among th
minor figures was Jean Louis de Lolme, a native of Geneva, who arrive
in England in 1769 at the age of twenty-seven and at once embarke
upon preparations for *Constitution de l'Angleterre*, published in Amster
dam in 1771 and translated with great success into English in 1775. I
went through edition after edition, and has been much quoted.[25] But th
secret of de Lolme's success is by no means the penetration or insigh
which he demonstrated or the subtlety of his analysis: it is the grotesqu
flattery with which he bombarded his English readers. As an assessmen
of the working of the constitution it was absurd. The English wer
congratulated that their constitution had 'contrived to find a remedy fo
evils which, from the very nature of men and things, seem to b
irremediable'. There is little interest at all in the practical working of th
constitution. Much was borrowed from Blackstone, who was himsel
condemned by Bentham as a smug conservative; by comparison with d
Lolme, Blackstone was a severe critic. Blackstone's discussion of th
representative system at least conceded that it was a 'misfortune' that th
deserted boroughs had retained representation and suggested the nee
for 'a more complete representation of the people'. De Lolme, in ;
perfunctory chapter, succeeded in omitting any reference at all to rotter
or pocket boroughs, or to the fact that Birmingham, Wolverhampton
Leeds, Sheffield and Manchester were unrepresented. The most remarkable feature of the criminal code was, in his opinion, its mildness. He wa:
struck by the forbearance and lenity of the persons of power and th
'constant attention of the legislature in providing for the interests and
welfare of the people'. He presumed an absurd division of powers. One
secret of success was that the people who make the laws 'are excluded
from all share in the executions of them' – a strange comment on the JPs
and the Lords Lieutenant in both houses. He concluded on a note o
sustained panegyric: 'The Philosopher, when he happens to reflect on
what is the constant fate of civil societies amongst men, and observes
with concern the numerous and powerful causes which seem, as it were,
unavoidably to conduct them all to a state of incurable political slavery,

---

[25] After the translation in 1775, there appear to have been subsequent editions in 1776, 1777, 1781,
1784, 1789, 1796, 1800, 1807, 1810, 1814, 1816, 1820, 1822, 1834, 1838 and 1846. There were
French editions in 1788, 1790 and 1791, and a German edition published in Leipzig in 1776.

akes comfort in seeing that Liberty, has at last disclosed her secret to mankind, and secured an asylum to herself.' The Hanoverian upper classes found this very persuasive, and, coming from a foreigner, quite disinterested. People like Junius, a critic of society, were as impressed as others. 'M. de Lolme's performance', declared Junius, was 'deep, solid and ingenious.' I think it was more 'ingenious' than Junius realised.

It would be foolish to suggest that the authority of classical writers or the admiration of ingenious foreigners could do more than reinforce the prejudices in favour of the constitution which so many of the English possessed. There were not, for most of the century, many persons in England advocating profound changes, but one result of the chorus of approbation from abroad was to make it marginally more difficult for them to gain a hearing. Of course foreign praise was not mere hallucination: there were many features of Hanoverian England – trial by jury, religious toleration and greater freedom of the press – which, by comparison with some continental standards, were liberal and worthy of imitation. Reformers in England had to face the charge, not merely that the whole machinery of state was so delicately adjusted that any change might wreck the balance, but that they were wilfully blind to the beauties of a system that even foreigners could discern.

No theory, however plausible, would have had much effect were it obviously at variance with the facts. The need for a balance of power within the constitution seemed to many to have been amply demonstrated by the events of the seventeenth century. In the 1640s a runaway House of Commons had shaken off the restraints of the other branches of the legislature and abolished, first the Established Church, then the House of Lords, and then the monarchy itself. The result, as classical commentators had predicted, had been a slide first into anarchy and disorder and then into military dictatorship. Forty years later, the Lords demonstrated their role in restraining a runaway monarchy, hell-bent on introducing popery and despotism. The Glorious Revolution was a conservative revolution, aimed at restoring the correct balance of the constitution, and carried out under the auspices of the aristocracy. The Lords spiritual and temporal had spoken for the country.

For decades, political life was dominated by fear of any resurgence of the commonwealth and admiration for the achievements of 1688. 'The principles of 1688' became a kind of intellectual bromide, a safe way of winding up any parliamentary oration. Once the complications arising from the dynastic problem were settled, the country could enjoy its new-found prosperity and prestige. First Marlborough, then Clive and

Wolfe, gave military glory on an intoxicating scale; the royal navy slowly established its grip upon the waters of the world, the way marked by Anson's circumnavigation and Hawke's victories. Defenders of the traditional order pointed out, with considerable truth, that these successes could not be divorced from the political and constitutional arrangements.

It did not, of course, go unremarked that the House of Lords was, in itself, scarcely capable of sustaining the central role sketched out for it in constitutional theory; nor, indeed, that the influence of the peers was bursting the banks of the Upper House and seeping into the Commons. All commentators were agreed that only eternal vigilance could preserve the delicate balance of the constitution, and its health was monitored in an obsessive fashion. The very concept of a balance suggests, not inertia but adjustment. But there was much less agreement from which side the danger to the balance would originate. It is perhaps difficult for us, aware of the vast gains in the power of the Commons made in the course of the nineteenth century, to understand how informed observers could have imagined that the balance might have swung the other way. Certainly a number of people argued that the Lords were gaining in influence, and there was a constant stream of complaint at their haughtiness, interference in elections, and so on. But the more common opinion was that the power of the crown needed to be watched. In part this is because people then and now, tend to read the future in terms of the past; partly because the crown, after its humiliations in 1649 and 1688, had shown remarkable resilience; but mainly because of the difficulty eighteenth-century writers experienced in distinguishing between the government and the monarchy – indeed, it was a distinction that could hardly be made since government remained royal in a very real sense. The standard charge was therefore that the Lords were already hopelessly subservient to the crown, and that the steady increase in the military, naval and administrative establishment was enabling the crown to subvert the House of Commons as well by introducing a body of tame placemen. The author of *The Detector detected: or the danger to which our constitution now lies exposed* warned that the country was in the 'utmost danger' from the aggrandisement of the crown: 'every commission, every post, every office, every employment, from the highest to the lowest, contributes to the corrupt influence of the crown'.[26]

---

[26] *The Detector detected* (1743), 10, 15. See also *A proper answer to the bystander* (1742), for another exaggerated view of the crown's influence.

Some of this evidence is, of course, suspect. Denunciation of monarchical power had a good popular appeal and place bills were part of the stock in trade of opposition from the time of Walpole to the 1780s. But David Hume in 1741 came to similar conclusions: the tide had flowed strongly for popular liberties in the previous decades and perhaps was now turning in favour of the crown.[27] Horace Walpole, in the 1770s, wrote in like fashion: 'It must be remembered at the same time that while any two are checking, the third is naturally aiming at extending and aggrandising its power. The House of Commons has not seldom made this attempt like the rest. The Lords, as a permanent and as a proud body, more constantly aim at it. The crown always.'[28] The theory of royal aggression was given almost semi-official approval when the House of Commons, on 6 April 1780, to the anguish of the first minister, resolved that the influence of the crown had increased, was increasing and ought to be diminished.[29] Fear of a resurgent monarchy was given further impetus by the melodramatic events of 1783/4. After their crushing defeat at the hustings in April 1784, many of the coalitionists came to believe that prerogative would run out of control. The overweening influence of the crown became even more an *idée fixe* of the Foxites, and was used to justify their secession from Parliament itself in 1797, on the grounds that the Commons was too subservient to make attendance of any utility. In 1801, Fox confided to Charles Grey his conviction that the House of Commons would soon be of no consequence at all.[30] This deep and abiding suspicion of the crown undoubtedly helped to maintain support for the Lords as a surviving barrier against despotism, just as similar fears in France – with rather more justice if we are to believe recent historians – rallied support behind the *parlements*.[31]

How was this argument to be reconciled with the evidence of their lordships considerable and growing influence in the Lower House? With some ingenuity, it was argued that this was one of the adjustments necessary to be made to the balance if the machine was to run smoothly.

[27] *Whether the British government inclines more to absolute monarchy or to a Republic.*
[28] Quoted Brooke, *King George III*, 57.
[29] Dunning's motion, intended as the foundation for a programme of economical reform.
[30] *Memorials and correspondence of Charles James Fox*, III, 341. Even after he had left the Foxites, Burke wrote in 1796 that the constitution 'had been founded upon the principle of jealousy of the crown . . . and it must keep alive some part of that fire of jealousy eternally'. *Letters on a regicide peace*, v, 78.
[31] The tendency of recent historical writing on France has been to question the purely class nature of the *parlements*, to confirm the autocratic tendencies of the monarchy, and so to take more seriously the claim by *parlement* to be an essential barrier to despotism. See, for example, W. Doyle, *Origins of the French Revolution*.

An anticipation of the argument can be traced as early as 1731 when D
Sherlock, bishop of Bangor, incurred the wrath of the parliamentar
opposition to Walpole by objecting to a pensions bill on the grounds tha
the working of the constitution demanded that the other two branches o
the legislature should have some influence over the Commons: 'a
independent House of Commons, or an independent House of Lords
was as inconsistent with our constitution as an independent, that is
absolute king'.[32] David Hume followed a similar line in his *Politica
essays*, published in 1741. He began by admitting that the share of powe
accorded to the House of Commons was so great that it 'absolutely
commands' the other branches of the constitution, yet its surviva
depended upon some balance being maintained. 'How therefore shall w
solve this paradox?' Crown influence, Hume argued, which if on
wished one could call by 'the invidious appellations of corruption an
dependence' was essential to the preservation of the mixed form o
government.[33]

The argument that there had to be some overlap between power
became the standard defence of the influence of both crown and lord
in the Commons in the later eighteenth century. James Boswell
ever anxious to provoke Johnson to further ratiocination, demanded t
know, on the way to St Andrews, how the influence of the Lords in th
Commons could possibly be justified. Johnson saw it as bowing to th
inevitable: 'influence must ever be in proportion to property and it is
right it should'.[34] In 1782, Thomas Pitt, proprietor of Old Sarum and a
future peer, turned the argument rather skilfully against any reform of
Parliament, then, moved by his young cousin William Pitt:

What, sir, but the weight of property (I will speak out, for I am not to be
discouraged by hard words, or the misrepresentations that may render me
unpopular without doors), I will say, the aristocratical weight of property,
which, increasing in this House, has enabled it to stand against the increasing
influence of the crown. The circumstances under which the other House exists at

[32] *Parliamentary history*, VIII, 844–57, debate of 20 Feb. 1731. All bishops had voted against the place
bill. The opposition retorted by bringing in in the following month a bill to prevent the
translation of bishops as a means of destroying government's control over the bench, *HMC.
Egmont*, I, 153. Sherlock was himself transferred to Salisbury in 1734, offered the sees of York
and Canterbury, and in 1748 became bishop of London.

[33] *On the independency of Parliament*. Samuel Squire made the point in *An historical essay upon the
balance of civil power in England* (1748), p. xviii. 'An exclusive place bill . . . would indeed render
the parliament entirely independent of the King . . . what, in fact, are the blessed effects of a
similar inconnection between the King and the Diet of Poland?'

[34] *Life*, V, 56. This was not really a direct answer to Boswell's point, that the influence of the Lords
ought to be exerted in their own House rather than in the Commons.

resent, perhaps it would not be decent for me minutely to describe; let me only
y, that such a counterpoise would hardly be thought sufficient to rely upon;
e barons are no longer the barrier against the encroachments of the crown.[35]

y depriving the lords of their boroughs one would risk destroying
ather than reforming the constitution.

Paley, when he came to defend the influence of the Lords over the
Commons, took up a line similar to Johnson's – that it was mere
rudence, and helped to keep the government of the country in the
ower House, 'in which it would not perhaps long continue to reside, if
powerful and wealthy a part of the nation as the peerage compose were
xcluded from all share and interest in its constitution'.[36]

Francis Jeffrey, editor of the *Edinburgh Review* in the 1800s developed a
ightly different version of the argument – viz., that overlapping
fluence was needed to prevent total confrontations between the
ifferent branches of the legislature, which would lead to 'dreadful
onvulsions' and constitutional impasse. Consequently the influence of
he Lords was deterrent in character and the celebrated balance of the
onstitution was now exercised within the House of Commons itself.
his was the more necessary since the royal veto had obviously fallen
nto abeyance. But the very different circumstances of the 1800s – and the
xtent to which supporters of the constitution were now being thrown
n to the defensive themselves – is revealed in an apologetic aside: that
his influence, being unrecognised by the law of the land, had to be
xercised 'in a sort of covert and underhand manner . . . this gives an
ppearance of guiltiness to the thing itself, which naturally embarrasses
hose who are called upon to defend it'.[37]

Until the French Revolution, there was little sustained attack in England
on the wisdom of the constitution, the role of the House of Lords, or the
hierarchical nature of society.[38] Proposals in the 1760s and 1770s
oncentrated almost completely upon reform of the House of Commons
nd the electoral system, and were argued within the context of

[35] *Parliamentary history*, XXII, 1427.   [36] *An essay upon the British constitution* (1792).
[37] 'Cobbett's *Political Register'*, 412; 'Parliamentary reform', *Edinburgh Review* (July 1809), 304.
For a discussion of the evolution of this rather novel twist to the argument, see J. A. W. Gunn,
'Influence, parties and the constitution: changing attitudes 1783–1832', *Historical Journal*, XVII
(1974), 301–28.
[38] James Millar's lectures on *The origin of the distinction of ranks*, delivered at Glasgow in the 1760s,
were from a man with a reputation for advanced thinking. They are remarkable, however, for
their lack of interest in social inequality and their absence of any analysis in class terms. This gentle
piece of comparative sociology on the lines of Montesquieu was far behind the speculation of
contemporary continental *philosophes*.

renovating the original constitution. Criticism of the Lords was rare
Charles Churchill, in *The Farewell* and *Independence*, both published i
1764, warned against 'titled upstarts'; Regulus, writing in the *Politic*
Register for 1768, had some sharp things to say about the *grandee*
Catherine Macaulay denounced Burke's *Thoughts on the cause of th*
present discontents as an apologia for an aristocratic faction; and Jame
Burgh's *Political disquisitions*, published in 1774, complained of the undu
power of the Lords. But these were on the radical fringe of politic:
Wilkes' skirmishes with the House of Lords were tactical rather tha
strategic. The most popular reform proposal, embraced by Chatham an
later by Wyvill, was for an increase in county representation which, i
the conditions of the time, could only have led to a further extension c
the influence of the aristocratic and landed classes.

A more important indication of the beginning of a shift of opinion wa
Jeremy Bentham's *Fragment on government*, published anonymously i
1776. A lively, youthful and irreverent work, it directed its sarcasm
more at Blackstone than at the constitution itself. Bentham was scornfu
of the way in which Blackstone had accepted the classical view tha
certain forms of government had particular qualities. Why, in any case
asked Bentham, should it be assumed that a mixed form of governmen
should necessarily combine the virtues of each – suppose it combined th
vices? As for the 'piety, birth, wisdom, valour and property' with whicl
Blackstone amiably credited the House of Lords, why should it hav
reached 'boiling point' in 1712 when Anne had created her twelve peers
Bentham regarded Blackstone's analysis as jaded, mystical and compla
cent and his avowed intention was to overthrow that authority whicl
had so often been called in to resist change of any kind. Bentham'
Fragment attracted only passing interest however. In his preface to th
second edition, he claimed that the *Fragment* has caused a 'sensation', bu
much of the interest waned as soon as it was established that the autho
was not an eminent politician but an obscure scholar; and the gap o
forty-eight years between the first and second editions scarcely suggest
that public interest was at fever pitch.

Bentham's *Fragment* was a modest and cerebral work, of interes
mainly to lawyers, and reaching, at most, a few hundred persons. Th
declaration by the National Assembly of France on 19 June 1790 that al
hereditary titles were forthwith abolished was, in contrast, a dramati
public repudiation of the old order. The result was soon apparent
Opinions which in the past had been only muttered or hinted at in
England were proclaimed boldly. Paine's *Rights of Man* came out in

March 1791 and attacked the whole concept of a House of Lords in the most direct terms: 'The idea of hereditary legislators is as inconsistent as that of hereditary judges or hereditary juries; and as absurd as an hereditary mathematician, or an hereditary wise man; and as ridiculous as an hereditary poet-laureate.' 'A friend to the people', the rather sinister pseudonym adopted by the author of *A review of the constitution of Great Britain*, dismissed the lords as 'political monsters' and 'mere creatures' of the crown. The British people, he insisted, were in worse plight than the subjects of the Sultan:

In Turkey, the tyger Despotism springs upon his single victim, and gluts himself with carnage; but in England, the monster, Aristocracy, extending over the devoted million her ten thousand fangs, sucks from every pore of the people, a never ceasing stream of blood . . . In England the people appear to have lost every natural criterion of right and wrong; they cannot tell whether they are oppressed or not, without consulting certain musty records, which form the basis of what they call their constitution.

He went on to ridicule 'a very mysterious story about the miraculous balance of the three powers, that wonderfully promote the purpose of political harmony, by running counter to each other'.[39] For a while these ideas seemed to spread like wildfire. Joel Barlow, the following year, in *Advice to the privileged orders*, questioned the assumption that the state should provide for 'all indigent noble children'. The members of the Stockport Society of the Friends of Universal Peace asked whether 'the grievances arising from the aristocracy can be redressed while the House of Lords retains its present authority in the legislature?'.[40]

These criticisms and strictures were given a philosophical framework in 1793 with the publication of William Godwin's treatise *Enquiry concerning political justice*. Through Godwin, English readers were introduced, many for the first time, to the egalitarian ideas of the French Enlightenment, though presented in highly personal form.[41] Criticisms of privilege, of primogeniture, of barbarous punishments, of the hereditary principle, even of private property and of the family were brought together in a kind of radicals' *vade-mecum*. Book v dealt in successive sections with 'Hereditary Distinctions', the 'Moral Effects of Aristocracy', 'Titles' and 'The Aristocratical Character' and there was not a lot to please earls and viscounts. The hereditary principle itself was

---

[39] A copy of this rather rare pamphlet is in the Cambridge University Library.

[40] *A complete collection of State Trials*, ed. T. B. Howell, xxiv, 388.

[41] Godwin, son of a Dissenting minister and himself a minister, lost his faith as a result of reading French polemicists. His early Calvinist beliefs may be traced in his insistence on 'necessity' and disbelief in free will.

'an insult upon reason and justice', titles were 'ludicrous and absurd, mere gaudy exhibitions', the privileges of the aristocracy guaranteed that they would be not the best but the least useful of men while their advantages inevitably marked them out for a life of 'flattery and effeminate indulgence'. Many contemporaries were shocked at Godwin's advanced views on marriage and scandalised by the complexities of his private life. His dismissal of all forms of government as 'brute engines' and 'regulated force' seems peremptory, undiscriminating and naive. Yet he was capable of passages which still sting:

There is no mistake more thoroughly to be deplored than that of persons sitting at their ease and surrounded with all the conveniences of life who are apt to exclaim, 'We find things very well as they are' and to inveigh bitterly against all projects of reform, as 'the romances of visionary men, and the declamations of those who are never to be satisfied'. Is it well that so large a part of the community should be kept in abject penury, rendered stupid with ignorance, and disgustful with vice, perpetuated in nakedness and hunger, goaded to the commission of crimes, and made victims to the merciless laws which the rich have instituted to oppress them? Is it sedition to enquire whether this state of things may not be exchanged for a better?

In the face of these attacks, the upper classes began to close ranks. Charles Fox chose the occasion of a debate on the Quebec Government Bill on 11 May 1791 to urge the ministers to introduce aristocracy into Canada:

Nor could any government be a fit one for British subjects to live under, which did not contain its due weight of aristocracy, because that he considered to be the proper poise of the constitution, the balance that equalised and meliorated the powers of the other two extreme branches, and gave stability and firmness to the whole. (A loud cry of Hear, Hear!)[42]

There were moments in the 1790s, with the war against Revolutionary France going badly, disaffection in Ireland and an upsurge of radicalism in England when it began to look a close-run thing. Gibbon, in May 1792, wrote from the comparative security of Switzerland to warn his friends of the terrible example of the French nobility: 'they are crumbled into dust; they are vanished from the earth'.[43] Even Pitt's nerve seems to have momentarily shattered at the time of the 'dagger plot' and he was reported to have declared that by tomorrow 'they

---

[42] *Parliamentary history*, XXIX, 409–10. For Fox's aristocratic views generally, see Dinwiddy, 'Charles James Fox and the people', 342–59. For the application of his views on aristocracy as a working principle, on which tactics were to be formulated, see letter to Holland, 1792, *Memoirs*, III, 130 explaining why the Whigs must join with the reformers.
[43] *Letters*, ed. J. E. Norton, III, 258.

night not have a hand to act nor a tongue to utter'.[44] Remorselessly and incessantly Burke protested that the wars were totally different in character from any previous wars in human history, that the social order and civilisation itself was at stake. In his *Letters against a regicide peace* he rallied his last strength to warn that such a peace must inevitably mean the destruction of the old order in Britain: 'The moment the struggle begins, it ends. They talk of Mr Hume's Euthanasia of the British constitution, gently expiring without a groan in the paternal arms of a mere monarchy. In a monarchy! fine trifling indeed. There is no such Euthanasia for the British constitution.'

By the time Burke died, the worst was over. The measures taken by Pitt's administration crushed the reform movement and the excesses of the French Revolution disenchanted many of its erstwhile supporters. Patriotic sentiments came to the rescue of the aristocracy and the constitution became once more a symbol of national unity and purpose. By 1801 Godwin could write that the reform societies were extinct or moribund: 'the days of democratical declamation are no more: even the starving labourer in the alehouse is become a champion of aristocracy'.[45] Gone, too, was Godwin's moment. For a few years his reputation blazed in the sky and he was the *guru* of romantic and radical intellectuals: then, as Hazlitt put it, he sank below the horizon.[46]

The challenge from France in the 1800s was less ideological and more nationalist. But a problem remained – whether the aristocratic governments of the old order could overcome the new French meritocracy under Napoleonic leadership without adopting, to a great extent, the chief weapon of its adversary, the career open to the talents. The failure of the Duke of York as Commander-in-Chief in 1794–5 and again in 1799 posed the question whether appointing the king's son was necessarily the best way to beat the French: his successful opponent in 1799 had been General Brune, a printer in private life. Russians and Prussians began to perceive that a less rigid structure was needed to deal with the new

---

44 Quoted in my *The Whig ascendancy*, 116.
45 *Thoughts occasioned by the perusal of Dr Parr's Spital Sermon.*
46 *The spirit of the age* (1825 edition), 31. Godwin had a considerable influence upon the young Wordsworth, who wrote: 'I disapprove of monarchial and aristocratical governments however modified. Hereditary distinctions and privileged orders of every species I think must necessarily counteract the progress of human improvement. Hence, it follows, that I am not among the admirers of the British constitution.' Letter to W. Mathews, June 1794, *The early letters of William and Dorothy Wordsworth*, ed. E. de Selincourt, No. 42.

menace.[47] France, declared Jeffrey in the *Edinburgh Review*, had 'triumphed by the free and unlimited use she has made of the talents of her people' and Britain would have to do the same.[48] The trouble was that, either way, revolutionary principles were likely to triumph, by conquest or by imitation. Jeffrey returned to the theme in July 1809, suggesting that one consequence of the revolution had been to 'render hereditary rank and pretensions less imposing and respectable than formerly in the eyes of the people':

> The diadem of Bonaparte has dimmed the lustre of all the ancient crowns of Europe; and her nobles have been outshone, and outgeneralled, and outnegotiated, by men raised by their own exertions from the common level of the populace. The ancient and hereditary rulers of states, in short, have made but a poor figure in the contest with their plebeian antagonists; and it is impossible that the people of this country should have been spectators of the struggle without feeling an abatement of that habitual veneration for rank and dignity.[49]

Jeffrey was writing at a dark moment, with Bonaparte triumphant, and Britain powerless to stop him. Six years later, after the Battle of Waterloo, things looked different. Bonaparte was on St Helena, the Bourbons were restored, and moderate men congratulated themselves that the British constitution had stood the test. For good measure, the two great war heroes, Nelson and Wellington, had been incorporated into the nobility, adding their lustre and reputation to its protection.

Jeffrey, in the excitement and preoccupation of the moment, placed the blame for the decline of respect on the wars. But although the wars speeded up the process of change, they were not its cause. The cause, as far as any cause can be identified for so gradual and complex a development, was the Enlightenment. Like all shorthand phrases, this one is apt to produce as much misunderstanding as clarification. It is still sometimes used in an old-fashioned sense to mean a specific group of writers or even a common body of doctrines peculiar to the mid-eighteenth century. But, more properly understood, it represents the gradual spread of education, of literacy, of sophistication throughout most parts of Europe, and it took place over centuries rather than decades. One

---

[47] Best expressed perhaps by Gneisenau: 'one cause above all has raised France to this pinnacle of greatness. The revolution awakened all her powers and gave to every individual a suitable field for his activity. Why do not the courts take steps to open up a career to [genius] wherever it is to be found, to encourage talents and virtues whatever the rank . . . The other states must appropriate the results of the revolution.' Though the analysis is somewhat exaggerated, there was enough truth to give France for years an edge in the struggle. G. H. Pertz, *Das leben des Feldmarschall's Grafen Neithard von Gneisenau*, I, 301.

[48] 'The Dangers of the Country', *Edinburgh Review* (April 1807), 18.

[49] 'Parliamentary reform', 294.

onsequence of the revised, and in my view improved, definition is that it
emoves England from a footnote in a chapter devoted to Voltaire,
Rousseau, Grimm and Beccaria and places it in the very forefront of the
rocess as a country where these developments had some of their earliest
nd most profound effects.[50] Although, in 1815, the menace of French
Revolutionary infection had been dealt with, the seeds of change were
ative to each country, and could not be sterilised. For all the fury of
Burke, they were not 'French' principles but principles of universal
pplication. No country was immune.

One of the contemporaries who saw most clearly what was happening
vas William Cobbett, perhaps because he had been through a painful
rocess of self-enlightenment. By 1811, no longer the hammer of the
acobins, he was capable of seeing the development in full perspective:

here is a change *in the mind of man*, of which the leaders in revolutions have been
nerely the *expositors*. The writings of Paine and Condorcet have been the effect
nd not the cause of this change, which has been gradually taking place, which
radually advances in its progress, and which cannot be arrested in that progress
ny more than human power can arrest the progress of nature in any of her
perations . . . Whether it be better or worse for mankind that *rank* and *birth*
hould fall into contempt is a question which is beyond my humble capacity to
nswer; but, it is a fact, that they have fallen and are daily falling into contempt.
What has been and is going on, is an insurrection of talents and courage and
ndustry against birth and rank. Men have not, at bottom been contending about
orms of government. Writers and orators have; but the mass of nations do not
nter into such theories; they look to the practical effects. They have been
eeking such *a change* as will render their lives more happy and less humiliating,
vith little regard as to *names* and *forms*.[51]

One cannot document a revolution, least of all a revolution in men's
ninds. Nevertheless, there seems to me one writing in which the conflict
netween the old order and the new and potentially subversive doctrine of
he career open to the talents is fought out. It is in the most unlikely, yet
he most likely place – the mind of Edmund Burke: unlikely, because he
vas the most articulate, devoted and passionate defender of the old order,
with a profound hatred of the principles of the revolution – the death-
lance of democracy he called it; likely, because he was, in himself, a
narvellous example of the career open to talent. It was Johnson who said
f Burke that, if one fell into five minutes' casual conversation with him
while held up by a drove of oxen, you would say, *this is an extraordinary
man*. The document was Burke's *Letter to a Noble Lord*, written in 1796 at

---

[0] See some excellent comments on similar lines in 'The Enlightenment in England' by Roy Porter.
[1] Cobbett's *Political Register*, xx, 585–7.

the end of his life, as a bitter reply to the attack upon his pension made i
the House of Lords by the thirty-year-old radical Duke of Bedford
Burke reminds Bedford of his services in the cause of aristocracy:

There is one merit of mine which he, of all men living, ought to be the last to ca
in question. I have supported with very great zeal, and I am told with som
degree of success, those opinions – or if His Grace likes another expression bette
those old prejudices which buoy up the ponderous mass of *his* nobility, wealt
and titles. I have omitted no exertion to prevent him and them from sinking t
that level, to which the meretricious French faction his Grace at least coquet
with, omit no exertion to reduce both. I have done all I could to discountenanc
their enquiries into the fortunes of those, who hold large portions of wealt
without any apparent merit of their own. I have strained every nerve to keep th
Duke of Bedford in that situation, which alone makes him my superior.

If this was a defence of the old order, did it need attack? And, as Burke'
rage got the better of his prudence, he spelt out the message in languag
of which Tom Paine might have been proud. The fortunes of the Hous
of Russell, he reminded Bedford, came from the spoliation of th
monasteries and the old nobility:

The first peer of the name, the first purchaser of the grants, was a Mr Russell,
person of an ancient gentleman's family, raised by being a minion of Henry th
Eighth . . . His grants were from the aggregate and consolidated funds o
judgements iniquitously legal, and from possessions voluntarily surrendered by
the lawful proprietors with the gibbet at their door. The merit of the grante
whom he derives from, was that of being a prompt and greedy instrument of
levelling tyrant.

As for the 1790s, Burke declared:

I am really at a loss to draw any sort of parallel between the public merits of hi
Grace, by which he justifies the grants he holds, and these services of mine, on th
favourable construction of which I have obtained what his Grace so much
disapproves . . . It would not be gross adulation but uncivil irony to say that h
has any public merit of his own to keep alive the idea of the services by which hi
vast landed pensions were obtained. My merits, whatever they are, are origina
and personal: his are derivative.

It seems to me that Burke won by a knock-out in the second round but, in
typical fashion, knocked out not merely his opponent but the referee as
well, and smashed up the ring at the same time.

What with the French Revolution and the elevation of Lord
Carrington to face, it is surprising that the aristocratic principle survived
as well as it did. In fact, it had a long life ahead of it still. It was once mor
considered to be in grave danger during the Reform crisis of 1831, when
the House of Lords was threatened with abolition by the radicals and

masculation by the Whigs. The repeal of the Corn Laws fifteen years later was hailed as the death-knell of the old order, and the misfortunes of the Crimean War called up fresh and bitter denunciations of aristocratic bungling. But, like a creaking door, aristocracy held on. The beginning of the twentieth century saw the Marquis of Salisbury at Number Ten. The retreat was slow, steady and unspectacular.

It is remarkable to what extent the nobility, after 1815, succeeded in restoring their position and no one would suggest that Victorian aristocrats worried that they might be murdered in their beds. But although the hurricane of the French Revolution had blown itself out, the questions it had raised did not disappear. The upper classes did not succeed in exorcising Tom Paine to the extent that, in the eighteenth century, they had exorcised Lilburne, Winstanley and the commonwealth men. 'The Duke of Richmond', Paine had observed, 'takes away as much for himself as would maintain two thousand poor and aged persons.'[52] It did not cease to be true. Why, Burke had demanded in his remorseless way, why should the poor not cut the throats of the rich and share out their property?[53] Gratifying though it was that he had provided an answer, it was a question which, perhaps, the upper classes would have preferred not to have been raised.

There were very few in Dorset and Lincolnshire, Herefordshire and Wiltshire in the eighteenth century who read Hume and Blackstone and even fewer of those who did were likely, in any case, to wish to subvert the social order. We have drifted, inevitably, into an over-cerebral attitude towards the problem, and to redress the balance it is necessary to stress how aristocratic values and the assumption of aristocratic superiority dominated everyday life. The great majority of English people formed their impressions not from books but from events and circumstances, which reinforced the notion of aristocratic pre-eminence, benevolence and inevitability. Thousands of them were employed on the great estates, hundreds of them were shop-keepers, inn-keepers, attorneys in small market towns, directly dependent upon the nobility for custom. Many thousands of others were caught up in the detailed and intricate network of patronage and connection. Cobbett talked of 'a chain of dependence running through the whole nation, which, though not everywhere seen, is everywhere felt. There is not one man in one thousand who does not feel the weight of this chain.'[54] But although

---

[52] *Rights of Man*, ed. H. B. Bonner, Part II, 205.   [53] *Thoughts and details on scarcity* (1795).
[54] Cobbett's *Political Register*, XIV, 585–6.

Cobbett, for political purposes, described it as an incubus or burden, t
many people it seemed more like a life-belt or a safety-net.

Aristocracy was not perceived separately but as a part, albeit a
important one, of the great system of authority and subordination whic
formed the context for men's lives. Nowhere, for example, wer
distinctions of rank of more importance than in the servants' hall of
great house: at Cannons, the mansion of the Dukes of Chandos, ther
were four tables for the domestics, carefully graded. Under thes
circumstances, envy was more likely to be directed at those immediatel
above one in the system than at those infinitely remote. In one sens
danger came when aristocracy could be perceived separately and whe
men could conceive that aristocratic privilege might be abolishe
without society at once falling into dissolution and ruin. In th
nineteenth century, it was increasingly argued that a stable society coul
well be formed on non-aristocratic principles and that it would be bot
cheaper and more efficient. Samuel Johnson, an old-fashioned man fror
a small provincial town, could scarcely conceive of such a society:

He again insisted on the duty of maintaining subordination of rank. 'Sir, I woul
no more deprive a nobleman of his respect than of his money. I consider myse
as acting a part in the great system of society . . . There would be a perpetu
struggle for precedence were there no fixed invariable rules for the distinction c
rank.'[55]

I suppose we now live in such a society and have grown so accustomed t
the perpetual struggle for precedence that it has become our natura
habitat. We no more question it than the majority of our forebears in th
eighteenth century questioned their own ordered and hierarchica
society. But Johnson might have been nonplussed to comprehend th
rationale behind our own society in which wealth beyond the dreams o
avarice goes to pop stars, television personalities and bad-tempere
tennis players.

It is worth reminding ourselves – if only as an intellectual exercise -
that there is a respectable case to be made for aristocracy, at least ir
theory. One would have to be very perverse not to wish to be governe
by the best. The difficulty is in obtaining the necessary guarantees. Unde
what system could one be certain that one would be ruled by the best -
the wisest, kindest and most disinterested – and not merely by the mos
ambitious, ruthless, cunning or plausible. And for how long, in thi
wicked world, would the best, entrusted with power, remain the best

[55] *Life*, I, 447.

That aristocracy meant the rule of the best was a message assiduously expounded in eighteenth-century England. Patents of nobility spelt out the exemplary services that noblemen had performed, and though equal services were scarcely to be expected from subsequent generations, the theory of noble blood insisted that peers were naturally disposed to gallant conduct and prudent advice. The author of *Common sense* in 1742 described them, majestically, as 'the Valiant and the Wise', and argued that aristocrats 'must be strangers to those vicious falsehoods and corruptions which necessity first, and then habit, puts men upon practising, whose lives are spent in pursuit of their fortunes'.[56] It was buttressed by the more prosaic argument that the wealthy, having most to lose, must always act most responsibly. 'Such men', wrote *An Old Whig*, 'are formed by their education, interested by their property, and bound by their conscience . . . to exercise the glorious privilege of mediating between the throne and the people.'[57] Expressed in its simplest form, the theory advised ordinary people to leave government to their betters. As for the lower orders, nothing much could be expected from them: 'It must indeed be granted, that the *base-born*, because *ill-begotten* progeny of *wicked parents*, may from the infelicity of their birth derive stronger dispositions to vice.'[58]

The upper classes, consequently, were sensitive about the effect of disgraceful actions by their members and the monarch was usually easily persuaded to rescue indigent peers from total penury. Philip Thicknesse, a notorious eccentric, was hitting at the whole social order when, to spite his son, the 19th Baron Audley, he advertised 'Boots and shoes mended, carpets beat, etc. by P. Thicknesse, father of Lord Audley.'[59]

From time to time, considerable concern was expressed at the harmful effects of the portrayal of noblemen on the stage or in novels as vicious or vapid. It is not difficult in the novels of the period to find specimens of the nobility – Lady Bellaston in *Tom Jones* or Lord Oxmington in *Humphry Clinker* – held up to satire or ridicule. But the most recent historian of the eighteenth-century novel insists that there was no general challenge to the class structure or the social order.[60] Although, in a number of novels,

---

[56] No. 272, reprinted in *Gentleman's Magazine*, XII (1742).

[57] *The present state of the British constitution deduced from facts* (1793). This was a reformist pamphlet but was here describing 'the spirit of the constitution'.

[58] *Reflections upon the moral state of the nation* (1701), quoted J. Hopes, 'The debate on the English theatre, 1690–1740', Ph.D. thesis, Newcastle upon Tyne University (1982), 372.

[59] Lord Audley had succeeded to the title through his mother, the eldest daughter of the 4th Earl of Castlehaven and second wife of Philip Thicknesse.

[60] H. J. Shroff, *The eighteenth century novel: the idea of the gentleman.*

the author presents a character of apparently humble antecedents, ye
honest and resourceful, and even at times observes that blood is of n
consequence, the *dénouement* is often a weak surrender to orthodoxy
revealing that the character is, in fact, of good or even noble birth. Thus
Tom Jones is not, after all, the bastard of a servant girl Jenny Jones, no
Joseph Andrews the son of Gaffar and Gammer Andrews, nor Humphr
Clinker a mere broken-down ostler, while Roderick Random's father
believed dead, returns improbably as Don Rodriguez, a Spanish *grandee*
Though the mechanics of the plot sometimes demanded that th
character be a natural son or daughter of a man of rank and position, thi
merely confirmed that blood is of more consequence than legitimacy

The trappings of power and rank were much in evidence. Bells rang
when his lordship arrived home or at the Bath. The main tavern in th
village or town was, and still often is, the Rutland Arms, the Newcastl
Arms, or the Radnor Arms. The town hall and perhaps the school and
almshouses were gifts from the local patron. The duke's name stood a
the top of the list for every charitable collection. Local newspaper
recorded with care each distribution of food or coal to the poor, each
bequest to debtors in prison, each act of condescension and benevolence
The great house overwhelmed visitors with its grandeur and elegance
And, in the close-knit communities of Hanoverian England, there wa
often much genuine kindness from rich to poor.

Few aristocrats needed Addison's advice to take pains to make their
rule acceptable. Though there are some grotesque examples of
overweening pride, like Charles Seymour, 6th Duke of Somerset, who
sent outriders ahead of his coach to clear the streets so that the vulgar
should not gaze on him, and some gloomy tyrants of the hall, like the 1st
Earl of Lonsdale, the majority wished to be respected, if not loved.[61]
Arthur Young complained that the desire for popularity in their local
community inhibited landlords from charging economic rents and thus
slowed down agricultural progress.[62] Newcastle's coming-of-age cele-
brations in Sussex in 1714 cost £2,000 and he continued to spend large
sums on casual entertainment despite his appalling financial difficulties.
By comparison, the Duke of Rutland's coming-of-age celebration at
Haddon Hall in 1799 was very inferior junketing. It cost a mere
£618.12.6¾. Nevertheless, the assembled throng got through four oxen,

---

[61] Somerset was perhaps a pathological case. 'His whole stupid life', wrote Horace Walpole, 'was a
series of pride and tyranny.' To Mann, 26 Dec. 1748, *Corr.* xx, 18. One of his daughters was sent
to Coventry for more than a year for allowing him, in old age, to roll off a sofa.

[62] R. A. C. Parker, *Coke of Norfolk*, says the Holkham estate pursued a conciliatory policy on rents
and at times of difficulty, arrears were enormous.

sixteen sheep and forty hogsheads of ale. Music was provided by sixteen members of the band of the Sheffield Volunteer Corps. One hundred and thirty gentlemen and ladies were at the ball, two hundred and fifty tenants dined at table, and the general populace milling around was put at ten thousand. 'I believe', wrote one participant, 'all who wished to be drunk were so, which comprised a considerable number.' One of the tenants composed and sang a tribute in suitably execrable verse:

> No paltry distinctions appeared at their board,
> Their servants sat swigging as big as their Lord.[63]

Equally impressive, in more sombre fashion, were the vast funeral processions, devised to impart awe and solemnity. The ritual of the hunting-fields brought together many others of the rural population, as onlookers if not riders, though Munsche notes that more generous hunting-rights tended to be withdrawn later in the century, when poaching affrays were beginning to sour relations.[64]

The features of Hanoverian society which shock modern readers are not necessarily those which troubled contemporaries. The ferocity of the criminal code and the multiplication of capital offences are aspects which we find peculiarly offensive. Yet Fielding, in his pamphlet on *The late increase of robbers* opened with the assertion that British punishments were 'the mildest and the most void of terror of any other in the known world', and one of his proposals for improvement was for a sharp reduction in the number of pardons. It should be remembered that most crime was perpetrated, then as now, not by the poor against the rich, but by the poor against each other. And the very harshness of eighteenth-century life introduced a degree of brutal equality into a society profoundly unequal. Duchesses and drabs died in childbirth, and when the great Duke of Chandos, that poor rich man, the prey to quacks, found his sight going, he bathed his eyes patiently in a mixture of Portuguese snuff, urine and viper's fat. I have never had the heart to find out what effect it had.

One does not doubt that there was muttering, resentment and discontent. In times of dearth, it burst out in sharp and worrying riots. But, for the most part, dissatisfaction was helpless, isolated geographically and intellectually. One could not write to the papers or start a new party. In the end, the old order was not swept away: it subsided. In the vast and growing industrial towns of nineteenth-century England, these

---

[63] *HMC. Rutland*, IV, 257–9.
[64] P. B. Munsche, *Gentlemen and poachers: the English game laws 1671–1831*, 109–15.

constant reminders of aristocracy were largely absent, and more and more the nobility came to look like an expensive irrelevance. It was hard to live in Woodstock or Alnwick or Petworth or Arundel and believe, with Tom Paine, that titles were 'mere foppery'. I dare say it still is. But in Merthyr Tydfil, Stockport, Barnsley and Middlesbrough, it seemed a more plausible proposition.

CONCLUSION

I began the work upon which these Lectures have been based with no specific hypothesis in mind, but a general uneasiness, a collection of unformed doubts and reservations about the degree of social mobility at the highest level in Hanoverian England. These misgivings were reinforced by what I knew of work being published on the social structure of other European countries, which seemed to reveal greater mobility than had been commonly supposed. My analyses slowly crystallised – perhaps congealed would be a more appropriate word – into two rather simple theses: that a comparatively small number of peers controlled to a great extent the commanding heights of political and social life and that, contrary to much presumption, aristocratic influence strengthened as the century progressed.

No two people would agree in drawing up a balance-sheet of the aristocratic regime. I have already praised the political acumen and sense of national interest. The aristocracy ran the country well, won its wars, fostered its trade and industry, and extended its empire. Not until the last quarter of the eighteenth century, with the loss of the American colonies, was the first set-back experienced, and even that was surmounted with surprising ease. To this we should add that, under patrician patronage, the eighteenth century set standards of taste in architecture and landscape gardening, in painting and music, in porcelain and furniture and dress, seldom, if ever, equalled. But there is a less attractive side. That it was a regime of bleak oppression is scarcely plausible. But there was a great deal of greed and pomposity. George I, on his arrival in England, is said to have expressed surprise that noblemen 'who possessed such large fortunes were so assiduous and covetous of office'.[1] The presumption that English peers, unlike their continental brethren, did not fret or fume

---

[1] Egmont Diary, Add. MS 47027, fos. 352, 354.

over matters of precedence is another of our comforting myths.[2] It is true that the French peerage behaved at times so curiously that most other nobilities seem sane by comparison. At the great crisis of the *ancien régime* on the death of Louis XIV, the Duc de Saint-Simon was totally obsessed with preserving the privilege of the bonnet and the subsequent experiment of the *polysynodie* showed the depths to which the French peerage had sunk. But the Prussian nobility does not give a comparable impression of effeteness, while the English peerage, collectively and individually, could be absurdly tenacious of their rights. They proferred a pointed insult to the Scottish peerage after the Act of Union by refusing to allow a Scots peer, also holder of a British peerage, to take his seat in the House of Lords, and throughout the 1730s there was a tedious running battle with the Irish peerage about precedence on state occasions.[3] Every first minister cursed the importunity of peerage hunters. During the American War, the king and Lord North sometimes gave the impression that the malignity of the rebels was as nothing compared with that of disappointed peerage aspirants. The unpleasantness caused by the remainder for the Duke of Montagu in 1776 drove the king to describe himself as 'in the greatest state of uneasiness I ever felt': he took refuge in the closet, refusing to see 'any mortal' until the matter had been sorted out.[4] Two years later Lord North, admittedly in one of his despondent moods, found peerage claims the last straw: he begged to be allowed to resign 'as I really shall not be able to stand the storm and violence which the candidates for the peerage will bring upon me'.[5] Promotions in the peerage were particularly delicate and provided an almost ideal formula for offending as many people as possible. Far from exhibiting gratitude for the grant of an earldom in 1784 (when his family had previously held only a barony), Sir James Lowther threatened to go into opposition because John Robinson's grandson would take precedence as Earl of Abergavenny.[6] When Baron Curzon was promoted viscount in 1802, his elder brother Baron Scarsdale wrote most bitterly to complain of the personal affront he had suffered as head of the family: 'The precedency of a younger brother and his family over me and mine is so painful to us all that I am greatly afflicted . . . it wounds me to the soul to think I must go

---

[2] L. G. Pine, *The story of the peerage*, 187–8, remarked that the English peerage 'preserved a sense of humour about such matters'.

[3] The Scottish case was that of the Duke of Hamilton. For a lengthy account of the struggle with the Irish peers, see Lord Egmont's diary, *HMC. Egmont*, I, 405–77; II, 43–63; III, 138.

[4] *The correspondence of King George III*, III, No. 1880.

[5] *Ibid.*, IV, No. 2309.   [6] *The House of Commons, 1754–90*, III, 59.

down to the grave with a dreadful undeserved stigma on *my* name.'[7] The pride of the 1st Marquess of Abercorn (Viscount Hamilton in the British peerage) was so great that he is reported to have gone shooting in his blue ribbon and to have insisted that his maids wore white gloves when making his bed.

The disagreement which I expressed in my Introduction with the Marxist interpretation of modern English history may have been prompted by its cruder manifestations, though there would be little difficulty in providing examples from current writing. The identification of a 'bourgeois revolution' in the mid-seventeenth century has, in my view, caused Marxists to postulate a vast chronological misplacement, anticipating developments by two hundred years or so, and ignoring the nature of the eighteenth-century political regime. They have been misled by the presumption that fundamental political shifts can be effected only by violent upheaval. 'Force', declared Marx authoritatively, 'is the midwife of every old society pregnant with a new one':[8] perhaps nineteenth-century midwives were like that. It has led some of his followers to exaggerate the importance of military and political convulsions and, curiously, to under-estimate the importance of social and economic evolution. Hence they are inexorably attracted to the proposition that the English Civil War must have been of decisive significance, since it is the grandest upheaval in sight, despite much evidence that it decided very little.[9]

But I have to admit that the problem that has worried me – the comparative absence of resentment of aristocratic supremacy in the eighteenth century – may also be, in part, one of my own invention. However much one has been warned – and, indeed, warned others – of the need to divest oneself of twentieth-century assumptions when investigating the past, it is not easy to do so in practice. More than a century of Marxist influence leads us to expect to find class conflict and disposes us to believe that class loyalties are the most potent. But, in fact,

---

[7] *The later correspondence of King George III*, IV, No. 2702.

[8] *Capital* (1970 English edition), Chapter 31. They also follow Marx more directly in identifying 1648 as the crucial European breakthrough of capitalism. 'The Bourgeoisie and the Counter-Revolution', *Neue Rheinische Zeitung*, 11 Dec. 1848.

[9] An engaging attempt to square the Marxist circle is made by Christopher Hill in his article 'A bourgeois revolution?', in *Three British revolutions: 1641, 1688, 1776*, ed. J. G. A. Pocock. In order to retain the concept of a bourgeois revolution in the 1640s, Hill argues that this does not mean a revolution *made* by the bourgeoisie, or even in accordance with their desires, and it may even be a revolution made by other people *against* the bourgeoisie. I think that it takes more than the authority of Lenin as an historian to persuade us that this is a step forward in methodology and an aid to clear thinking. Perhaps one may mildly suggest that if one's thesis requires such elaborate semantic exegesis, there may be something wrong with it.

religious, family or national loyalties may well be more decisive, possibly today and certainly in the eighteenth century.

The 'middling orders' of Hanoverian England were in no position to offer a sustained, coherent or united challenge to aristocratic rule, even if they had wished to. Any sensible definition of the middling orders must include a vast number of farmers and gentry, who were more likely to identify with the landed interest, including the nobility, than with commercial and professional men in the towns. For that matter, many brewers, bankers, coal-owners and merchants, having made their pile, were only too anxious to purchase a country estate and turn gentlemen. Successful professional men were too dependent upon aristocratic patronage to discern a separate or rival interest, however much they may have been enraged by patrician nonchalance in paying bills. Since many peers, as we have seen, participated in commercial and industrial undertakings, there was no very obvious reason why they should have seemed obstacles to a capitalist development or an industrial revolution.

The minority who did wish to see profound changes in government and society were, for most of the century, without mechanisms to bring them about, or even to exert much influence. Perceptive aristocrats were right to see long-term dangers in the spread of 'associations' in the later 1770s, and Rockingham, though willing to make use of them for party purposes, tried hard to head off any radical tendencies. But the habit of association persisted. In 1785 Josiah Wedgwood and Samuel Garbett formed the General Chamber of Manufacturers of Great Britain to bring provincial industrial opinion to bear on Westminster. Though the General Chamber collapsed in 1787, an even more ominous development was the establishment in 1792 of the London Corresponding Society, organised by working men, and dedicated to obtaining manhood suffrage and annual parliaments.

But, in the mid-eighteenth century, there was little to suggest what form an alternative regime might take. A democratical and levelling system, which had briefly in the 1640s appeared a possibility, was tainted with religious fanaticism and was as unlikely to appeal to commercial and industrial magnates as to landed ones. The example of the Dutch republic, where finance and commerce held sway, might have beckoned. But the blaze of Dutch success was transitory and, by the mid-eighteenth century, the Dutch were certainly in political and possibly in economic decline. In any case, from 1747 onwards, aristocratic and dynastic influence, in the shape of the Orange family, had reasserted itself. For the most part men conceived the alternative to aristocratic rule to be some form of royal absolutism. But the folly of James II had discredited arbitrary government for ever and the practice of capricious repudiations and bankruptcies in Spain and France did nothing to promote the cause of royalism with financiers and men of business. They were better off with a parliamentary regime and a guaranteed National Debt.

But we must do more than explain why aristocratic ascendancy was unchallenged for so long. We must seek to understand how this regime presided over those industrial and financial developments on which an effective challenge to its own position could be based. I have already expressed doubt whether the degree of social mobility, at the highest level, can have been sufficient to offer motivation to thousands of entrepreneurs, though belief in the possibility might have done so. But the political contribution to industrialisation seems to me to have been understated. This contribution was the creation, for a few vital decades, of a society sufficiently stable to afford encouragement to investment and industry, free at last from coups and revolutions and civil wars, and free also from government intervention. For the unobtrusive government, which suited the aristocracy very well, suited entrepreneurs also. Adam Smith's the *Wealth of nations*, published in 1776, was not merely a call for free trade and *laissez-faire*: it was to a great extent a reflection of the policy that English governments had followed for many years. Hence the race for industrial breakthrough went, in the end, not to the *dirigiste* vigour of Colbert's France nor to the frenetic state enterprises of Peter the Great, but to aristocratic England.

Three factors combined to usher in the challenge to the old aristocratic order. First, the beginnings of that transformation into an industrial society which changed the balance of wealth in the community and made an alternative power structure a possibility. Second, the slow but relentless impact of the spread of information and knowledge, of humane and liberal values, in a country much affected by the Enlightenment. Third, the discernment of the aristocracy, not as part of the natural and inevitable order of things, but as a separate group, pursuing its own interests, and the dawning recognition that the influence of that group was, if anything, increasing. The author of the *Black book* in 1820 complained that the aristocracy had 'swallowed up, not only the rights of the people and the prerogatives of the crown, but also the immunities of the church. At no former period was the power of the aristocracy more absolute.' The chronology is doubtful, the case exaggerated and the language melodramatic, but it would be a mistake to dismiss it as no more than radical rhetoric.

INDEX

Peers are entered under their titles, thus: Ailesbury, Thomas Bruce, 2nd Earl of